Espen Aarseth, Stephan Günzel (eds
Ludotopia

Espen Aarseth, born in 1965, is Professor of Game Studies at the IT University of Copenhagen. He is the Editor-in-Chief of *Game Studies*, a journal he co-founded in 2001. In 2016 he received an ERC Advanced Grant for the project "MSG – Making Sense of Games".

Stephan Günzel, born in 1971, is Professor of Media Theory at the University of Applied Sciences Europe and currently head of the Media Studies Master Program at the Technical University of Berlin. He co-founded the Digital Games Research Center at the University of Potsdam in 2008.

ESPEN AARSETH, STEPHAN GÜNZEL (EDS.)

Ludotopia

Spaces, Places and Territories in Computer Games

[transcript]

Supported by European Research Council's grant agreement No 695528 'Making Sense of Games'.
Funded by the Insitute for Design Research
at the University of Applied Sciences Europe.

Bibliographic information published by the Deutsche Nationalbibliothek
The Deutsche Nationalbibliothek lists this publication in the Deutsche Nationalbibliografie; detailed bibliographic data are available in the Internet at http://dnb.d-nb.de

Cover layout: Maria Arndt, Bielefeld
Cover illustration: Screenshot from 'DayZ'
Proofread by Ida Kathrine Hammeleff Jørgensen, Naomi Seeling
    and Ryan Christopher Wright
Printed by Majuskel Medienproduktion GmbH, Wetzlar
Print-ISBN 978-3-8376-4730-3
PDF-ISBN 978-3-8394-4730-7
https://doi.org/10.14361/9783839447307

Content

III. Territories

Introduction
Space – The Theoretical Frontier

Even before game studies was a recognized research field, space has been a recurring, core topic of debate on the new cultural form of videogames. Digital games do share aspects of spatiality with other (audio-)visual forms – in particular film, as well as painting, photography, and literature – but due to the dynamic nature of simulations, space was acknowledged as a constitutive factor of designing and playing games; their sine-qua-non.

We coined the term 'Ludotopia' as an adequate expression for the dialectical entanglement of games and space. Here we hark back to the original Latin word *ludus*, meaning games and play in general, before Roger Caillois attempted to oppose it with the Greek *paidia* – the two words have more or less the same meaning. On the other hand, *topos* for 'place' stresses the fact that any experience of space, in games as well as in real life, is rooted in a relation to location(s) or an activity transforming places, whether in the sense of Martin Heidegger, who claims that "spaces receive their being from locations," or in the sense of Michel de Certeau, who defines: "space is a practiced place."

This volume is the result of two workshops that were held at the IT University Copenhagen and the University of Salford in Manchester, organized in cooperation with the Digital Games Research Center at the University of Potsdam. The participants at these workshops as well as additional authors were invited to contribute to this volume. Their contributions cover the three subtopics 'spaces,' 'places' and 'territories,' including the relevance of maps and cartographic representation for digital games.

The first section on 'spaces' begins with a contribution from Stephan *Günzel*, who calls for an understanding of "Computer Games as Spatial Concepts," by arguing that a basic misunderstanding of representation can be diagnosed, by which videogames no longer need to be considered as denotations of an actual space, but rather are exemplifications of ideas about space. Stephan *Schwingeler* then, in his article "Construction of Perspective in Videogames" applies the art historian's terminology of 'artificial perspective' to computer games, exploring the various ways in which the view of the virtual camera can become a constitutive moment of gameplay. Karla *Teilhaber*, in her article, "Spatial Concepts in 'Portal' and 'Echochrome,'" argues that previous approaches to digital games transgressed contemporary design conventions, which conceptualized three-dimensional game space as 'natural,' passive background; instead, in contemporary games, space itself becomes an active subject. By looking at "Artistic Practices of Presence in Narrative Media" from the standpoint of literary criticism, Teun *Dubbelman* reconstructs the complex debates in narrative theory to highlight the difference between the 'implicit author' and the character being present in the game world; in doing so, he argues that the concepts of presence and immersion are subject to the intended design of games. Following up on this, Sebastian *Domsch* in his contribution, "Space and Narrative in Computer Games," argues that the narrative potential of videogames is still about to be discovered, whereby the potential lies particularly in their spatiality.

The section on 'places' starts off with Espen *Aarseth's* chapter on what he terms "Ludoforming in Game Worlds," which is a discussion of the strategies used and the resulting game landscapes when game designers are trying to use an existing, historical or fictional landscape for ludic purposes. Daniel *Vella*, in his contribution on "Dwelling and Being at Home in Digital Games" turns away from game studies' typical focus of travel and movement, and towards ludic conceptions of the home, paying special attention to 'Animal Crossing' and 'Minecraft.' In "Videogame Wastelands as (Non-)Places and 'Any-Space-Whatevers'" Souvik *Mukherjee* deploys Augé's concept of a 'non-place' and Deleuze's of the 'any-space-whatever' to analyse the post-apocalyptic landscapes of 'S.T.A.L.K.E.R.,' 'Fallout 3,' and others. Bjarke *Liboriussen*, in "The Game and 'The Stack'" jumps off of Benjamin Bratton's recent and influential internet-theory to augmented reality games, especially 'Pokémon Go,' and assesses its relevance to game studies. Finally, Michael *Nitsche* closes the section with "No End of Worlds," an interface-related take on the dialectic between game space and real space; asking what happens when gameplay moves out of their digital 'windows' and into our living spaces?

The third and final section, on 'territories,' is opened by Mathias *Fuchs* in his contribution on "visual itineraries and written itineraries," which links the ancient tradition of drawing and writing roadmaps to the ways in which traditional computer games, but also location-based games, support wayfinding and orientation by virtue of design features. In a unique approach to "Defining the Play Space" Sebastian *Möring* then uses the proxemic concept of 'distance' as well as the existentialist notion of 'fear' to look at games in the way that they confront users with the necessity to keep up the play space amidst the threats of the 'game over.' By using "Lotman's Spatial Semantics as a Method for Analysing Videogames" Niklas *Schrape* analyses the serious game 'Global Conflicts: Palestine' with a narratological approach – almost forgotten by game studies – that essentially distinguishes between the topology and the topography of a semantizised space.

Following up on this, Paul *Martin* describes the interconnection of "Morphology and Meaning in 'Castle Wolfenstein 3D,'" by looking into the swastica-architecture of the respective game's level 6-3 with the focus of spatial syntax as it has been developed in urban planning by Bill Hillier and Julienne Hanson. The closing entry of the book by Mark *Wolf* gives "A Brief History of Procedurally-Generated Space in Videogames," from 'Rogue' to 'Minecraft' with special attention to the development of hardware, by which the spatiality of this particular genre turns out to be one of the most elucidating when it comes to the interdependency of a game's territory and the means of design.

The editors want to thank Ida Kathrine Hammeleff Jørgensen and Ryan Christopher Wright from the IT University Copenhagen, Naomi Seeling from the University of Applied Sciences Europe and Laura Lackas from the Technical University of Berlin for editing and proofreading, Mathias Fuchs for hosting the second Workshop in Manchester at the University of Salford, Jakob Horstmann and Annika Linnemann from transcript-publisher for acquisition and lectorate, the Institute for Design Research in Berlin for funding the online version of this volume as well as the European Research Council, whose support of the project 'Making Sense of Games' made the finalization of this publication possible; and last but not least: all authors for participation – and patience in the process...

Berlin and Copenhagen, Summer 2019

I. Spaces

What Do They Represent?
Computer Games as Spatial Concepts

Stephan Günzel

Since the late 1980s a so called 'spatial turn' affected the arts and humanities, foremost cultural studies. Also, computer game studies took a turn towards space, if they were not from the very beginning always about analyzing the spatiality of digital games (Günzel 2010). Nevertheless, this contribution investigates not only spatial theories, but suggests a further possible turn within the spatial turn and look at computer games themselves *as spatial concepts*. This means that in as much as spatial theory can be used in game studies to describe their objects in structure and appearance, games do *enact* spatial concepts.

Henri Lefebvre and the Spatial Turn

To understand this new approach, it nevertheless is crucial to go back to the origin of the current debate about the spatial turn, which can be traced back to 1974, when Henri Lefebvre published his book *La production de l'espace*. Yet in the 1970s the relevance for a spatial account of culture has not been recognized yet. It took almost two decades, until – by reason of the English translation of Lefebvre's (1991) book – neo-marxist and postmodern theorists began to discover the relevance of a spatial approach in sociology and urban studies. During the 1980s the focus lay on what Fredric Jameson (1998) called the 'cultural turn', i.e. the critical notion of capitalism incorporating culture for means of profit (Jameson 1984). Spatial thinking was present only implicitly, most prominently in Michel Foucault's (1998 and 1977) research on heterotopology and panopticism.

Lefebvre's thoughts were finally introduced to a broader audience when the geographer Edward Soja (1996, 53-82) published his reading of *The Production of Space*. The monograph was the follow-up to Soja's (1989, 39) publication *Postmodern Geographies*, in which the term "spatial turn" was coined for the first time (diagnosing a turn of Western Marxism towards spatial aspects of culture). As the title of the following book, *Thirdspace*, suggests, with Lefebvre, Soja calls for an understanding of a society as a synthesis of first space and second space.

In line with modern philosophical approaches by Charles Sanders Peirce, Gottlob Frege, and Karl Popper the difference between first and second space in Lefebvre could be understood as the material or present space in opposite to the logic or a conceptual space: Peirce (1984, 56) called it the 'indexical' as opposed to the 'iconic' sign, Frege (1960) called it 'reference' in contrast to 'imagination' and Popper divided the 'physical' from the 'psychological' world. In addition all three of them claimed that there is another realm or a third 'world' that has to be taken into consideration: Peirce named it the 'symbolic' sign, which gains its meaning only from interpretation, and Frege (1956) termed it 'thought' (*Gedanke*), which is very close to Popper (1980, 144), who described the third sphere as "the products of the human mind", to which "languages; tales and stories and religious myths; scientific conjectures or theories, and mathematical constructions; songs and symphonies; paintings and sculptures" belong.

The reason why Lefebvre also insists on a third realm or 'space' is not only because he, like Popper, thinks of the symbolic space as being a human product, but – following Karl Marx (Elden 2004) – claims that production takes place at any of the three stages (fig. 1): Physical space to Lefebvre is as much produced as imaginations are: landscapes are reworked nature and social or architectural utopias are manmade ideas. Both are in a dialectical relation and the outcome of their concurrence is the social space. Therefore, Soja subsequently addresses cultures as 'thirdspaces' – a term originally coined in postcolonial studies (Bhabha 1990, 211) – spaces that are 'real-and-imagined places' alike.

Fig. 1: Triad of Space according to Lefebvre and Soja

Spaces	Forms	Modalities	Equivalents
1st	**Spatial practice** [*pratique spatiale*]	**perceived** [*espace perçu*]	subjective | real everyday live/nature
2nd	**Representations of space** [*représentations de l'espace*]	**conceived** [*espace conçu*]	objective | imaginary urbanism/cartography
3rd	**Representational spaces** [*espaces de représentation*]	**lived** [*espace vécu*]	collective | symbolic lifeworld/culture

Going even beyond Lefebvre's idea of a dialectical production of space, Soja speaks of a 'trialectics of spatiality', and this for at least two reasons: One is that the results of the imaginary (re-)production of physical space as culture again feeds back into the first (as well as the second) space by which the first space is already affected by the third (and second); the other reason is that Lefebvre describes each of the spaces as two-fold, hence as dialectical in themselves. ('Dialectics' – based on the Greek word *logos* for 'spirit', 'speech' or 'meaning' – does not literally designate a movement between only 'two', since the prefix is derived from *dia-*, for 'through' and, and not from *di-*; '*tri*-alectics,' as Soja names the process, therefore is almost a nonsensical term.)

Production of space on the first level takes place as an everyday spatial practice, in which space is at the same time not only acted out or performed, but also individually perceived: it is the aspect of a *phenomenology* of space. Production of space on the second level takes place due to the representation of (perceived) space in architecture, geography, urbanism and so forth, but is also objectively conceived: it is the aspect of an *epistemology* of space. Production on the third level takes place as the constitution of 'representational spaces' (as Lefebvre calls them) or 'spaces of representation' (as Soja calls them), i.e. *culturally significant places* which are significant due to the collective production as an interpretation or a collective reproduction as preservation of certain traditions; both of which are called the 'lived space' by Lefebvre.

Lefebvre's (or Soja's) triad of space has become very popular in the recent discussions and been used for describing the various modes of cultural production. However, confusions occurred about the model. This is not only due to the latter term of the 'lived space', which is hard to separate from the 'spatial practice' of the first level (indeed, the confusion was Lefebvre's intention as he wanted space not to be conceptualized as static, but as a process). The confusion was also because the second and third space are both attributed as 'representations.' It is especially this duplication or bifurcation that can be used to have a different look at the medium in question: computer games.

Lefebvre and Space in Game Studies

In computer games studies, Lefebvre's approach has just been used shortly after Soja's reading in 1996: In a paper entitled *Allegories of Space*, which initially was published online, the Norwegian hypertext-theorist Espen Aarseth (1998) referred to Henri Lefebvre, which makes him first to mention the theory of spatial production regarding games. However, Aarseth's paper is not the first one to discuss games in terms of space: Just the year before, in 1997, the US-American film theorist Mark J.P. Wolf published an article on *Inventing Space*. This paper, four years later also published as a revised version, can be seen as the origin of the understanding of computer games in their spatiality, even though Wolf does not mention Lefebvre at all.

Inspired by formalistic film analysis – in the tradition of the so called Wisconsin School (Bordwell 1985) – Wolf (2001) refers to the opposition of space 'on screen' and space 'off screen', invented by Noël Burch (1981) in the 1960s: He in turn is following an idea introduced shortly before by André Bazin (1967, 166), who claimed that the "frame" of a painting "is centripetal, the screen centrifugal." Thus, Burch defined moving images not only by what is present to a spectator in the frame (*cadre*), but also to what is absent and lies outside the frame, by which its function turns into that of a cover (*cache*). The off screen-space(s) (fig. 2) is/are not identical with the space off stage in theater (the backstage and auditorium), but still belong(s) to the narrative or 'diegetic space' (Souriau 1951).

Fig. 2: Six 'off-screens'-spaces adjacent to the space on screen

However, in applying the dynamics of space 'on screen' and space 'off screen' to computer games, Wolf faces two problems, of which the second also is to be found in Aarseth's Lefebvrian approach. The first problem in Wolf's approach is the *difference between visibility and interactivity*: Computer games are not only 'representations' on the screen, but can be actively manipulated by the user. Due to the progress of computer graphics real-time rendering, it is hardly obvious nowadays that the possible manipulation of onscreen-representations matches the interactive space completely: Parts of the visible game-world might be interactive, but not everything that is digitally generated is a direct object of manipulation on the side of the user. This is more obvious in early games, like *Pong* (Atari 1972), in which the interactive onscreen-space is only a vertical line for each player, in which the representation of the ping-pong paddle on screen can only be moved up and down, but not sideways. (With the most popular phenomenon amongst this visual-interactive dissonance being the "invisible wall" [Juul 2005, 165].)

The other and for the debate at stake here more severe problem is Wolf's (1997, 11) use of the term 'representation,' in that he considers the "content" of games to be "largely representational." In line with most film-scholars anything happening on the screen is conceived of a repetition of something that has been present elsewhere (in physical space). When this understanding is applied to computer games, it leads to the almost instant conclusion that these representations lack a 'real' correspondent. Similar to films, in which the representation might have an actual basis – the actors, the stage etc. – but the fictional world itself does not exist other than in the film.

In this regard, a contradictive part in Wolf's is the passage, in which he identifies maps as a distinct spatial modality of computer games and does call them 'representations', too (ibid., 21). Thus, implicitly Wolf deals with two understandings of representation: a *first order representation* and a *second order representation*: The image on the screen and the map-mode within the game, representing the first one as an offscreen-depiction 'on screen'. Obviously both kinds of representations differ from each other different in an almost ontological way: The latter is a representation of the imaginary world, which itself would be a 'null'-representation.

Even though Wolf does not explicitly reflect on the deviating meanings of 'representation,' they hint at the two usages of the term 'representation' in Lefebvre's dialectics of space. Wolf's denomination of in-game maps as representations correlates with what Lefebvre calls 'representations of space' (on the imaginary level of production). A map (as second space) can represent a space of practice (as first space) and either help humans to orient themselves in the world or let them 'get a picture' of the space around them. On the contrary, what Wolf called 'representations' in the first place is exactly the space to which maps (in games) refer to: the first space of practice. This space rests upon the third or 'representational' space, but is not identical with it.

As opposed to Wolf, whose parallel to Lefebvre is not intentional, Espen Aarseth (2001a) in his text (published in print not until three years after its online-appearance) as well as in the simultaneous German translation (Aarseth 2001b), and as a later shortened version (Aarseth 2007), explicitly refers to Lefebvre, following the popular reading of the three spaces as firstly the physical, secondly the abstract and thirdly the social space. Aarseth hereby claims that the spatial practice in games – i.e. the first space as (simulated) *physical space* – derives from a relational space of navigation – i.e. the second space as (imaginary) *abstract space* – as well as from what Aarseth calls an 'aesthetic space' – i.e. the third space as (conventional) *symbolic space*.

At this point Aarseth's approach opens the possibility to also link the theory of computer games space with Ernst Cassirer's (1969) triad of 'mythic,' 'aesthetic' and 'theoretical space,' as the practical, the symbolic and the relational aspect of games (just as Lefebvre's original triad matches Jacques Lacan's [1978] psychoanalytic differentiation of 'real', 'imaginary', and 'symbolic'). Thus, according to Aarseth, games are allegorical representations of space; in other words: They are metaphors of space, and not space itself. 'Representation' hereby again (just like in Wolf) means an incomplete copy or an ontologically deviant 'image' of the real world. It is 'only' a representation; and games can never depict space as it is perceived fully as it exists 'in real life.'

Since Aarseth's article on game space, Lefebvre's triad of space has been used quite a lot in game studies, notably without following Aarseth's interpretation: The first case is a paper on *Virtual Real(i)ties* that was presented for the first time on a conference in 2001 by Shawn Miklaucic (2006), who discusses *SimCity* (Maxis Software 1989) in quite a negative way as an example for a second space, i.e. as an abstract space or the representation of space. In his view the representation dominates the first as well as the third space likewise: To him there is no 'lived' (or perceived) space in *SimCity* to be found, but only its (cartographic) representation. Miklaucic hereby faces a similar problem that Wolf does when talking about 'representations' and uses the term for in-game representations and the reference of the image alike. Furthermore, Miklaucic does not seem to be aware of the fact that in *SimCity* the first space is not a map at all, even though the game world is visible in a top-down view. A map does occur in the game, too, but only as a miniature that represents the frame or cover of the first space, that is: the border between on- and offscreen space. On the contrary, the primary view is the first space of the game – the lived space of *SimCity*.

A second example is Axel Stockburger's Dissertation (2006) on *The Rendered Arena*, in which the three modalities of space are used to differentiate between the first space of the physical medium of the game device(s), the second space as the narrative as well as rule-based representations of space on the computer-screen, and the third space as the realm, constituted by the players' kinesthetic actions. An aspect that is affirmed more and more by recent approaches due to the success of alternative motion control devices, e.g. Kinect, and consoles, e.g. Wii (Juul 2009).

Another author using Lefebvre's schema in a similar way is Michael Nitsche in his book on *Video Game Spaces* from 2008: Just like to Stockburger two years before him the representation of space to Nitsche is the visible space on screen as second space. However, Nitsche separates the rule-based space – which Stockburger includes in the second space – and identifies it with the first space as the set of rules underlying secondary visual space. 'Representation' thus is understood as the visualization of otherwise invisible space. Like Aarseth, Nitsche takes into consideration the dialectic of aesthetics and knowledge (symbolic space and relational space in Aarseth), or fiction and rules (in Juul), from which the spatial constitution of a particular game arises. And like Stockburger, Nitsche (2008, 16) also incorporates the aspect of the social as a third space and claims that the 'third-space' is the "combination of fictional, play, and social spaces".

As can be seen from these examples Lefebvre's triad of space is a very stimulating heuristic model for a rich description of computer games (not to speak of the possibility to easily apply Lefebvre to his original subject-matter: the urban space which now is pervaded by the virtual game space). Nevertheless, the following tries to offer another reading of Lefebvre in regard to computer game spaces, which is quite different to the ones mentioned above: *games as spatial concepts*.

Representation as Denotation and Representation as Exemplification

To do so, a closer look at what a 'representation' is (or could) be, must be taken: Besides its *ideological* meaning, in which a representation is always suppressive and dogmatic, and also besides the *ontological* understanding of representation as something that lacks reality or materiality, representation has a *semiotic* dimension. Indeed, Lefebvre himself, as indicated earlier, seems to have all three dimensions in mind, when he does not only refer to a *phenomenological dialectics* (in respect to the ontologies of space: perceived, conceived, and lived) and an *ideological dialectics* (in respect to the ways of social reproduction: biology, knowledge, and culture), but also to a *semiotic dialectics*: with respect to the first space where the lived, cultural space feeds back into the individual perceived space, Lefebvre refers to it as the realm of 'performance', i.e. where meaning is acted out. This idea originally invented by John L. Austin (1975), who insisted on differentiating between 'performatives' and 'constatives', or the *how* something is said and *what* is being said (as the content of an utterance).

Thus, the relation between the first and second space in respect to semiotics could be understood as Nitsche does: as the dialectics between the (rule-based) performance and the (onscreen) representation. Still, the question remains, what then is the difference between a representation in the second space and a representation in the third space if not understood ideologically or ontologically? Semiotically one could argue for two ways of representation. A whole book has been devoted to the problem of representation by Nelson Goodman, who in *Languages of Art* from 1968 tried to outline a semiotic approach that avoids any ontological understanding of sings. By this, images as 'mere representations' are no longer considered to 'lack reality'.

Goodman (1976, 52-57) distinguishes between representation as 'denotation' and representation as 'exemplification', being the two ways of using a sign in specific contexts: When *denotating* something, what is used to refer to an object or the 'content' of the sign, has not to be like what is referred to in respect to its appearance. For example, most words humans use to designate have nothing in common with the referred object. There are some onomatopoetic words which might resemble an object or an aspect of it: like sounds of animals used as common nouns for the species in question. But those examples are rare; most words are symbolic in the sense that they have nothing in common with the object and thus are also not lacking its ontological status.

Another way of representation, i.e. to represent something is *exemplification*. In the act of exemplification something is used to refer to something that shares the same properties; or some of them that are relevant for the context of the act of reference. For example, when going to a hardware store, because running out of nails, one might ask for a certain type by naming them properly, this would still be an act of denotation; but if one has forgotten about the name or type, one could just show a remaining nail and ask the salesperson to hand out a(nother) package 'of those.'

Speaking in terms of diagrammatic topology, the nail presented as a sign for other nails belongs to set of objects that share properties like size or hardness, whereas they might vary in other respect from each other, concerning color or brand. Thus, a denotation is an *asymmetrical* representation (the signifier does not share the properties of the signified), and an exemplification is a *symmetrical* representation (the signifier does share the properties of the signified).

One could even say that the difference between denotation and exemplification is the pragmatic reformulation of the (ontological) difference between a sign and an image, or the semiotic (and also ontological) difference between an index and an icon: An exemplification is an image or an iconic sign insofar as it is (used) 'auto-referential(ly)' and is presented due to aspects of its appearance; a denotation is a sign or an index insofar it is used to refer to something else than what is. The symbol (as a possible act of representation) according to Goodman then is the set of all 'iconic' images (exemplifications/symmetrical) and 'indexical' signs (denotations/asymmetrical).

Poetics and Iconology of Space

With Goodman it is possible to look at computer games differently and not only conceive of them as allegories of physical space (or 'metaphors' only), which – as asymmetrical representations in the sense of denotations – do lack the 'real-being' of space, but that are symmetrical representations of theories of space, i.e. *the game exemplifying a spatial concept*. And with Lefebvre, this means taking into consideration representations of space as conceived not only as representations of physical space as perceived, but also as representations in relation to 'thirdspaces', i.e. the culturally produced space, that in which symmetrical and asymmetrical representations together constitute the 'symbolic' space, which is lived.

Gaston Bachelard, in *The Poetics of Space* from 1957, had quite a similar project to Lefebvre almost two decades later, only Bachelard starts off with the spaces produced on the cultural level, especially those described by literature (directly or structurally). To Bachelard it is also due to this poetic spatiality that new spaces are produced at all and different perceptions of space are envisaged actively. According to Bachelard (1994), modern poets are especially aware of this power and produce alternative spaces to those inherited by the tradition. (For instance, he speaks of 'spirals' that Henri Michaux and others oppose to common literary images of rooms as container-spaces.)

Thus, philosophies of space are – in Lefebvre's schema – not only located on the conceptual level, like Geography and Physics as sciences of space, but are already the transition or from second to third space or do define the dialectics in between representations of space and spaces of representation. With Goodman a philosophy of space may exemplify a contemporary conceptualization of space, which the same time denotates (and likewise produces) physical space. Philosophical concepts of space then are not about a 'true' or 'false' *representation of nature*, but are the *expression of culture*.

This is an approach that has also been claimed by iconology, namely by Erwin Panofsky (1955), in the early twentieth century: They only called the difference between denotation and exemplification that of *iconography* (what is shown in a picture) and *iconology* (how it is shown in a picture). If philosophies are understood in the latter way as a structural resemblance of scientific conceptualizations, they offer a much deeper insight into cultural processes than they do on the level of their own argumentation. One of the first to look at philosophies that way was Michel Foucault; he conceived of philosophical concepts as diagrams, as identical in their structure to the cultural space of an epoch (Deleuze 1999). In fact, as another form of the sign, the diagram was already considered by Peirce: Something is a diagram when it is used as an iconic sign, not by resembling the appearance or visible Gestalt, but the structure or internal relation; or in Lefebvre: Something that is (used as) an image on the level of the first space is looked upon in cultural studies of thirdspaces as a diagram.

In the light of a diagrammatic reading René Descartes' (1996) dualistic ontology then is less relevant in respect to what is being said (on the performative level of a described first space) about the ego and the reflections about whether god exists or not, but how the Cartesian ontology resembles or exemplifies (on the structural level of an implied third space) the configuration of the classical era, which is characterized by a separation of reason and madness (Foucault 1965). This spatial separation is the same time present as madhouses, pestilence-colonies, hospital or prisons and structurally as the claimed separation between the *res cogitans* and *res extensa*, with the first being an intelligible non-space and the latter being the realm of pure matter. Following up this diagnosis, to Foucault (1989, 3-18) Diego Velazquez' painting *Las Meninas* then is a representational space *par excellence* as it does not only exemplify a certain ontology of space, but the same time expresses the transition from one cultural space (the classical age of representation itself or dualisms in general) to another (the modern age of the human sciences and transcendental structures).

Games as Spatial Concepts

All in all, the proposal now is to look at computer games not necessarily as a critique of our epoch and its understanding of space, which indeed could be done. Understandings of *Tetris* (Pajitnov 1984), like Janet Murray's (1997, 144) reading, which conceive of it as a (critical) resemblance of contemporary capitalism, do work that way. But computer games could be attempted to be understood as exemplifications of spatial concepts, i.e. symmetrical representations of asymmetrical denotations or, in short, as thirdspaces or representational spaces. Computer games then are not conceived of as designating a certain space or place, but as demonstrating how a certain (historically contingent) truth of space can look like. So it is not the *what?* of space or the *where?* of place, but the *how?* of space; or its 'likeness'.

The task for an interpretation of games as representational spaces therefore is to use spatial theory for analyzing games, insofar as they express or enact spatial concepts as well as possibly contradict them. Jon Cogburn and Mark Silcox (2009, 20-21) in their book on *Philosophy through Video Games* included a chapter discussing the success of Nintendo's Wii-console from 2006 in contrast to Microsoft's Xbox 360 and Sony's PlayStation 3. They apply a similar idea to the one presented here, when they argue that very few people predicted the success of the Wii because nearly everybody's view of the human-computer interface presupposed the truth of *phenomenalism*. According to this philosophical theory, people do not directly perceive the actual world, but instead experience a realm that is a function of their own private sensory manifolds. [...] By contrast, *enactivist* theories of perception hold that human beings do directly perceive the world. According to enactivism, this direct perception is a function of the way we physically manipulate ourselves and our environments. Unlike phenomenalism, enactivism provides a compelling explanation of why Wii game-play is more realistic.

Even though the final claim of 'realism' should be doubted in the long run, Cogburn and Silcox propose the possibility that already on the level of the hardware different exemplifications of philosophical world-views are to be found: rationalistic dualism (in the style of Descartes) and embodiment (as it was brought forth by Phenomenology in the early twentieth century).

'Tetris' as Topic Space

From the Greek classical antique until the middle-ages prevailed a negative concept of space (in the modern sense). Such conceptualizations have been since characterized as resting upon a *horror vacui*, when experimental demonstrations of an empty space as 'vacuum' had been carried out in the seventeenth century by Blaise Pascal or Otto von Guericke (Grant 1981). The dominant spatial concept of antiquity rested upon the idea that the divinity of the cosmos does not allow for space to be empty ('without god'). Even though there were concepts like the Platonic *chora* (which originally designated the acre outside the city-walls), which could be understood as 'open space' or 'absolute space', this basically is a modern projection of Newton's physics onto ancient concepts (Derrida 1997). The dominant interpretation of physics can be found in Aristotle's *Physics*, where he assumes that every object has its own place (*topos*), i.e. the object occupies 'a space'; from which derives the belief, that – as there is no empty space – even air and other natural media are objects or elements (Algra 1995).

However, those topoi are not part of a greater space as an encompassing *topos* that would be prior to the objects, as Plato suggested, but that all places are 'attached' to things. In this perspective one could conceive of the game *Tetris* as an exemplification of topic space as well as of the related *horror vacui*: Even though there is something like an 'empty' space, in which things seem to move freely, that space is defined only by the shape of the objects themselves that do block out space occupied by 'air'. Each possible location is already defined and there is no way to have the tetraminos 'placed' other than in these *topoi* (fig. 3).

Fig. 3: Aristotelian space in Tetris

Even though it looks like they would fall due the force of gravitation, once they are placed, they do not move anymore, even when they would naturally fall over. In the light of the exemplification of a spatial concept, the variation *Not Tetris* (Staby-ourself 2010) then demonstrates, how *Tetris* would perform when it is an exemplification of Newtonian space (fig. 4): Blocks have no predefined places, but fall over due to gravitation. – Thus, the possible variations of the gameplay of *Tetris* is to try to enforce the modern understanding of space against the ancient.

Fig. 4: Newtonian space in Not Tetris

'Advent' as Relational Space

In difference to the topic space of the antique physics the relational space is a topological concept that stems from graph-theory, which dates to the early eighteenth century, namely the Russian-Swiss mathematician Leonhard Euler, who himself used games like chess to raise mathematical problems. In case of chess: how to calculate the possible moves with the knight and touch every square on the board, but all of them only once. Another game Euler (1995) discussed is 'Seven Bridges of Königsberg', in which the quest was to cross all seven bridges of the capital city of Eastern Prussia over the river Pregel and return to the starting point without using one of them twice, but using *all of them once*. As Euler demonstrated (fig. 5), this is impossible due to the situation of the bridges. He gave a proof for the impossibility by reducing the topography of the city's inner island, the canals and shores to a pure space or relations of points, i.e. a topological net, system or labyrinth. For such a labyrinth to be 'unicursal' always two connections (or edge) are necessary between every knot (or vertex) of the graph to constitute a walk in which a return to the starting point is possible.

Fig. 5: Euler's topological drawing of the seven bridges of Königsberg across the river Pregel

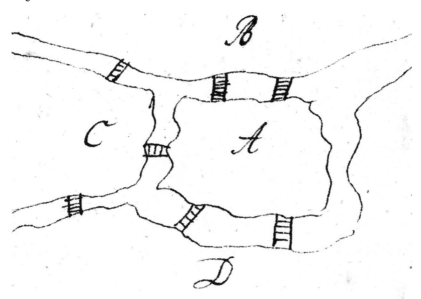

Even though there is a digital game about *The Seven Bridges of Königsberg* (Grossbart 2015) that reenacts as well as varies the mathematical problem, there have been other ones earlier that already exemplified its specific spatial task: *Adventure* (Crowther/Woods 1976) and the successor *Zork* (Infocom 1980) as well as other 'text-only' adventure games do exemplify a relational space in which the task is not only to find the way to the final knot, but to also find the most efficient walk between the starting point and the ending point (as this is what is counted by the game in order for the users to compete). In fact, Newtonian space is present in *Zork* (fig. 6) as the illusion of a world, too, but mainly on the side of the pre-given descriptions and not on the side of players' actions, who can mainly give topological orders like typing "n" for 'going north'.

Fig. 6: A fan's drawing of Zork's topological space

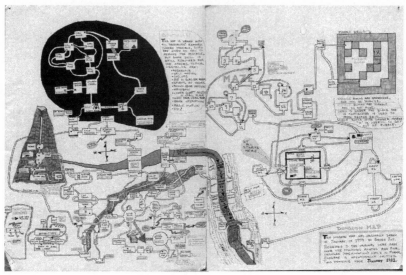

'Portal' as Curved Space

Closely linked to the concept of relational space in mathematics is the physical idea of curvature, which was considered in theories of relativity in the twentieth century and initiated by nineteenth-century Non-Euclidian geometry: As the assumption of parallels in Euclidean space could not be proven, a need for an alternative geometry gave rise to new concepts of space: Whereas for Euclid a plane was defined as the (nonspatial) surface of an object, Carl Friedrich Gauss (2005) defined a plane as a spatial object that could be curved, i.e. be in itself three dimensional (with a 'flat plane' being the special case). Applied to three-dimensional object-space itself, this means that it could be conceived of as curved within the fourth dimension (fig. 7).

Fig. 7: Curved (outer) space with portal or 'wormhole'

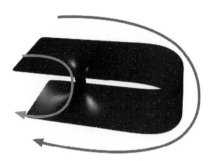

But as opposed to the curvature of the plane in three dimensions the curving of space itself cannot be perceived by humans, but becomes an object of speculation (Henderson 2013). Since Edwin A. Abbotts novel *Flatland* from 1882 artists as well as scientists were looking for a demonstration of four-dimensional space – not to be confused with the problem of time being an additional dimension of space, hence spacetime. One way to demonstrate this is to show the consequences of the folding or bending of space and not the curvature as such. This is exactly the situation in *Portal* (Valve Software 2007), where three-dimensional space is (hypothetically) folded back onto itself, without giving the visual impression of a curvature (fig. 8).

Fig. 8: Portals in Portal

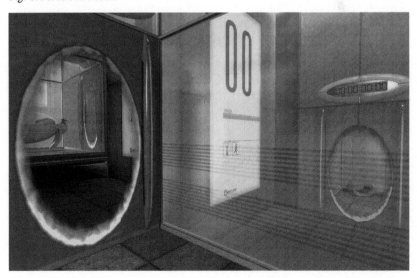

'Mirror's Edge' as Hodological Space

According to the 'topological' approach of the German psychologist Kurt Lewin (1936) Euclidian space hardly ever can be experienced by human beings, since (built) physical space never allows for following a straight line from 'A' to 'B'. Instead the human 'life-space' (*Lebensraum*) is constituted by several paths (gr. *hodos*) through space. Just before seeking exile in the United States, Lewin coined a term that never reappeared in his later English publications: 'hodological space'. To Lewin (1934) it is defined by directions within a given 'field', defining accessible and inaccessible areas (fig. 9).

Fig. 9: Structure of a hodological space according to Kurt Lewin

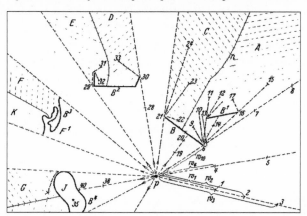

Without referring to Lewin, Espen Aarseth (1997, 1) in his book on *Cybertext* fosters a similar understanding in order to substitute the notion of digital games and similar phenomena, usually addressed as a given 'text' with the notion of dynamic literature:

During the cybertextual process, the user will have effectuated a semiotic sequence, and this selective movement is a work of physical construction that the various concepts of 'reading' do not account for. This phenomenon I call ergodic, using a term appropriated from physics that derives from the Greek words *ergon* and *hodos*, meaning 'work' and 'path.' In ergodic literature, nontrivial effort is required to allow the reader to traverse the text.

Just like Aarseth, Lewin is interested in the actual engagement with space, yet he wants to focus on the spatial result itself as the constitution of an 'environmental psyche', less on the concrete, single and more or less random path, taken within a game. Lewin's (and Aarseth's) understanding of space seems relevant to almost all – at least action based – games, yet, there are games that do make use of the 'hodos' in particular. In difference to strictly topological game-spaces (like in text-based adventure games) the way as a certain kind of space 'in use' can be found in games that deliberately refer to the spatial practice of Parkour or Freerunning. One of the first and the most prominent example is *Mirror's Edge* (DICE 2008).

Fig. 10: Following the marked path in Mirror's Edge

In this game the path literally is 'the goal' since the foremost task of the game is to master the untypical control of the avatar, running up walls of jumping over cliffs between skyscrapers in the city's space (fig. 10). Therefore, within the game the path is marked red to show the user the ideal course. At this point, Lewin's original idea is even turned upside down, since it can be considered an approach to Euclidian space, constituted by the shortest line between starting- and endpoint. But this is not a contradiction at all: Euclidian space is the special case of hodological space, in which the straight line becomes the actual path. In his respect, it can be argued that *Mirror's Edge* is a decent simulation of actual Parkour (invented by the French soldier Raymond Belle and his son David in the 1980s), since its spatial practice also aims at using the shortest way possible between two given locations. – In the terms of Michael de Certeau's (1988, 100 and 117) seminal study on *The Practice of Everyday Life* freerunning(-simulations) can be considered the spatial practice *par excellence*:

There is a rhetoric of walking. The art of 'turning' phrases finds an equivalent in an art of composing a path (*tourner un parcours*). Like ordinary language; this art implies and combines styles and uses. [...] In short, *space is a practiced place*. Thus the street geometrically defined by urban planning is transformed into a space by walkers. In the same way, an act of reading is the space produced by the practice of a particular place [...].

'Assassins' Creed' as Horizonal Space

Before Lewin introduced his idea of hodology he in 1917 wrote a piece during his time at a military hospital, where he stayed due to an injury from a battle in the First World War. The text is titled *The Landscape of War* and is a quite irritating piece of phenomenological reflection on space. The disturbing aspect of the text is that Lewin (2009) does not address any of the cruelties happening in war, but tires to bring forth a 'neutral' understanding of spatial modalities. In particular, he differentiates between the spatial experience of a landscape in times of peace and in times of war. When in combat, space appears to have certain 'directions.' especially those of the 'front' and the 'back.' The front is, where the enemy is located, the back is where you can seek shelter within friendly troops. Quite commonly this early text is considered to be the earliest conceptualization of hodological space, yet with an interesting difference: Looking at the later concept from this early idea, the hodological structure of space would call for the absence of peace or: using space hodological is like being at war.

A peaceful space to Lewin on the contrary is a space in which all directions are equal, and the spectator is located in the center of the space from which the surroundings are contemplated. Instead of a designated 'front' the landscape at peace appears to have an 'horizon'. Whereas directed spaces can be found in a lot of computer games, most likely in first-person shooter, 'horizonal' spaces are quite uncommon. Nevertheless, there are some instances, in which space is structured a-directional. One example are instances in *Assassin's Creed* (Ubisoft Montreal 2007) when Desmond Miles climbs a tower in the city. When reaching the top, the virtual camera starts rotating around the character (fig. 11).

Fig. 11: Roofing in Assassin's Creed

Even though, *Assassin's Creed* is another example for a freerunning-simulator at this very moment it becomes another game(-space); comparable to the practice of 'roof(topp)ing', which presumably originates in Russia. Other than Parkour this method does not aim at 'practicing place', but – to rephrase de Certeau – at 'practicing space'. Roof(topp)ers do not look for the shortest connection between two given locations in the urban space, but at an experience of space as a totality.

'Doom' as Threshold-Space

As already mentioned, the directed space (of the war landscape) is the structural significance of basically all first-person shooters. But to some games of this genre there is another aspect even more typical: the threshold. As a spatial concept it was described already in 1909 by the French ethnologist Arnold van Gennep in *The Rites of Passage*. In his research van Gennep discovered a kind of constant in all human cultures: the crossing of a passage, accompanied by certain 'rites' (as the title of his book explains). Throughout history the passages become more 'metaphorical' and disconnected from their original location. The most prominent example being the rite to carry the bride over the threshold of the main entrance in the husband's home. The threshold, however, is a marker for a state of being 'in between,' especially between two countries 'on the border.' Such "zones of indiscernibility" (Deleuze/Guattari 1987, 101) used to be extended spaces in themselves, when borders where not yet marked with walls or fences. As van Gennep (1960, 19) puts it: "The neutral zone shrinks progressively till it ceases to exist except as a simple stone, a beam, or a threshold."

Fig. 12: Doom 3

Doors and other kinds of spatial (dis-)connections are to be found throughout the history of computer games (Wolf 2011). The spatial experience of a threshold, however, is very prominent in computer games that rely on scripted events. Being the embodiment of the whole genre, the *Doom*-series particularly is a paradigmatic exemplification of the threshold-structure of space, with *Doom 3* (id Software 2004) being the first one to include also (scripted) story-elements that were located specifically at passages. In most cases the threshold is marked by a door(step), which to cross is activating the combatants on the other side. In most cases the door then gets blocked and the reverse movement is impossible (fig. 12) (just as it is the case with ritual crossings into the next 'state of being').

'Ghost Recon' as Intentional Space

Speaking of first-person shooters one could argue that already before the emergence of computer games the subjective perspective as the typical European mode of depiction in art since the Renaissance (Kemp 1990) is an exemplification of what towards the end of the 19th century has been called 'intentionality'; namely the directedness toward the object, by which the distortion of pictorial space is in compliance with. The main protagonists of this approach to space as a foremost perceptional being can be found in the Phenomenological movement and its leading figure Edmund Husserl. From his teacher Franz Brentano Husserl (1999) adopted the idea that the way things are perceived differs from the way they are in the physical world. Under the premise of perception being only accessible to the subject, Brentano (1973, 102) names the *"intentional in-existence* [...] a distinguishing characteristic of all mental phenomena"*, with intentionality being defined as "the reference to something as an object" (ibid.). This means, that to Phenomenology consciousness is structures as an orientation towards a thing immanent to perception. The most famous illustration of that insight was drawn by Ernst Mach (1914, 18-19) shortly after Brentano, alongside a corresponding description:

Fig. 13: Ernst Mach's first person-point of view

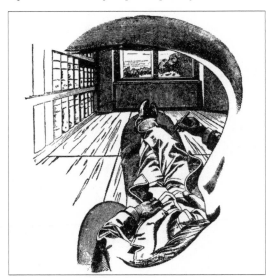

My body differs from other human bodies beyond the fact that every intense motor idea is immediately expressed by a movement of it, and that, if it is touched, more striking changes are determined than if other bodies are touched by the circumstance, that it is only seen piecemeal, and, especially, is seen without a head.

Mach's image entails an important hint on a strange doubling that appears in many – if not most – visualization of the first person's point of view: Like in a regular first-person shooter in Mach's drawing it is the central item in the hand of the ego: Mach holding a pencil or the shooter holding a gun. This common, yet disturbing inconsistency lies in the duplication of the object being an object (or 'content') of perception, but at the same time its precondition. In the case of Mach's drawing the right hand is holding a pen that seems to be drawing exactly the image one looks at (being Mach's point of view), but the paper on which the image is drawn is not visible in the image, other than being the background of the drawing itself (by which the pen would need to be between the viewer and the head of Mach).

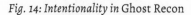

Fig. 14: Intentionality in Ghost Recon

The same applies to first-person shooters, which usually exemplify depict a hand with a gun, whereby the same time the image itself is the view through the gun or the gun's crosshair (by which the gun itself would not be visible). Henry Jenkins and Kurt Squire (2002, 65) therefore describe the first-person view in shooter games as the "through-the-gunsight perspective". The – almost – consistent depiction of the subjective view being intentionally related to the object in sight (and not to the seeing subject) can be found in the sub-genre of sniper-games or in tactical first-person shooters like *Tom Clancy's Ghost Recon* (Red Storm Entertainment 2001), where the seeing ego itself is not its on (intentional) object of perception (fig. 14); the only, typically (Galloway 2012), contradicting moments being the elements of the interface, like the mini-map and the health-bar.

'Max Payne' as Heautoscopic Space

The contradictions to the interface as well as the paradox of the hand can be subsumed under what in narratology, following Gerard Genette, is called "metalepsis" (Galloway 2006, 34). However, it is not the traditional kind of metalepsis that can be found in novels, theatre or movies, when a protagonist addresses the audience directly by breaking the 'fourth wall' – even though this phenomenon occurs in computer, too, like for example in *Zork*, when the user is addressed directly as 'you,' whereby he or she is telling the avatar the same time to do something as a disjunct person (Neitzel 2008). In computer games as exemplifications of spatial concepts the metalepsis occurs in particular as the disjunction of the point of view, of the user or the image per se, and the *"point of action"* (Neitzel 2005, 238), of the avatar controlled by the user.

This is the case in most of the so-called 'third-person shooter,' which attribution actually is misleading: The particularity of this genre is not the third-person view as such – something that is the case in platformers, when controlling a character like Mario – but the mix of a first-person experience with a "following camera" (Nitsche 2008, 96). This mix usually is not witnessed as a disjunction, but can occur as a disturbance, when the character is injured or intoxicated and not only the avatar on screen is tainted in blood of moves strangely, but also the screen turns red or becomes blurred. One of the games, where the effect (fig. 15a-b) can be found is *Max Payne 2: The Fall of Max Payne* (Remedy Entertainment 2003).

Fig. 15a-b: Heautoscopis space in Max Payne 2

Without being mentally deranged, users of games here can look at the possibility of a psychopathological experience that Karl Jaspers (1997, 92) addresses as "heautoscopy": in difference to regular autoscopy the patient hereby does not only view him- or her-self from outside (as looking at another person), but still has the bodily sensations of the first person (especially pain). This worst of all out-of-body- or *Doppelgänger*-phenomena is neither caused by this kind of games, nor can it fully be simulated. Nevertheless, it exemplifies the typical – schizoid – spatial structure of this form of perception.

In regards of the history of philosophy it can further on be observed that this kind of splitting of the self is a concept that occurred in the epistemology of the 18th century, namely in Immanuel Kant, who thinks of the subject as a, as Michel Foucault (1989, 347) put it frankly, "empirico-transcendental doublet": Just like the hand of Mach's ego or the gun of the shooter is content and precondition of the spatial representation the same time, the subject here is the (empirical) matter of experience and the same time the (transcendental) precondition of perception as such. Again, this is neither a claim for Kant's concept of the self being true for all human beings or being true only for psychopathologies, it only is claimed that computer games can exemplify philosophical concepts – maybe more accurate than any other medium.

References

Aarseth, Espen J. (1997): *Cybertext: Perspectives on Ergodic Literature*, Baltimore, MD/London: Johns Hopkins UP.

– – – – (1998): Allegories of Space: The Question of Spatiality in Computer Games, web.archive.org/web/20080430070251/http://www.hf.uib.no/hi/espen/pap ers/space/Default.html.

– – – – (2001a): Allegories of Space: The Question of Spatiality in Computer Games, in: *Cybertext Yearbook 2000*, ed. by Markku Eskelinen and Raine Koskimaa, Jyväskylä: Research Centre for Contemporary Culture, 152-171.

– – – – (2001b): Allegorien des Raums: Räumlichkeit in Computerspielen, in: *Zeitschrift für Semiotik* 23/1, 301-318.

– – – – (2007): Allegories of Space: The Question of Spatiality in Computer Games, in: *Space Time Play: Games, Architecture, and Urbanism – The Next Level*, ed. by Friedrich von Borries, Steffen P. Walz and Matthias Böttger, Basel/Boston, MA/Berlin: Birkhäuser, 44-47.

Algra, Keimpe (1995): *Concepts of Space in Greek Thought*, Leiden/New York, NY/ Cologne: Brill 1995.

Austin, John L. (²1975): *How to Do Things with Words*, Cambridge, MA: Harvard UP [1962].

Atari (1972): *Pong*, Arcade: Atari.

– – – – (1979): *Asteroids*, Arcade: Atari.

Bachelard, Gaston (1994): *The Poetics of Space*, Boston, MA: Beacon [1958].

Bazin, André (1967): Painting and Cinema, in: id.: *What is Cinema?*, Vol. 1, Berkeley, CA/Los Angeles, CA/London: University of California Press, 164-169 [1959].

Bhabha, Homi (1990): The Third Space: Interview, in: *Identity: Community, Culture, Difference*, ed. by Jonathan Rutherford, London: Lawrence & Wishart, 207-221.

Bordwell, David (1985): Space in the Classical Film, in: id., Janet Staiger and Kristin Thompson: *The Classical Hollywood Cinema. Film Style and Mode of Production to 1960*, London: Routledge, 50-59.

Brentano, Franz (1973): *Psychology from an Empirical Standpoint*, London: Routledge & Kegan Paul [1874].

Burch, Noël (1981): *Nana*, or the Two Kinds of Space, in: id.: *Theory of Film Practice*, Princeton, NJ: Princeton UP, 17-31 [1961].

Cassirer, Ernst (1969): Mythic, Aesthetic, and Theoretical Space, in: *Man and World* 2/1, 3-17 [1931].

de Certeau, Michel (1988): *The Practice of Everyday Life*, Berkeley, CA/Los Angeles, CA/London: University of California Press [1980].

Cogburn, Jon/Silcox, Mark (2009): *Philosophy through Video Games*, New York, NY/London: Routledge.

Crowther, William/Woods, Don (1976): *Colossal Cave Adventure*, PDP-10: Crowther/Woods.

Deleuze, Gilles (1999): Topology: 'Thinking Otherwise', in: id., *Foucault*, London: Athlone, 45-123 [1986].

—–—/Guattari, Felix (1987): *A Thousand Plateaus: Capitalism and Schizophrenia*, Minneapolis, MN: University of Minnesota Press [1980].

Derrida, Jacques (1997): Chora, in: *Chora L Works. Jacques Derrida and Peter Eisenman*, ed. by Jeffery Kipnis and Thomas Leeser, New York, NY: Monacelli Press, 15-32 [1987].

Descartes, René (1996): *Meditations on First Philosophy: With Selections from the Objections and Replies*, Cambridge: Cambridge UP [1641].

DICE (2008): *Mirror's Edge*, Xbox 360: Electronic Arts.

Elden, Stuart (2004): *Understanding Henri Lefebvre: Theory and the Possible*, New York, NY/London: Continuum.

Euler, Leonhard (1995): From the Problem of the Seven Bridges of Königsberg, in: *Classics of Mathematics*, ed. by Ronald Calinger, Englewood Cliffs, NJ: Prentice Hall, 503-506 [1736].

Foucault, Michel (1965): *Madness and Civilization: A History of Insanity in the Age of Reason*, New York, NY: Pantheon Books [1961].

—–— (1977): *Discipline and Punish: The Birth of the Prison*, New York, NY: Vintage Books [1975].

—–— (1989): *The Order of Things: An Archaeology of the Human Sciences*, London/New York, NY: Routledge [1966].

—–— (1998): Different Spaces, in: *Essential Works of Foucault 1954-1984*, Vol. 2: *Aesthetics, Method, and Epistemology*, ed. by James D. Faubion, New York: New Press, 175-185 [1984].

Frege, Gottlob (1956): The Thought: A Logic Inquiry, in: *Mind* 65/259, 289-311 [1918]

—–— (^{2}1960): On Sense and Reference, in: *Translations from the Philosophical Writings of Gottlob Frege*, ed. by Peter Geach and Max Black, Oxford: Blackwell, 56-78 [1892]

Galloway, Alexander R. (2006): Gamic Action, Four Moments, in: id.: *Gaming. Essays on Algorithmic Culture*, Minneapolis, MN/London: University of Minnesota Press, 1-38.

—–— (2012): The Unworkable Interface, in: id.: *The Interface Effect*, Cambridge/Malden, MA: Polity Press, 1-53 [2010].

Gauss, Karl Friedrich (2005): *General Investigations of Curved Surfaces*, Mineola, NY: Dover Publications [1827].

van Gennep, Arnold (1960): *The Rites of Passage*, Chicago, IL: University of Chicago Press [1909].

Goodman, Nelson ([2]1976): *Languages of Art: An Approach to a Theory of Symbols*, Indianapolis, IN: Hackett [1968].

Grant, Edward (1981): *Much Ado about Nothing: Theories of Space and Vacuum from the Middle Ages to the Scientific Revolution*, New York, NY: Cambridge UP.

Grossbart, Zack (2015): *The Seven Bridges of Königsberg*, iOS: Iapps Technology.

Günzel, Stephan (2010): The Spatial Turn in Computer Game Studies, in: *Exploring the Edges of Gaming: Proceedings of the Vienna Games Conference 2008-2009 – Future and Reality of Gaming*, ed. by Konstantin Mitgutsch, Christoph Klimmt and Herbert Rosenstingl, Vienna: Braumüller, 147-156.

Henderson, Linda Dalrymple ([2]2013): *The Fourth Dimension and Non-Euclidian Geometry in Modern Art*, Cambridge, MA/London: MIT Press [1983].

Husserl, Edmund (1999): *The Idea of Phenomenology*, Dordrecht/Bosten, MA/London: Kluwer [1950].

id Software (2004): *Doom 3*, PC: Activison.

Infocom (1980): *Zork*, PC: Infocom.

Jameson, Frederic (1984): Postmodernism, or The Logic of Late Capitalism, in: *New Left Review* 146, 53-92.

– – – – (1998): *The Cultural Turn: Selected Writings on the Postmodern 1983-1998*, London/New York, NY: Verso.

Jaspers, Karl (1997): *General Psychopathology*, Vol. 1, Baltimore, MD/London: Johns Hopkins UP [1913].

Jenkins, Henry/Squire, Kurt (2002): The Art of Contested Spaces, in: *Game On: The History and Culture of Videogames*, ed. by Lucien King, London: King, 64-75.

Juul, Jesper (2005): *Half-Real: Video Games between Real Rules and Fictional Worlds*, Cambridge, MA/London: MIT Press.

– – – – (2009): *A Casual Revolution: Reinventing Video Games and Their Players*, Cambridge, MA/London: MIT Press.

Kemp, Martin (1990): *The Science of Art: Optical Themes in Western Art from Brunelleschi to Seurat*, New Haven, CT/London: Yale UP.

Lacan, Jacques (1978): *The Four Fundamental Concepts of Psychoanalysis*, New York, NY: Norton [1973].

Lefebvre, Henri (1991): *The Production of Space*, Oxford/Cambridge, MA: Blackwell [1974].

Lewin, Kurt (1934): Der Richtungsbegriff in der Psychologie: Der spezielle und allgemeine hodologische Raum, in: *Psychologische Forschung* 19/3-4, 249-299.

– – – – (1936): *Principles of Topological Psychology*, New York, NY/London: McGraw Hill.

– – – – (2009): The Landscape of War, in: *Art in Translation* 1/2, 199-209 [1917].

Mach, Ernst (1914): *The Analysis of Sensations and the Relation of the Physical to the Psychical*, Chicago, IL/London: Open Court [1886].

Maxis (1989): *SimCity*, PC: Maxis.

Miklaucic, Shawn (2006): Virtual Real(i)ty: SimCity and the Production of Urban Cyberspace, in: *Game Research: The Art, Business and Science of Computer Games*, game-research.com/index.php/articles/virtual-reality-simcity-and-the-pro duction-of-urban-cyberspace.

Murray, Janet H. (1997): *Hamlet on the Holodeck: The Future of Narrative in Cyberspace*, New York, NY et al.: Free Press.

Neitzel, Britta (2005): Narrativity in Computer Games, in: *Handbook of Computer Game Studies*, ed. by Joost Raessens and Jeffrey Goldstein, Cambridge, MA/ London: MIT Press, 227-245.

———— (2008): Metacommunicative Circles, in: *Conference Proceedings of the Philosophy of Computer Games 2008*, ed. by Stephan Günzel, Michael Liebe and Dieter Mersch, Potsdam: Potsdam UP, 279-294.

Nitsche, Michael (2008): *Video Game Spaces: Image, Play, and Structure in 3D Games Worlds*, Cambridge, MA/London: MIT Press.

Panofsky, Erwin (1955): Iconography and Iconology: An Introduction to the Study of Renaissance Art, in: id.: *Meaning in the Visual Arts: Papers in and on Art History*, Garden City, NY: Doubleday, 26-54 [1939].

Pajitnov, Alexey (1984): *Tetris*, Electronica 60: Pajitnov.

Peirce, Charles S. (1984): On a New List of Categories, in: *The Writings of Charles S. Peirce: A Chronological Edition, Vol. 2: 1867-1871*, ed. by Edward C. Moore, Bloomington, IN: Indiana UP, 49-59 [1867].

Popper, Karl R. (1980): Three Worlds, in: *The Tanner Lectures on Human Value*, ed. by Sterling McMurrin, Salt Lake City, UT: University of Utah Press, 141-167.

Red Storm Entertainment (2001): *Tom Clancy's Ghost Recon*, PC: Ubisoft.

Remedy Entertainment (2003): *Max Payne 2: The Fall of Max Payne*, PC: Rockstar Games.

Soja, Edward W. (1989): *Postmodern Geographies: The Reassertion of Space in Critical Social Theory*, London/New York, NY: Verso.

———— (1996): *Thirdspace: Journeys to Los Angeles and Other Real-and-Imagined Places*, Cambridge, MA/Oxford: Blackwell.

Souriau, Etienne (1951): La structure de l'univers filmique et le vocabulaire de la filmologie", in: *Revue international de Filmologie 7-8*, 231-240.

Stabyourself (2010): *Not Tetris*, Browser: Stabyourself.

Stockburger, Axel (2006): *The Rendered Arena: Modalities of Space in Video and Computer Games*, Dissertation, University of the Arts, London, stockburger.at/fil es/2010/04/Stockburger_Phd.pdf.

Ubisoft Montreal (2007): *Assassin's Creed*, Xbox 360/PS3: Ubisoft.

Valve Software (2007): *Portal*, PC: Electronic Arts.

We Create Stuff (2007): *Portal: The Flash Version*, Browser: We Create Stuff.

Wolf, Mark J.P. (1997): Inventing Space: Toward a Taxonomy of On- and Off-Screen Space in Video Games, *Film Quaterly* 51/1, 11-23.

––––– (2001): Space in the Video Game, in: *The Medium of the Video Game*, ed. by id., Austin, TX: University of Texas Press, 52-75.

––––– (2011): Theorizing Navigable Space in Video Games, in: *DIGAREC Keynote-Lectures 2009/10*, ed. by Stephan Günzel, Michael Liebe and Dieter Mersch, Potsdam: Potsdam UP, 18-49.

Playing with Sight
Construction of Perspective in Videogames

Stephan Schwingeler

Speaking with Espen Aarseth (2001, 161) every videogame is about space; it is the "raison d'être" of digital games. Every game is about manipulating configurations of space the player mainly perceives in the form of images. This paper explores the history and the unique characteristics of these images. Although current videogames can include all kinds of spatial modes, any method of graphical projection and a vast variety of visual styles, the focus lies on imagery as seen in contemporary 3D-videogames: "And scientific perspective is the kind on which most modern 3D videogames are constructed" (Poole 2004, 205).

Fig. 1: Check-pattern in Wipeout

Fig. 2: Check-pattern in Paolo Uccello's Christian Woman Selling a Consecrated Host to a Jewish Moneylender, 1465-69

The images perceived while playing a videogame like *Wipeout* (Psygnosis 1995) are part of a long tradition of images and, of course, the history of art. The mathematical and geometrical principles of perspective were formulated during the Renaissance. The three-dimensionally constructed images we perceive as spaces are constructed in the same way (fig. 1) a Renaissance artist would have constructed a painting in the middle of the 15th century (fig. 2). Current three-dimensional computer graphics use the same mathematical and geometrical principles as Renaissance painters – namely the principles of perspective.

Renaissance painters had to calculate on their own, whereas the videogame's new images are generated automatically by algorithmic computation; hence their digital nature. In a robust analogy, one could easily say these algorithms behave very much like Renaissance painters who paint a correctly constructed perspective image 60 times a second or even faster. The technique of perspective could be described as a constructional recipe or an algorithm itself. Despite being deeply rooted in art history, these images have developed unique qualities that clearly differentiate them from traditional images. There are major differences and new qualities concerning these new 'space-images' (Günzel 2008) or "navigable spaces" (Manovich 2001, 245).

Images in general have three basic medial modes: first, they can be static as in painting, various graphical techniques or photography. Second, they can be dynamic and moving as in film, traditional animation or pre-rendered CGI and third, images can be interactive simulations (Günzel 2009b, 51/Wiesing 2009). As Peter Weibel (2004, 187) stated these interactive simulation pictures can be described as post-industrial versions of the 'moving image' [*bewegtes Bild*]. Weibel described them as 'living images' [*belebte Bilder*]. Consequently, spectators become users: they are able to navigate images in real-time and perceive the manipulation of the images as being an interactive experience. Videogame images "present artificial navigation" (Günzel 2008, 172).

The paper is structured as follows: In a first step, a short overview is given over the history of linear perspective as formulated in Italy in the 15th century to build the groundwork for the understanding how spatial configurations are shown in pictures. In this context, the term *perspective* is understood as graphical projection: the entirety of means by which an image of a three-dimensional object or space is projected onto a planar, two-dimensional surface. Important contributions to the theory of perspective are shortly reflected in a second step in order to provide a historical framework and to place the current videogame image in the tradition of art history. Linear perspective is characterised as a mathematical *model of sight* and it is emphasized that perspective images have a special relationship to the spaces and objects. In this context, they hint at the discussion about the relationship between *seeing* and *perceiving*.

In a next step it is retraced, that the principles of perspective have been built into devices – namely, photographic cameras and graphics processing units that are able to generate perspective images automatically. In this coherence, linear perspective is identified as a cultural code, a paradigm of depicting space. Because of its independence from the exposure to light and its ability to depict seemingly realistic but conceived spaces, videogame imagery is then marked as being 'hyper-realistic'.

The new qualities of videogame images based on linear perspective are addressed by comparing traditional perspective with the automatic perspective processed by videogames, manipulated by the player. From that argumentation the term 'arbitrary perspective' is deduced, which firstly signifies the player's ability to deliberately control the viewpoint in videogames. The different notions of arbitrariness are then addressed in a last step. It can be stated that the usage of linear perspective for the construction of game space is only one option, considering a canon of different (even non-optical) spatial modes and points of view developed by the videogame as an expressive (and even artistic) medium in its history. Although linear perspective can be defined as a non-conventional construction principle based on natural laws, its application in the context of videogames is conventional and, therefore, arbitrary.

Renaissance Perspective: Translation into Mathematical Space

The invention of linear perspective was the foundation for the development of sim-ulated space we see in most 3D-videogames today. Perspective – as a theory based on mathematical and geometrical principles – begins in the early 15th century in Florence. Art history has a name connected to its invention: "linear perspective was invented by Filippo Brunelleschi" (Kemp 1990, 9) in the year 1413. Brunelleschi was an architect who discovered the basic optical principles that could be used to depict space perceived by individuals with two eyes in three dimensions on two-dimensional, flat planes.

In contrast to non-optical parallel projection, three-dimensional objects are not projected along parallel lines, but along lines emerging from a single point, the centre of projection. Perspective construction correctly represents the light that passes from objects or scenes to a viewer. The assumed *rays of sight* are con-centrated and bundled in one point: the viewer's eye, i.e. the centre of an individ-ual's viewpoint. If an imaginary rectangle (e.g. a canvas) is inserted, a flat plane is created. One could define the image as an intersection of this assumed visual pyr-amid with its tip pointing directly towards the viewer's eye as the centre of pro-jection (fig. 3). This new paradigm of sight, developed in the Renaissance by Leon Battista Alberti (a Renaissance humanist, polymath and perspective theorist), can be understood as an orientation of the whole era towards objective principles of science and as a metaphor for the blossoming role of the subjective individual and a symptom of humanism in the same degree.

Fig. 3: Illustration from Brooke Taylor's New Principles of Linear Perspective, 1719

Alberti coined a metaphor for the perspective image in his treatise *On Painting* from 1435. He compares the image with an 'open window' [*finestra aperta*], the viewer's line of sight is positioned to gaze out this open window and behold depicted space. Clearly this metaphor has influential power until today, relating to overlapping windows of the computer's GUI that open the gaze into virtual worlds (Friedberg 2006).

Brunelleschi's discovery and Alberti's theory fundamentally changed how space is depicted in images. Before knowing the principles of perspective painters kept trying to depict seemingly realistic, three-dimensional space using certain tricks of craftsmanship and their experience. For the first time, Brunelleschi managed to put depictions of space in scientific terms. Linear perspective – fully developed as *costruzione legittima* or 'scientific perspective' – became a "beguilingly simple means for the construction of an effective space in painting" (Kemp 1990, 7). Further it evolved into a "standard technique" to create "a systematic illusion of receding forms behind the flat surface of a panel, canvas, wall or ceiling" (ibid.). Because scientific perspective is based on the optical principles of sight the images have a special relationship to the objects they represent, they are considered 'realistic'. Eventually, due to this invention, the painter's status fundamentally changed: he became an artist. Perspective always corresponds to the individual viewer. Vanishing points are relative to the subject's vision. (This new paradigm of sight can be understood as a metaphor for the role of the individual in Renaissance society and a symptom of the development of humanism in general.)

Erwin Panofsky's essay *Perspective as Symbolic Form* from 1927 has a major influence on theories of perspective. Fact is that perspective images describe the optical principles of human eyesight in a correct manner: they copy human vision. In his seminal essay Panofsky (1991, 29) criticises that the technique of perspective is a mathematical-geometrical bold abstraction from human perception. The illusion of three-dimensional space is created on a two-dimensional surface by using the means of perspective.

Panofsky argues that in reality – within the actual, subjective, visual impression of an individual – spatiality is perceived with two eyes whereas one of the basic principles of perspective is the assumption of monocular sight. (To further conceptualise reality, Panofsky introduces the term 'psychophysiological space' to describe the actual space perceived by an individual.) Further the human eye is a sphere: the correct depiction of subjective vision creates a picture that is sharp in the middle and growing more out of focus tending towards the edges in a circular manner. According to Panofsky, this distortion is tacitly corrected in perspective images. Therefore, every perspective image is an idealised image that is thought of as realistic due to its similarity to the perceived world. In general, it is not a correct representation of the actual perception of a human being but the representation of mathematised spatiality. Perspectival images are not naturalistic depictions of reality but *constructions of a possible space* that seem plausible and convincingly realistic to the spectator.

In this context, it is necessary to hint at the discussion about the relationship between 'seeing' and 'perceiving'. As Klaus Rehkämper (2002) made clear, there is an important difference when he states that we cannot err while *seeing* a picture – but we can while *perceiving* it. The act of seeing deals with the way light takes from an object towards the eye. Visual perception is based on seeing, but strongly permeated by cognitive processes. Rehkämper (2006, 186) points out that in literature on perspective theory this differentiation often is not separated clearly enough which eventually leads to a 'fatal leap' in Panofsky's biased argumentation.

Panofsky's negative bias towards perspective images is, that they do not show the world as *perceived* – that they are abstractions from reality. Rehkämper on the other hand pointed out that this is not the function of perspective images at all. Perspective images do not mimic perception, but they describe the distance light covers from an object to the eye in a correct manner. They, therefore, represent correctly how an individual does *see*. Perspective can reproduce the act of *seeing* and is not conflicting with optical principles. Perspective images correctly depict space as we see it because the underlying construction principle is a mathematical and geometrical model of sight. Rehkämper confronts the underlying critique of perspective theory that images are not 'true' and do not show 'reality' by quoting Albert Flocon and André Barre (1987, 110): "Thus an absolute image does not exist. Only a relative image is possible."

However, of course there is a dichotomy identifiable between 'perceived' and 'represented space'. Gernot Böhme (2004, 129-141), for instance, differentiates between the space of bodily presence and space as a medium of representation. The space of bodily presence can be described as subjective whereas represented space can be called objective. Böhme identifies a second dichotomy – a dichotomy of scientific fields or disciplines associated with the different spaces: He assigns phenomenology to the subjective *space of bodily presence* whereas mathematics is assigned to the objective *represented space*.

Indeed, depiction of space on two-dimensional planes is most closely connected to mathematical, geometrical and optical principles. These principles are the groundwork for scientific perspective as 'legitimate construction' [*costruzione legittima*]. Consequently, perspective itself can be described as a rational instrument, an abstract, mathematical principle producing depictions of space that are rational, abstract and mathematical in their very nature. The invention of perspective as symbolic form is a symptom of an era that is oriented towards rationality, blossoming science and objectivity in general. According to Panofsky (1991, 66), by the means of perspective in the Renaissance, a translation of space was achieved: "The result was a translation of psychophysiological space into mathematical space; in other words, an objectification of the subjective".

A new idea of humanity is reflected in perspective with its assumed visual pyramid pointing to the individual's eye. On the one hand, perspective *objectifies* space by mathematical abstraction; on the other hand, it is inextricably related to an individual's *subjective* viewpoint. This makes perspective a "two-edged sword" (ibid., 67) oscillating between the subjective space and the mathematised objective represented space.

For the purposes of this paper, then, the optical principles of perspective and the images constructed upon these are designated as 'objective'; whereas the spectator's or player's realm is designated as 'subjective'. Considering videogames in particular, different planes can be divided in *rule-based space* and *mediated space* on the objective side and fictional-, play- and social space on the subjective side (Nitsche 2008, 15-17). Following Alexander Galloway (2006) the objective side is called the 'machine's moment' whereas the subjective side is the 'operator's moment'.

Automation of Sight: Photographical and Geometrical Traditions

The translation of space into mathematical space – the invention of perspective and the formulation of its mathematical, geometrical and optical principles – is the fundament for the development of automatically generated perspective images; images we see in 3D-videogames today. Consequently, the creation of perspective images was handed over from illustrators and painters to devices.

Fig. 4: Woodcut from Albrecht Dürer's Four Books on Measurement, 1525

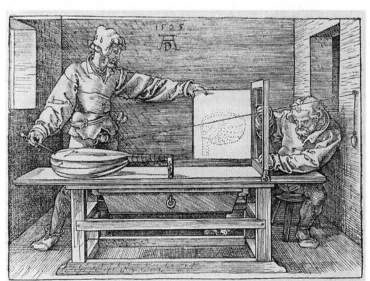

Historically such devices range from early auxiliary means such as diffusing screens, to the *camera obscura*, and photographic cameras (fig. 4). The mathematised space Panofsky described consequently became the digitized space of current videogame imagery automatically created by algorithms. This process can be described as 'rationalization of sight' (Ivins 1975), 'rationalization of mimesis' (Büttner 1998) or as a last step for the time being 'automation of sight' (Manovich 1993, 132-146). Lev Manovich – basing himself on the preliminary work of William M. Ivins – pointed out, that the process of automation has two dominant historical development directions:

> Modern designers, scientists or engineers, of course, do not simply use perspective as it was formulated by Alberti in the fifteenth century; they use more sophisticated techniques. According to Ivins, the rationalization of perspectival sight proceeded in two directions. On the one hand, perspective became the foundation for the development of the techniques of descriptive and perspective geometry which became the standard visual language of modern engineers and architects. [...] On the other hand, the photographic technologies automated the creation of perspectival images. Both were accomplishments of the nineteenth century; in fact, both were developed more or less simultaneously. Indeed, as Ivins points out, Niépce and Talbot, the founders of photography, were con-temporaries of Monge and Poncelet, decisive figures in the development of descriptive and perspective geometry. (Ibid., 117)

Both development traditions are based on perspective principles with one major difference: The photographic direction is dependent on exposure to light (Friedberg 2006, 72) whereas the geometrical direction is not. Joseph Nicéphore Niépce was the creator of the first known photographic image that shows a gaze out of his study's window around 1820. He called his invention 'heliography' (meaning 'writing with the sun'). This fact even has not changed with the digitalization of photography. Photography is still dependent on the exposure to light. This has the consequence that photographic images can only show objects that physically reflect light – objects that exist in the *space of bodily presence*.

Videogames and Realism: Hyper-Realistic Power Culture

The field of computer graphics – and therefore videogame imagery – is associated with the geometrical tradition of perspective images. This result in computer graphical images that are independent from the exposure to light and consequently can depict spatial configurations and objects that are conceived and fictional but plausible and seemingly realistic at the same time: "In this sense, a videogame camera shares a relationship much closer to painting than the photographic arts'" (Thomas/Haussmann 2005, 2).

Although the construction of videogame imagery is closer to painting than to photography, we can observe that the spaces and objects represented in most modern 3D-games are oriented towards remediating photographic and cinematic techniques considering their aesthetics and concept of realism. Videogames tend to mimic analogue photographic aesthetics by integrating simulation of virtual cameras, lens flare effects, in-motion blurring, depth of field etc.

Lev Manovich (2001, 92) discussed how linear perspective was adapted by the photographic/cinematic image and how this is adapted again by human-computer interfaces as a cultural code; a paradigm of sight, originally developed in the Renaissance: "As a result, linear perspective became the default mode of vision in computer culture. [...] In short, what was cinema is now the human-computer interface." Building on that observation, David Thomas and Gary Haussmann (2005, 1) pointed out that the use of linear perspective in a sense of cinematic perspective is a "form of visual cliché" in modern videogames. This convention renders something as realistic because players are used to it from other media: "Videogame fans and critics still praise, 'realistic graphics' without a hint of irony or a whiff of history" (ibid., 3).

It can be observed that videogame imagery and its representation of space is often characterised as being *realistic*. Espen Aarseth (2001, 169) was of the opinion that "[c]omputer games, finally, are allegories of space: they pretend to portray space in ever more realistic ways, but rely on their deviation from reality in order to make the illusion playable". This (eventually industry driven) tendency to be "ever more realistic" was accurately characterised as a "hyper-realistic power culture" by Gerrit Gohlke (2003, 105). In this coherence computer generated imagery in general has been described as 'hyper-realistic': images depicting spaces and objects that have no reference in the *space of bodily presence* and therefore do not exist but seem plausible and convincing. Still, an avatar has no reflection in the mirror.

Linear Perspective in Videogames: Playing with the Viewpoint

Because of their independence from the exposure to light and their digital nature, videogame images can be navigated in real-time offering an interactive experience to the player. Consequently, spectators become users. In videogames users begin to manipulate the images, they choose the viewpoint, move the visual pyramid. As stated by Günzel, videogame images present 'artificial navigation': "Videogames are actions. [...] One plays a game. And the software runs" (Galloway 2006, 2).

About the new qualities of the videogame image and the artistic relevance of gaming technologies (Schwingeler/Lohoff 2009) – Mathias Fuchs (2003) claims: "Computer games are more innovative in so far as the view-point of the viewer must not necessarily be predetermined by the medium." The player herself chooses the viewpoint. Depending on the chosen viewpoint, the image is generated almost in real-time based on the principles of perspective computed by algorithms: e.g., the player's hand moves the mouse in the *space of bodily presence*. Because of and dependent on this movement, a new image is created in *represented space*.

Klaus Rehkämper (2002, 4) coined the term 'p-shape' [*P-Gestalt*]. A p-shape is the objective depiction of an object or space based on the principles of perspective. In Panofsky's sense, this would be the objectivization of the subjective. Dependent on different viewpoints, pyramids of sights and vanishing points an object or space can have infinite p-forms in theory because one perspective image shows exactly *one* p-shape of its denotatum. Videogames as computer programs are able to render these p-shapes depending on the player's input in theoretically unlimited different ways.

Fig. 5 and 6: Changing the viewpoint arbitrarily in God of War

This phenomenon is known as 'free look'. It can be described as a simulation of the alteration of the player character's viewpoint, like staring at the ceiling (fig. 5) and to the ground (fig. 6) in *God of War* (SIE Santa Monica Studio 2018) nowadays. If the character is not getting killed, these images are persistent. These image phenomena are technically generated by perspective algorithms but produced by the player's *will* to change the viewpoint. The image is always connected to the player as a subject. The videogame image generated by first person shooter-games (FPS) for example can be characterised as follows: "In the simulation image the line of sight is centralized and fixed, and what is steered by the interface is the virtual space around it. The simulation picture of the first person shooter type thus visualizes intentionality and, furthermore, uses it as the major basis for interaction" (Günzel 2007, 6).

The player literally begins manipulating the image deliberately by choice: She is able to gaze at a represented sun or at a virtual wall and persist in this viewpoint of her own free will: "The computerization of perspectival construction made possible the automatic generation of a perspectival image of a geometrical model as seen from an arbitrary point of view – a picture of a virtual world recorded by a virtual camera" (Manovich 1993, 131).

Clearly, linear perspective used in videogames has added new qualities to the principles of perspective, made possible by the digital nature of the medium and the 'automation of sight.' The ambivalent relationship between subjectivity and objectivity concerning Renaissance perspective and perspective as used in videogames can be described as follows: As we have seen, the Renaissance perspective's purpose was to turn the *space of bodily presence* into *represented space*. Historically the main concept of representation was *mimesis* – the depiction of the world. By making human vision calculable the Renaissance perspective objectified the subjective, space was transferred into mathematical space – pictures seen by spectators. A picture is exactly one static intersection of the assumed visual pyramid.

Perspective as used in videogames turns the *space of bodily presence* into *represented space* as well. It is still a principle to project three-dimensionality onto planar surfaces. This process occurs automatically and almost in real-time. Its main concept of representation is simulation – the imitation of a world. By making human vision computable, this kind of perspective objectifies the subjective even more. The binary nature of code is more abstract than figures and formulas are. Spectators become users. The visual pyramid is movable by the user. While interacting with the images she can change her viewpoint dynamically. Therefore, an infinite amount of perspective images can in theory be generated. Metaphorically speaking, one could say the perspective image evolved from a window into a door (Weibel 2004, 190).

Paradoxically, perspective videogame imagery simulates subjective perception to a higher degree than perspective images in general: movement, interaction, simulation of physical laws and the phenomenon of hodological space (Günzel 2006/Schwingeler 2008, 144) can contribute to intensive subjective experiences while playing videogames. In videogames, then, perspective's *construction* is more objective in comparison to the Renaissance perspective, but its *reception* is more subjective. Steffen P. Walz (2009, 241) summarises:

So according to Manovich, geometric, i.e. algorithmic vision, is subject to automation. Perspective in videogames is simulated and fully mathematized. [...] Schwingeler suggests a name for this hyper-subjective view of the player in games: arbitrary perspective. [...] Manovich and Schwingeler, for their part, show that in comparison to Renaissance perspective, the construction of perspective in videogames engenders infinite possible points of view. This finding can, in turn, be related back to Salen and Zimmerman, [...] who commented that 'space, it seems, is in the eye of the beholder.'

Choosing from Arbitrary Perspectives in Videogames

The arbitrariness of perspective in videogames is not limited to changing the viewpoint and moving the visual pyramid. By doing so, perspective itself – the principle of construction – is not altered of course. Deliberately choosing an arbitrary viewpoint has always been a component of linear perspective: Historically the illustrator or painter chose a viewpoint first and then begins to construct the picture. The major difference between traditional, static images and interactive simulation pictures is of course that changing the viewpoint has immediate effects on the visual phenomenon perceived. This immediacy of the computer's reaction provokes the feel of interactivity.

Overall linear perspective may be the defining principle of videogame imagery, but it is still only one mode of depicting spatial configurations in videogames. This again brings the videogame closer to painting than to photography. Videogame spaces historically developed from being two-dimensional parallel-projections towards being true linear-perspective constructions. The spatial categories range from being text based, only 'described spaces', to contained spaces on a single screen, to fully developed interactive three-dimensional environments (Wolf 2001). Videogame imagery's independence from the exposure to light means that videogames can use all kinds of spatial modes and methods of projection besides linear perspective (Schwingeler 2008).

From Poole's (2004, 136) perspective as a game designer, the spatial mode is a major framework for gameplay and can be chosen arbitrarily: "Two-dimensional videogames live on, for example, in software for the Gameboy. The choice of spatial mode, of course, which includes the choice even of whether or how far to be representational at all (*Doom* versus *Tetris*), is bound up intimately with the question of what kind of game the designers want to make." Interestingly it can be observed that videogames that rely on two-dimensional mechanics and gameplay (x- and y-axis) have made use of linear perspective but stay in two dimensions regarding their gameplay. In their latest releases, the *Street Fighter*- and *Mortal Kombat*-series show characters, environments and objects in three-dimensional graphics, for example. Nevertheless, the use of three dimensions is purely cosmetic in *Street Fighter V* (Capcom 2016) and the ninth *Mortal Kombat* (NetherRealm Studios 2011).

The possibility to change the point of view is a standardised convention in digital games as well. In avatar-based games, it is possible to switch from a third-person- to a first-person-perspective. Here the use of the term 'perspective' is borrowed from literary theory describing the narrative mode of a text and the point of view. This does not refer to visual perspective in the first place, but can very suitably be transferred to videogame images, in order to describe what is seen on the screen.

Artist Julian Oliver (2005) even developed a game making use of an experimental second-person-perspective: The player controls the avatar labelled as me and is seen through the assumed eyes of an enemy controlled by the computer (labelled as 'you'). The *2nd Person Shooter* inverts the ego as the assumed subjective viewpoints of the player character and the enemies in a three-dimensional space: the player-controlled avatar is seen through the 'eyes' of the computer-controlled enemy as if it was an enemy. – The concepts of *me* and *you* are interchanged (fig. 7).

Fig. 7: The intermingled egos in Julian Oliver's 2nd Person Shooter

Often a change of projection mode is integrated in the game's mechanics: players can switch to topographical representation of game space when looking at a map for example. Arbitrariness of the projection mode even became a key element of gameplay in *Super Paper Mario* (Intelligent Systems 2007) which is a game with a true arbitrary perspective, in the sense that not only the viewpoint or point of view is changed by the player, but the whole graphical construction principle of the game world. At a certain point in the game, the player gains the "ancient secrets of dimensional flipping" from the NPC Bentovius– an ability to switch the spatial mode from a parallel projected 2D view (non-optical) to a three-dimensional, linear-perspective view (optical) which literally adds another dimension (z-axis) to the gameplay. Interestingly, *Mario* himself stays in his two-dimensional, flat form, resembling being made out of a piece of paper (fig. 8). The use of perspective here is truly arbitrary, because the player can switch the whole construction principle of the game world: from a parallel projected 2D view (non-optical) to a three-dimensional, linear perspective view (optical).

Fig. 8: Flipping dimensions in Super Paper Mario

Rehkämper (2002, 106) defined linear perspective as a non-conventional construction principle of visual representation because it is based upon natural, optical laws. Linear perspective is a scientific model that correctly shows how the rays of light behave in correspondence to the human eye. A perspective image exactly mimics this correspondence. As shown in videogames linear perspective behaves differently than in a static image because linear perspective is automated and can be played with: the player can move the viewpoint and manipulate the visual pyramid, which adds a feel of subjectivity. In theory, while playing the game, the player chooses between an infinite quantity of viewpoints. Whereas linear perspective is a non-conventional principle, its use in the context of videogames is very much a convention closely connected to a certain concept of realism – namely the simulation of cinematic aesthetics.

Like in painting the objective, mathematical laws of linear perspective can be deliberately broken or neglected in videogame imagery because it is independent from these natural laws hence its digital characteristics. This means videogames are independent from the paradigm of linear perspective as well: "Because the videogame camera is not an optical camera, it can be programmed to represent a potentially infinite number of perspectives beyond the classic, representational linear perspective" (Thomas/Haussmann 2005, 1).

Historically different spatial modes have been developed for the representation of space in videogames. Non-optical perspectives – like wraparound screens that describe the form of a torus when unwrapped for example – belong to the digital games' repertoire of spatial modes whereas linear perspective is only one possible construction principle of videogame imagery. All the spatial modes, that have become design conventions today, are still used and even become intermingled. As Aarseth (2001, 154) pointed out: "Computer games are essentially concerned with spatial representation and negotiation, and therefore a classification of computer games can be based on how they represent – or, perhaps, *implement* – space." The principle of perspective in digital games turns out to be an arbitrary one.

That means there is no method of projection and no kind of perspective that is better in a sense that it is capable to depict representations that are closer to reality. The different kinds of spatial modes (or the intermingling of spatial modes) do not have to be *representational* or *realistic* at all. All kinds of experiments are possible, like (future) cubist games or games based on M.C. Escher's impossible drawings – such as *Echochrome* (SCE Japan Studio 2008) – like Steven Poole (2004, 369) suggested. Interestingly art history shows that – after perspective has been fully mastered by artists as a technique and means of expression – modern painting begins to experiment with and reflect its laws and principles; experiments range from impressionism, to cubism and radically neglecting perspective in abstract painting (Hofmann 2003/Gombrich 2006). In this context, Julian Oliver's *2nd Person Shooter* and *Super Paper Mario* could be described as modern games in the art historical sense of the word.

In this connection one might ask, what lies beyond three-dimensional graphics? – The 'games' *Tetris 1D* (Dawn of Play 2010) and *Wolfenstein 1-D* (Wonder-Tonic 2011) humorously comment on and reflect about the three-dimensional paradigm by demaking the original games in one dimension only: *Tetris 1D*'s 'gameplay' is restricted to the y-axis; blocks keep falling, the player's only possible action is to make them fall faster (fig. 9). The original FPS *Wolfenstein 3D* (id Software 1992) has been converted to a one-pixel line with its 'gameplay' unfolding strictly on the x-axis (fig. 10).

Fig. 9 and 10: Demakes of Tetris *and* Wolfenstein 3D *in one dimension*

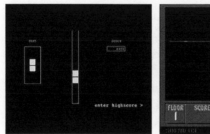 

The spatial mode determines the underlying principle of action (Günzel 2009b, 54). *Wolfenstein 3D* is a different game than *Tetris* (Pajitnov 1984) with different gameplay. *Wolfenstein 3D* is based on a certain representation achieved by the means of perspective whereas Tetris is a non-representational game with no simulation of a camera at all. It is important to emphasize that the first-person-shooter, as a genre, is linked to linear perspective's representational abilities as its visual style. Gameplay cannot unfold if the player does not see the game space depicted in a representational manner.

In this regard, the works of media-artists JODI show that a purely abstract FPS can be programmed, but not played in a meaningful way anymore (Günzel 2009a, 339). In JODI's (1999) artistic modification of *Wolfenstein 3D* – called *SOD* – the player does not recognise the graphics as a representational game space and is unable to act upon that basis (fig. 11). The original game has been stripped and abstracted to its very core, being a pure 'perspective engine':

> The starting idea was to find very basic forms like just a line or a square, just black and white, and attach these forms to the behaviour of the code so that we could have a better view on how such a game is driven, what are the dynamics of the game. So it's bringing those games back to the abstract dynamics of it and we were also trying to find out a little bit, how they do create the so-called 3-D space. That's the whole trick of these games, that they are perspective engines. All the time they create tunnels and illusions of a 3-D space and that's part of the 'kick' you have as the user, that you think you explore and you enter and you move into. In fact the only thing which is happening is a perspective which just is drawn all the time – so it's just about graphical tricks. (Hunger 2007, 154)

Its immersive power is exposed as being an interplay of graphical tricks. – *SOD* is a piece of interactive art, a paradox artefact: a FPS reduced to absurdity, a game that should be played with, but cannot be played with according to its intention.

Fig. 11: JODI's SOD

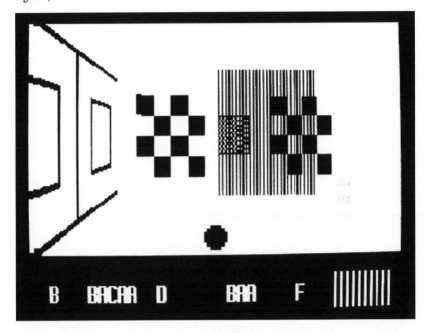

Overall, there is no hierarchy between a representational and a non-representational game. In opposition to a "hyper-realistic power culture" (Gohlke 2003, 105) of games developing "ever more realistic" (Aarseth 2001, 169) representations, Aarseth's (et al 2003) multi-dimensional typology of games provides an unbiased analytical tool to describe perspectives and space in videogames: Players either have an omnipresent or vagrant view; movement through space is either topological and discrete or geometrical and continuous; the environment is either static or dynamic.

The imagery of digital games is evolving and tends to reach further into space. Recent development considering the Nintendo 3DS' autostereoscopic capabilities and the rise of VR with Oculus Rift and similar products might be the next logical steps to add another tradition of visual representation to the videogame's canon of spatial modes and conventions. This does not mean – of course – that 'transplane images' (Schröter 2014) are closer to reality than other images. They only have different traditions and principles of construction: "For they are still images, when all is said and done, no more, but also no less" (Grau 2003, 323).

References

Aarseth, Espen (2001): Allegories of Space: The Question of Spatiality in Computer Games, in: *Cybertext Yearbook 2000*, ed. by Markku Eskelinen and Raine Koskimaa, Jyväskylä: Research Centre for Contemporary Culture, 152-171.

Aarseth, Espen/Smedstad, Solveig Marie/Sunnanå, Lise (2003): A Multidimensional Typology of Games, in: *Level Up: Digital Game Research Conference*, ed. by Marinka Copier and Joost Raessens, Utrecht: Universiteit Utrecht, 48-53.

Böhme, Gernot (2004): Der Raum der leiblichen Anwesenheit und der Raum als Medium von Darstellung, in: *Performativität und Medialität*, ed. by Sybille Krämer, München: Fink, 129-141.

Büttner, Frank (1998): Rationalisierung der Mimesis. Anfänge der konstruierten Perspektive bei Brunelleschi und Alberti, in: *Mimesis und Simulation*, ed. by Andreas Kablitz and Gerhard Neumann, Freiburg i.Br.: Rombach, 55-87.

Capcom (2016): *Street Fighter V*, PS4: Capcom.

Dawn of Play (2010): *Tetris 1D*, Browser: Dawn of Play.

Flocon, Albert/Barre, André (1987): *Curvilinear Perspective: From Visual Space to the Constructed Image*, Berkeley, CA: University of California Press.

Friedberg, Anne (2006): *The Virtual Window: From Alberti to Microsoft*, Cambridge, MA.: MIT Press.

Fuchs, Mathias (2003): Mirrors, syl-eckermann.net/fuchs-eckermann/fluID/fluID.html.

Galloway, Alexander R. (2006): Gamic Action: Four Moments, in: id.: *Gaming: Essays on Algorithmic Culture*, Minneapolis, MN: University of Minnesota Press, 1-39.

Gohlke, Gerrit (2003): A Fledgling Genre: Computer Game Art as a Counter-Draft to Technology-Alienated Art, in: *Games: Computerspiele von KünstlerInnen*, ed. by Timan Baumgärtel, Frankfurt a.M.: Revolver, 104-111.

Gombrich, Ernst H. (2006): *The Story of Art*, London et al.: Phaidon [1950].

Grau, Oliver (2003): *Virtual Art: From Illusion to Immersion*, Cambridge, MA/London: MIT Press.

Günzel, Stephan (2006): Bildtheoretische Analyse von Computerspielen in der Perspektive Erste Person, in: *Image* 4, bildwissenschaft.org/image/ausgaben?function=fnArticle&showArticle=89.

———— (2007): The Irreducible Self: Image Studies of First Person Perspective Computer Games, Paper presented at the Second *Philosophy of Computer Games Conference* in Reggio Emilia, game.unimore.it/Papers/Guenzel_Paper.pdf.

———— (2008): The Space-Image: Interactivity and Spatiality of Computer Games, in: *Conference Proceedings of the Philosophy of Computer Games 2008*, ed. by id., Michael Liebe and Dieter Mersch, Potsdam: Potsdam UP, 170-188.

–––– (2009a): Simulation und Perspektive: Der bildtheoretische Ansatz in der Computerspielforschung, in: *Shooter: Eine multidisziplinäre Einführung*, ed. by Matthias Bopp, Serjoscha Wiemer and Rolf Nohr, Münster et al.: Lit, 331-352.

–––– (2009b): Das Computerspielbild als Raummedium, in: *The Ludic Society*, ed. by Stephan Schwingeler and Ulrike Gehring, Kromsdorf: Jonas, 51-56.

Hofmann, Werner (2003): *Grundlagen der modernen Kunst: Eine Einführung in ihre symbolischen Formen*, Stuttgart: Kröner.

Hunger, Francis (2007): Perspective Engines: An Interview with JODI, in: *Videogames and Art*, ed. by Andy Clarke and Grethe Mitchell, Bristol et al.: Intellect, 152-160.

id Software (1992): *Wolfenstein 3D*, PC: Apogee Software.

Ivins, William M. (1975): *On the Rationalization of Sight*, New York, NY: Da Capo.

Intelligent Systems (2007): *Super Paper Mario*, Wii: Nintendo.

JODI (1999): *SOD*, Browser: Jodi.

Kemp, Martin (1990): *The Science of Art: Optical Themes in Western Art from Brunelleschi to Seurat*. New Haven: Yale UP.

Manovich, Lev (1993): *The Engineering of Vision from Constructivism to Computers*, PhD Diss., University of Rochester.

–––– (2001): *The Language of New Media*, Cambridge, MA: MIT Press.

NetherRealm Studios (2011): *Mortal Kombat*, PS3: Warner Bros. Interactive Entertainment.

Nitsche, Michael (2008): *Video Game Spaces: Image, Play, and Structure in 3D Game Worlds*. Cambridge, MA: MIT Press.

Oliver, Julian (2005): *2nd Person Shooter*, PC: Selectparks.

Pajitnov, Alexej (1984): *Tetris*, Elektronika 60.

Panofsky, Erwin (1991): *Perspective as Symbolic Form*, New York: Zone Books [1927].

Poole, Steven (2004): *Trigger Happy: Videogames and the Entertainment Revolution*, New York: Arcade Publishing.

Psygnosis (1995): *Wipeout*, PS: Sony Computer Entertainment.

Rehkämper, Klaus (2002): *Bilder, Ähnlichkeit und Perspektive: auf dem Weg zu einer neuen Theorie der bildhaften Repräsentation*, Wiesbaden: DUV.

–––– (2006): What You See Is What You Get: The Problem of Linear Perspective, in: *Looging into Pictures: An Interdisiplinary Approach to Pictorial Space*, ed. by Heiko Hecht, Robert Schwarz and Margaret Atherton, Cambridge, MA/London: MIT Press, 179-189.

Salen, Katie/Zimmerman, Eric [Eds.] (2006): *The Game Design Reader: A Rules of Play Anthology*. Cambridge, MA: MIT Press.

Schröter, Jens (2014): *3D: History, Theory and Aesthetics of the Transplane Image*, London et al.: Bloomsbury [2009].

Schwingeler, Stephan (2008): *Die Raummaschine: Raum und Perspektive im Computerspiel*, Boizenburg: VWH.

– – – – /Lohoff, Markus (2009): Interferenzen: Eine kunsthistorische Betrachtung von Computerspielen zwischen Wissenschaft, Kommerz und Kunst, in: *The Ludic Society*, ed. by Stephan Schwingeler and Ulrike Gehring, Kromsdorf: Jonas, 16-39.

SCE Japan Studio (2008): *Echochrome*, PSP: Sony Computer Entertainment.

SIE Santa Monica Studio (2018): *God of War*, PS4: Sony Interactive Entertainment.

Thomas, David/Haussmann, Gary (2005): Cinematic Camera as Videogame Cliché, in: *Proceedings of DiGRA 2005 Conference: Changing Views – Worlds in Play*, digra. org/wp-content/uploads/digital-library/06278.52285.pdf.

Walz, Steffen P. (2009): Approaches to Space in Game Design Research, in: *DIG-AREC Lectures 2008/09: Vorträge am Zentrum für Computerspielforschung mit Wissenschaftsforum der Deutschen Gamestage/Quo Vadis 2008 und 2009*, ed. by Stephan Günzel, Michael Liebe and Dieter Mersch, Potsdam: Potsdam UP, 228-254.

Weibel, Peter (2004): Neurocinema: Zum Wandel der Wahrnehmung im technischen Zeitalter, in *Gamma und Amplitude: Medien- und kunsttheoretische Schriften*, ed. by id., Berlin: Philo, 166-195 [1996].

Wiesing, Lambert (2009): Virtual Reality: The Assimilation of the Image to the Imagination, in: id.: *Artificial Presence: Philosophical Studies in Image Theory*, Stanford, CA: Stanford UP, 87-101 [2001].

Wolf, Mark J.P. (2001): Space in the Video Game, in: *The Medium of the Video Game*, ed. by id., Austin: University of Texas Press, 51-77 [1997].

Wonder Tonic (2011): *Wolfenstein 1-D*, Browser: Wonder Tonic.

From Background to Protagonist
Spatial Concepts in 'Portal' and 'Echochrome'

Karla Theilhaber

Despite obvious differences in their representation and game principle all games discussed have one thing in common: the construction of space through movement. The basis is formed by theories focusing on movement, particularly the concept of hodological space and the role of perspective. Since it defines the position of character, player and the view they are holding, central perspective plays a dominant role in game play and the construction of space. After giving a short overview of theories relevant to this paper, I will then continue to look at three different games examining the handling of space and the discussed topics.

Using *Portal* (Valve Software 2007), *Super Paper Mario* (Intelligent Systems 2007) and *Echochrome* (SCE Japan Studio 2008) as an example, the paper looks at perspectives of the image presented and its meaning for the game and the construction of space using viewpoints – like in art practice. It is also relevant to consider the relation of the player and the character regarding the control mechanisms in a spatial context. Another central argument is the shift from a three-dimensional to a two-dimensional world, and vice versa. The aim is to point out a spatial concept that moves away from passive background graphics via an experience space to an active space including characteristics of an active subject of avatar. Thus, the construction of space is an active process, a part of the game.

Construction of Space

The connection between movement and space is important, and the role of perspective might be a relevant element in this relationship. Movement and space are clearly connected as the commands of the player are mediated through movement on the keyboard or the controller. As these commands are executed, the movement of the avatar is what determines virtual depictions of space. If the avatar is walking in a certain way and direction, the game space is depicted accordingly, that means the avatar's point of view and his environment is the game space. There are different concepts of space in computer games, but almost all of them include the movement of the player in the game.

Although I would like to look at the structure and the formal representation of a game in order to analyse the game space, it might be necessary at times to include the narrative elements, which mostly includes the game space. In *The Language of New Media* Lev Manovich describes computer games as navigable spaces that are based on a narrated journey such as the *Odyssey*. His term 'navigable space' proposes a spatial concept based on the Homerian story, thus a journey structured by several narratives. The hero of Homer and Manovich makes his way through stormy waters, past seductive sirens or murderous zombies. In both computer games and antique myths, the focus of the narration lies on the journey, the movement through a space. The story develops, as the hero/player is moving through space:

> In *Doom* and *Myst* – and in a great many other computer games – narrative and time itself are equated with the movement through 3-D space, the progression through rooms, levels, or words. In contrast to modern literature, theatre, and cinema which are built around the psychological tensions between the characters and the movement in psychological space, these computer games return us to the ancient forms of narrative where the plot is driven by the spatial movement of the main hero [...]. (Manovich 2001, 214)

This concept could be applied to most games, if we stay on the narrative level. Technically, though, the player does not move through space, he moves the space itself, as Günzel (2007) says:

> Factually, he or she does not move in space, but rather primarily moves space itself. In the simulation image the line of sight is centralized and fixed, and what is steered by the interface is the virtual space around it. The simulation picture of the first person shooter type thus visualizes intentionality and, furthermore, uses it as the major basis for interaction. And this interaction derives from the image's composition alone.

This statement focuses on the genre of first person-shooter games, but could be applied to other game genres as well. The significant difference between film and computer games is interaction. Images are not only seen, but made/produced. The journey of the player in the game is the key element in the production process of the digital-virtual computer image. Perspective is an important part in this construction process. The first person-shooter is dominated by the central perspective image, and as quoted, "the line of sight is centralized and fixed" and the player moves "the virtual space around it." However, even games that are not based on a first person-perspective depend on the perspective of the player on the game world: Either, the player continues her exploration of game space by scrolling or by moving an avatar in third person perspective, or the player remains the space defining instance in playing a game.

If we agree on the player's ability to construct and move the space within a game, there is one concept of space construction that is especially worth looking at: Michel de Certeau's concept of space in *The Practice of Everyday Life*. According to him, space is a location that you are doing something with. A space is constructed by actions or people telling stories about actions. Stories and the act of telling them are important to de Certeau's theory, which seems familiar from Manovich's concept of navigable space.

Narrations or oral descriptions of space are divided in two categories by de Certeau: *map* and *tour*. Both possibilities of descriptions are based on the corresponding verbs, actions. Describing a location from a certain point of view making the viewing process the center, the description has cartographic characteristics and therefore is a map. In contrast, walking through a location is a space constructing action:

> In other words, description oscillates between the terms of an alternative: either seeing (the knowledge of an order of places) or going (spatializing actions). Either it presents a tableau ('there are...'), or it organizes movements ('you enter, you go across, you turn...'). (De Certeau 2002, 119)

Walking through a game, playing it, constitutes the represented space. Seeing directly communicates with walking. Looking at the first person-shooter, the avatar moves because the player is altering the cross line and therefore the vanishing point of her perspective. The avatar seems to move by being steered up, down, forward, to the side, and thus, the view on the represented game world changes.

De Certeau's definition of a location or place resembles a spot; a still standing avatar could be defined as such. The visualized location is being manipulated while playing; it changes through movement (of the controller, cross hairs, direction) and becomes space. The player moves through this space and changes it continuously. Her commands trigger the creation of new spaces, and all of this happens in real time. Like de Certeau's walking people transform the street into a space through their movement.

De Certeau defines space as a web of mobile elements. In contrast to locations – constellations of fixed spots – spaces are constructed by movement in such a constellation. Spaces are not solid and steady, and they are rather a result of activity. This concept of space-constructing movement is very applicable to computer games. By moving her avatar in the game, the player creates the game space; or, as discussed before, by changing or moving her viewpoint onto the game space, the player creates space. Different viewpoints in a game situation create a particular space. The film camera is a perfect example to explain this situation. Angles, viewpoints and the moving camera are working together to create a convincing landscape, room or other setting.

At this point, I suggest again that there is a space in videogames constructed by the player's movement in the game world. The image of a videogame is determined by those movements. Besides the image space of a computer game, which can be divided into the perspective image space and the topographical space (that I have not talked about yet), there exists another space. This space is not based on images, but on the experiences whilst playing a game: the hodological space.

The experiences of the player while playing/walking through a game is included in the term of the hodological space (adopted from the Psychology of Kurt Lewin): Stephan Schwingeler (2008, 104) defines this as a 'line of events' that construct the experience of space for the player and enable a spatial experience. Stephan Günzel (2006, 8) draws a connection between the experience of space and the spatial experience, claiming that the experience of space is created through the interaction of both representations of space, perspective image and topographical space. The game experience is influenced by both types of representation. Adding to the images and their influences on the player, the game experience and space inside the player's mind is determined by the experiences she makes while playing the game. The hodological space experience plays an important role in all games discussed in the following text. Without the experience and the player's mind, the game does not function as it should.

Space as Game Object I: 'Portal'

The first person-shooter puzzle *Portal* inhabits a three-dimensional game world that follows a regular first person-shooter in terms of graphics, possibilities of movement and action, as well as the construction of space. The player/avatar is moving in a first person-perspective and within a game world consisting of three axes (X, Y, and Z). The first person-perspective is essential to this game, as it defines the player's viewpoint and determines the depicted space. It is constructed through the character's movements and the actual playing of the game, as it is usual in first person shooter games.

An equally important part in playing a game is the avatar, which is the connection between game and player. The contained first person perspective defines the game space, while the implicit character, mostly only visible through a gun or a hand holding a weapon, sustains a central perspective on the game space. This perspective corresponds with the position and viewpoint of the player sitting in front of the screen, thus creating the relationship between player and implicit character.

Yet in *Portal*, this almost intimate relationship between player and implicit avatar is broken up by the appearance of the avatar's body – when two portals are located in a specific angle (fig. 1). The body becomes visible and, therefore, comments on itself, the player and the usual game structure. This might be the first time when the game highlights its self-reflexivity. There will be more moments like this.

Fig.1: Portal, *Level 7*

The central perspective also navigates the person and the aim of the weapon. In contrast to regular shooter games, which aim for fighting and destroying enemies, *Portal*'s main goal is to conquer, explore and master the space by shooting portals in walls, ceilings or floors and navigating through them. There are no real, independently moving enemies, except robots (first appearance in level 12). The mission of each level includes navigating the spaces in order to get to an elevator that literally goes to the next level. Not only is the main task a spatial one, the structure of the game is also based on space. Here, structure is corresponding to the game principle, and vice versa.

Portal enables the player to activate viewpoints and see things that she cannot see immediately from her actual position. There is not only one perspective – that of the player and at the same time the avatar – but several different viewpoints created by locating portals in particular positions. If one positions both portals opposite of each other, they are endlessly mirrored (like in video-feedback). By shooting a portal into a wall and another one into the ceiling, one can see right through the wall, and depict the spatial situation situated below the ceiling. Thus, new viewpoints and spatial situations and representations are enabled. One could say, "I am installing new cameras by installing portals". Not only has the player the possibility to discover a perspective independent from her own, she can also install those viewpoints freely in any given position. The shooting becomes a (film-)shot. – So, the player explores the space by shooting portals, installing new viewpoints and, thus, experiences the space in a different way than a regular shooter. The handling of space as a tool to master a certain spatial situation hints to the space itself and its materiality. Teleportation via portals can be considered a self-reflexive way to deal with space in games.

In many games, it is possible to switch into a two-dimensional, topographical map to gain insight into achievable goals, persons or quests. Both spaces – the three-dimensional perspective space and the topographical space – communicate with each other and enable the player to solve problems. *Portal* does not have a map, the player explores the space by moving, that means by taking different viewpoints. There is no overview, no map, of the existing game world that could inform you about size, time or distance. The interface is reduced to the immediate view onto the space, yet including the weapon and cross hairs, towards which the objects in the game space are orientating.

On the other hand, there is a two-dimensional image giving information about the upcoming level to the player. At the beginning of each level, the player finds an illuminated sign that shows the level number (02, 08, 15, etc.) as well as one or more pictograms. These pictograms hint to the characteristics of the level, such as obstacles or enemies, and inform the player about actions necessary to solve certain situations. They are black and white icons showing complex situations in a simple style, like directing the fireball into a technical device (see central icon on top in fig. 2).

Fig. 2: Portal, *Level 8*

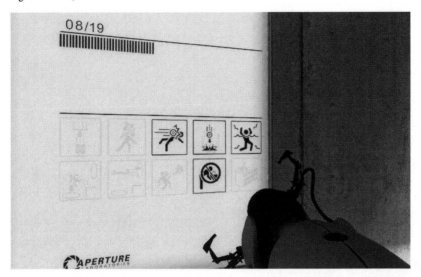

To conquer a huge wall, for example, the player has to remember the pictogram and use the two-dimensional graphic in the actual situation within a three-dimensional game world. Thus, the pictograms could be seen as an equivalent to the map in another game since they help to solve problems. Although *Portal* follows the construction of space in a first person-perspective, the game requires two-dimensional thinking and gameplay. The player orientates herself by moving around a three-dimensional space, the problems are only solvable applying a two-dimensional concept of space. This game principle becomes obvious when looking at *Portal: The Flash Version* (We Create Stuff 2007), which uses the same method to explore game space: teleportation through portals (fig. 3 a-d).

Fig. 3 a-d: Portal: The Flash Version, *Level 7*

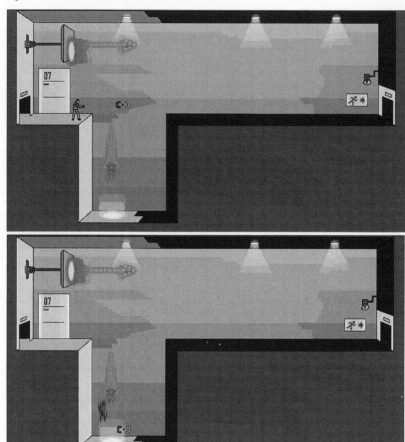

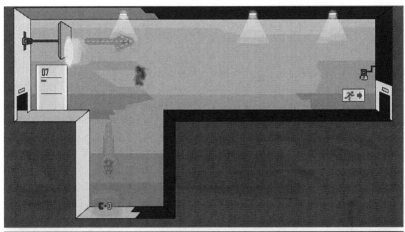

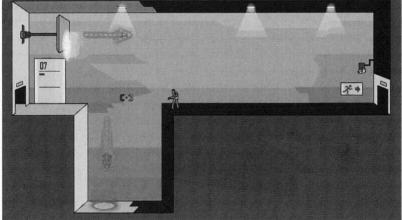

The use of the pictograms corresponds with a topographical representation, the depictions and their content, though, could be considered similar to a tour according to de Certeau: a discursive line of actions. There is no overview on structure and spatial characteristics, the player can only acquire information about dangers and ways to solve problems within the game space of a level. After observing at the icons, the player knows the necessary actions.

Space as Game Object II: 'Super Paper Mario'

Another game playing with multi-dimensional thinking is *Super Paper Mario*. In order to solve problems in a familiar Mario game world (only minimally changed to 3D-graphics), the player has to switch from the usual two-dimensional graphics to a three-dimensional world (fig. 4a-b). All levels are programmed in both worlds, the two- and the three-dimensional. Playing in a somewhat familiar game world, the player gets to a point where the conventional Mario methods are no longer applicable. If she switches to a three-dimensional representation, the qualities and characteristics of the world change as well and obstacles, enemies or situations are easily passable. The change of game world results in a different gameplay. Besides mastering the first level of the game, the two-dimensional game world – the player can switch back and forth between two- and three-dimensional worlds to try out different solutions for each game situation.

Fig. 4a-b: Super Paper Mario, *obstacle in 2D and 3D-solution*

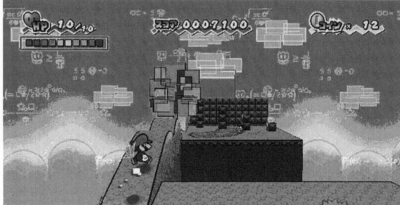

To play *Super Paper Mario* successfully, one has to be constantly conscious of the possibilities and changes in the 'other world.' The game space of *Super Paper Mario* is a variable space; however, the construction follows the conventional construction and graphics of space in two-dimensional games.

Space as Game Object III: 'Echochrome'

In this particular game, the player manipulates the space, so that the character can pass gaps, holes or obstacles by shifting the perspective from a three-dimensional world to a two-dimensional, flat view on certain elements. This switch between dimensions and the related way of thinking corresponds with the multi-dimensional gameplay in the two games discussed above. However, in *Echochrome* this action is only one of many ways to play successfully. The whole game is based on five laws concerning the perspective representation in the game, as the tutorial states. Basically, all rules follow this statement: "Change the perspective and create a path" (fig. 5 a-b).

Fig. 5a-b: Echochrome, *Tutorial: "Change the perspective and connect the path"*

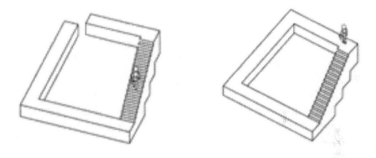

The player and the character have to find a path through the elements in space to collect Echoes, shadow-like figures standing in various changing positions. The perspective, the viewpoint, of the player is equally important and dominant for the gameplay as it is in a first person-shooter, although it does not coincide with the viewpoint of the character. The player changes the view onto the space, in which her character is walking; in return, the new perspective modifies the space itself. It is not only the perspective, but also the dimensionality in the game space that changes throughout the game. In some cases, the player needs to connect two elements to reach the Echo, and the entire game space (including all spatial elements) transforms from a three-dimensional representation into two dimensions. Depth disappears and a flat view makes the solution possible.

To play *Echochrome* successfully, one has to be able to think in multiple dimensions, three with an occasional jump into two dimensions. The switch between both ways of representation resembles the map in other games, like *World of Warcraft* (Blizzard Entertainment 2004), *Doom* (id Software 1993) etc., that are being activated to receive advantages in playing. The 'map' of *Echochrome*, though, has different qualities: There is no overview of the game world, and the player can only see a single one out of multiple perspectives. Echoes, partners or enemies are mostly not visible in this mode. By moving the spatial construction – at this point, the movement of the character is not of any interest – spaces or spatial situations are being created. Thus, the elements of the spatial construction (stairs, cuboids, holes, etc.) could be understood as single spots, which become a space through movement, following Michel de Certeau: only the execution enables the construction of space.

The conventional (game) story and the narrative so dear to de Certeau, however, takes a remarkable turn in *Echochrome*: The hero does not exist. Instead of defining the game space by moving through and exploring the space, the character – in this case a faceless doll – is rather a dull walking figure with no perspective of its own. The character can only be controlled minimally. When we start the game, the character starts its walk through the spatial construction. The player can make the character pause and think, while still moving the entire construction. Yet, time is running out and limits this break. Additionally, the player can manipulate the walking speed of the character, precisely, she can fast forward it. Generally, though, there is no intermediation between player and character. The moment in which player and character do the same thing – thinking – is limited and without any effect on the character's motion. The character only indirectly adds to achieving a goal. The direct point of action lies with the spatial construction, which immediately reacts to the commands of the player. The course of the game is influenced by directing the space, while the character continues unaltered in its walk.

The perspective and thus the power and control over the game space lies only in the player herself, therefore establishing a relation between player and character different from other perspective-based games, such as first person-shooter games. Firstly, the player might identify herself with the character; after all, it has a body, head and limbs. Nevertheless, differing from games with a character orientating itself and being controlled within the game space, like for example *Super Mario World* (Nintendo EAD 1990) or *Diablo II* (Blizzard North 2000), the assumed avatar does not react directly to the entered commands.

Perspective and positioning the space hold central roles in *Echochrome*. The spatial construction, and therefore the actual spatial situation, can be directed, manipulated and effectively altered. The character is walking through the directed space and reacts to changes. Space is not only background or playground; it significantly contributes to the experience of and success in the game. It becomes an active participant. This constellation implicates an interaction, even mediation, between player and movable space. The player might identify herself with the character; nonetheless, the actual control mechanisms relevant for the game lie with the spatial construction rather than the character.

Adding to this statement is the image of the spatial representation. There is no connection between perspective and character as we have seen in other games, especially perspective-based games like the first person-shooter. The walk of the character has no effect on the representation of space at all. The controlled space appears to be similar to an avatar in its relation to the player. In contrast to the continuously walking character, it forms the parameter that executes the commands given by the player. The spatial construction transforms from a spatial object, background or playing field, to an active subject, an agent, that represents the player, solves problems and acts as a projected spatial being. The overall perspective becomes that of a third person, and adds to the active spatial character.

Space as Game Subject: 'Echochrome'

Space is created through action: Action and interaction are essential to playing a game. The single elements in a game world (pixels, polygons, angles) come together and build a space through the motion of the player. Without action, the computer game image might depict a space, but it only becomes space by playing the game itself.

Playing with multi-dimensional representations within their game world, games like *Super Paper Mario* or *Portal* demonstrate certain self-reflexive usage of game space. Additionally, to the subtle irony in narration, *Portal* discusses the role of space, perspective and player character on a topological – structural – level. The construction of game space is literally experienced by shooting portals and using them to teleport the character from one location to another. To play a game like *Portal* successfully, the player creates a hodological space, an experience and knowledge that derive from the visual representations, the understanding of game physics and the act of playing. Space becomes a visible, and, thus, conscious main topic of the game.

This understanding of space as a main structure and theme in games is widely spread by now. Games such as the traditional analogue marble labyrinth find their equivalent on the iPhone, dealing with space as an important aspect in order to play successfully. Some of these games contain very simple graphics and focus on the understanding of construction and handling of space. This is very similar to processes taking place as discussed in *Echochrome*, whose simple black and white appearance is reminiscent of a drawing.

The construction of space through motion *is* literal in this game, as well as the function of perspective in this process. What makes it differ from other games reflecting game space, is the complete manifestation of an active space. The view on the game space is not limited, compared with, for example, *LocoRoco* (Sony Computer Entertainment 2006) where game space is visually still a background element of the game. The spatial object in *Echochrome* is fully visible, controllable and responsible for its actions. The player finds herself looking at the space in a third person perspective comparable with the avatar in games like *World of Warcraft*. The object obtains features, which are usually linked to an avatar in computer games; it becomes a game subject, an active figure that can be played with independently from the displayed (walking) character.

Motion and interaction separate the images of computer games from images in film, photography or painting. And still, they could all have one thing in common: The creation of a conscious subject within the space of the medium. Similar to the observer of a Baroque painting becoming an active part in the spatial construction, the player takes on the same role. In games like *Echochrome*, the player might identify herself with another conscious and active subject: space.

References

Blizzard Entertainment (2004): *World of Warcraft*, PC: Vivendi.

Blizzard North (2000): *Diablo II*, PC: Blizzard Entertainment.

de Certeau, Michel (2002): *The Practice of Everyday Life*, Berkeley, CA: University of California Press [1980].

Günzel, Stephan (2006): Bildtheoretische Analyse von Computerspielen in der Perspektive Erste Person, in: *Image* 4, gib.uni-tuebingen.de/image/ausgaben -3?function=fnArticle&showArticle=89.

– – – – (2007): The Irreducible Self: Image Studies of First Person Perspective Computer Games, Paper presented at *The Second Philosophy of Computer Games Conference*, Reggio Emilia, Jan, 25th-27th, tv.unimore.it/media/societa/computer_ games/26th/start26.html.

id Software (1993) *Doom*, PC: id Software.

Intelligent Systems (2007): *Super Paper Mario*, Wii: Nintendo.

Manovich, Lev (2001): *The Language of New Media*, Cambridge, MA/London: MIT Press.

Nintendo EAD (1990): *Super Mario World*, SNES: Nintendo.

SCE Japan Studio (2008): *Echochrome*, PSP: Sony Computer Entertainment.

Schwingeler, Stephan (2008): *Die Raummaschine: Raum und Perspektive im Computerspiel*, Boizenburg: VWH.

Sony Computer Entertainment (2006): *LocoRoco*, PS Portable: SCE.

Valve Software (2007): *Portal*, PC: Electronic Arts.

We Create Stuff (2007): *Portal: The Flash Version*, Browser: We Create Stuff.

The Art of Being There
Artistic Practices of Presence in Narrative Media

Teun Dubbelman

> In turning to films and books for inspiration, game writers seem to miss the true potential of the medium of games, in which the player becomes the arbiter of the character's fate through actions which, ostensibly at least, should reinforce or alter the moral compass of the character.
> Andy Dilks (Inbox *EDGE*, June 2007)

> A film is viewed externally, voyeuristically. A game, by contrast, exists to be interacted with. The player must feel that they are writing their own story as they go, and that their actions are actually having an effect on the ultimate outcome.
> Howell Davies (Inbox *EDGE*, December 2007)

For many years now, the topic of storytelling has been high on the agenda of game magazines. The popular periodical *EDGE* contains tons of articles, columns and letters discussing the particular ways in which games deal with stories. What these contributions often share is a profound belief in the new possibility computer games offer in terms of narrative. The exact interpretation of these new possibilities can however differ greatly. No general idea exists on the affordances of games in terms of storytelling.

The two quotes that are printed above are exemplary of this lack of consensus. Both have been from letters sent by readers to *EDGE*. When comparing the letters, they seem at first sight quite similar in the way they approach game stories. Both authors emphasize, either explicitly or implicitly, the interactive nature of games as something that separates the relatively new medium from older media such as films and books. However, on closer examination, it seems that the first letter approaches interactivity as something that allows the player to operate as the arbiter of the character's fate, while the second letter connects interactivity to the ability of players to experience their own personal stories within the games they play.

There seem to be two distinctive logics at work in the ideas of these writers. One focuses on the player as an implied author who guides the hero through his trials and tribulations. The player can intervene in the hero's faith by controlling him. The other focuses on the player as an embodied participant in the world of the story. In the former, the player closely follows the hero through his adventure; in the latter, the player becomes the hero and experiences adventures of his own.

The aim of this article is to make explicit the implicit logics that play their part in the ideas these letters put forward. How can we define these logics what are their characteristics and how do they differ from each other? Moreover, how do the two logics relate when co-existent in the design of one and the same avatar-based 3D-game. I believe that games exist in which one of the two logics is more prevalent. In games such as *Fahrenheit* (Quantic Dream 2005) or *Heavy Rain* (Quantic Dream 2010) the player becomes the implied author of an unfolding story. These games hand the player the power to alter the destiny of protagonists by making certain choices for them. Games such as *Half-Life* (Valve Corporation 1998) or *BioShock* (2K Boston 2007), on the other hand, seem put the player directly in the shoes of the main character, and try to blend the boundary between player and protagonist. (Although these types of games are often first-person games, examples exist of first-person games where the other approach is more dominant. One striking example is the game *Dinner Date* (Stout Games 2010) where the player hears – by controlling the protagonist's first-person view – the thoughts and anxieties of the protagonist while he is waiting for a date to show up. Similarly, there are also many examples of third-person games who aim to give us the sensation as if we are the main character, often by using a fixed over-the-shoulder-cam).

Between the four examples, many other games exist where it is not so clear which logic steers their design. Both logics can be apparent and can clash in interesting ways. This paper wants to investigate the implications of this co-existence concerning the *narratological* for the design of avatar-based games.

The Screen-Projected Avatar

One of the main reasons why both logics are visible in the design of many avatar-based 3D-games stems from their dependency on screen-projected avatars. On the one hand, 3D-games excel in giving players the feeling as if they themselves are walking around in the story world; this sensation of existing in a mediated environment is commonly called 'presence' (Ryan 2001; McMahan 2003; Carr

2006; Nitsche 2008; Tamborini/Skalski 2006) – and is possible only because of the avatar.

The avatar is needed in a computer-simulated and screen-projected space to mediate the feeling of presence. Rune Klevjer (2006, 10) has written extensively on this phenomenon in *What is the Avatar*, describing the relationship between player and avatar as "a prosthetic relationship; through a process of learning and habituation, the avatar becomes an extension of the player's own body." On the other hand, however, this screen-projected avatar also invites another design approach. As demonstrated by Bolter and Grusin (1999) in *Remediation*, games tend to remediate films because they look alike in their means of mediation. Computer games and cinema are both screen-dependent media. Because most popular films focus on the portrayal of the experiences of others, it is not so surprising that many 3D-games do the same.

Looking at the popular games sold today, one indeed sees how they foreground the avatar as both an extension of the player's body as well as a main character in a story to be told. *Grand Theft Auto IV* (Rockstar North 2008), for example, tells the story of Niko Bellic and his quest for revenge and allows players to experience their own stories as they rampage through Liberty City. Somehow, the availability of screen-projected avatars invites and allows both logics. Conceived of as protagonists, they allow game designers to communicate the adventures of imagined protagonists, similar to actors on a movie screen. Conceived of as an extension of the player, they allow game designers to build elaborate fantasy worlds where players can venture out in for themselves. Although this, mostly implicit, double logic in the design of game stories is not wrong per se, it does lead to an interesting aesthetic tension.

When the avatar is designed as a body belonging to the protagonist, but also as an extension of the body of the player, the experiential merits of the separate logics might clash. A particular event in a story may enrich me when I act as an implied narrator, but as an embodied player, I might not be affected positively at all. In the case of *GTA IV*, the scripted events Niko Bellic goes through in Liberty City tell an exciting tale of vengeance, but set many boundaries to my own bodily experience of the game world and its narrative context. An interesting story event to witness and control as distant observer can be very boring to experience first-hand, and vice versa. In 3D-game research this entanglement of embodied and story-based participation is one of the most pressing issues that need to be theoretically unraveled, as Klevjer (2006, 218) emphasizes in the conclusion of his thesis:

A dedicated study of the relationships between avatar-based play and avatar-based formats of storytelling would be an obvious next step in the analysis, particularly with respect to the contemporary 3D action adventure. The fusions, overlaps and tensions between embodied and story-based fictional participation in singleplayer computer games is a complex and diverse area of study.

My paper wants to make the next step Klevjer proposes with an elaborate theoretical exploration of the two logics at work in these 3D-games. For this purpose, the following paragraphs will critically review the representational concept of narrative as developed once in structuralist narratology and will develop an additional presentational conceptualization, applicable to both marginal narrative practices of the past as well as mainstream practices of the present.

Narrative as Representation

Although the scholarly interest in storytelling has a long history and can be traced all the way back to Plato's *Republic* and Aristotle's *Poetics*, the study of narratives as an autonomous academic discipline only came into existence in the 1960s. Termed 'narratology' by Tzvetan Todorov (1969, 10) in his work *Grammaire du Décaméron*, the theory of the narrato*logical* aims to present a logical and structural description of the way in which stories are told. The narratologist dissects the narrative phenomenon into its component parts and attempts to determine functions and relationships (Jahn 2005). As becomes clear from this description, the shared episteme of these first narratologists is strongly rooted in the discourses of French structuralism (e.g. Tzvetan Todorov, Roland Barthes, Christian Metz, Claude Bremond, Algirdas Julien Greimas, Gerard Genette) and Russian formalism (e.g. Vladimir Propp, Roman Osipovich Jakobson, Yury Tynyanov, Boris Eichenbaum, Viktor Shklovsky and Mikhail Mikhailovich Bakhtin).

While scholars in what often is referred to as structuralist narratology disagree about the exact definition of narrative, their work unanimously conceives narrative as representational in nature. As explained by Marie-Laure Ryan (2004, 13) in *Narrative Across Media*, these narratologists believe the standard conception of narrativity to be manifested in the act of "telling somebody else that something happened, with the assumption that the addressee is not already aware of the events." Also, the etymological root of the word narrative defines it as a form of recounting, as it derives in part from the Latin verb *narrare*, which means 'to recount.' A feasible definition of the structuralist concept of narrative, then, is given by Gerald Prince in his Dictionary of *Narratology*. According to Prince (1987, 58; my emphasis), narrative should be thought of as "the *recounting* [...] of one or more real or fictitious events *communicated* by one, two, or several (more or less overt) narrators to one, two, or several (more or less over) narrates." With this definition in mind, Prince subsequently argues that statements such as 'Mary is tall and Peter is small' do not constitute narratives, since "they do not *represent* any event" (ibid.; my emphasis). Similar definitions of narration can be found in the works of other prominent narratologists. Rimmon-Kenan (1983, 2; my emphasis) describes it for example as "a *communication* process in which the narrative as message is transmitted by addresser to addressee." Branigan (1992, 146) accordingly believes the concept of telling to involve "a 'narrator' who places the events of the narrative in the past, or creates some other non-present temporal modality."

What is distinctive about this particular conceptualization of narrative, then, is that it understands narrative as something that communicates real or fictitious events from the past. The concept of recounting implies that the events expressed (the story) already happened and find themselves re-presented in the present by some discourse, whether verbal, written, pantomimic, or any other form of narrative transmission (Chatman 1978). For structuralist narratologists, then, a narrative retrieves the there-and-then in the here-and-now, thereby suppressing (but not replacing) our direct experience of the here-and-now. The following statement by Christian Metz (1974, 22), taken from his *Semiotics of the Cinema*, is exemplary of this basic principle:

> Reality assumes presence, which has a privileged position along two parameters, space and time; only the here and now are completely real. By its very existence, the narrative suppresses the now (accounts of current life) or the here (live television coverage), and most frequently the two together (newsreels, historical accounts, etc.).

Leaving aside the epistemological question of reality, the words of Metz are typical for the representational approach to narrative. In this approach, the *modus operandi* of narrative is concerned with communicating or re-presenting events, not with staging new events. Stories concern the there-and-then and are solely expressed in the here-and-now.

Representation or Presentation?

Although structuralist narratologists study various forms of narrative transmission, their episteme has arisen mainly out of stories that are either told or written. Not surprisingly, it is in these narrative formats where one finds a strong representational logic:

> The states of affairs stipulated [...] in novels are at an evident remove from the stipulater's or reader's immediate context, so much so that classical narrative is always oriented towards an explicit there and then, towards an imaginary 'elsewhere' set

in the past and which has to be evoked for the reader through predication and description. (Elam 1980, 98)

The 19th century novel is exemplary here. Books of authors such as Charles Dickens or Jane Austen portray without exception the story as a thing recounted. This can be contributed largely to the presence of a narrator who, in telling the story to the reader, explicitly emphasis its 'pastness.' Narrators establish the story as something that happened in the past by using the past tense when discussing, summing up, and commenting on, the events pertinent to it and by employing specific temporal tropes (Rimmon-Kenan 1983: 110). The following famous sentence from *A Christmas Carol* illustrates this practice clearly: "Once upon a time – of all the good days in the year, on Christmas Eve – old Scrooge sat busy in his counting-house" (Dickens 1843, 5; my emphasis).

The representational approach to narrative becomes problematic however when applied to narrative formats without an explicit narrator. In cinema or theatre, for example the discourse does not always clearly acknowledge the 'pastness' of the story it expresses. We are presented with a sequence of images or gestures, and have the feeling as if the events projected or performed are happening right in front of us, in the here-and-now rather than the there-and-then. Elam writes: "Dramatic worlds [...] are presented to the spectator as 'hypothetically actual' constructs, since they are 'seen' in progress 'here and now' without narratorial mediation" (1980, 98). So, to what extent are these events still representational in nature as the audience witnesses the events unfolding directly in front of them? Is this representational logic still valid? In the second edition of *The Cambridge Introduction to Narrative*, Abbott (2008, 15) addresses this specific problem, he writes:

Those who favour Aristotelian distinctions sometimes use the word presentation for stories that are acted and *representation* (re-presentation) for stories that are told or written. The difference highlights the idea that in theatre we experience the story as immediately present while we do not when it is conveyed through a narrator. My own view is that both forms of narrative are mediated stories and therefore involved in re-presentation, conveying a story that at least seems to pre-exist the vehicle of conveyance. A good counter-argument to my position asks: Where is this story before it is realized in words or on stage? The answer, so the argument goes, is: Nowhere. If that is the case, then all renderings of stories, on the stage or on the page, are *presentations* not *representations*. [...] I will stick to the term 'representation.' I do this in part because the word is so commonly used in the way I am using it and in part because it describes at least the feeling that we often have that the story somehow pre-exists the narrative, even though this may be an illusion.

Like Abbott, I do not prefer to use the (actually already Platonic) distinction between 'telling' (*diegesis*) and 'showing' (*mimeses*) to designate the difference between representation and presentation. I do prefer however, unlike Abbott, to keep the distinction in practice: To me, the logics of representation and presentation provide valuable insights, not when used to differentiate between vehicles of narrative conveyance, but when used to address different ways in which every single one of these vehicles in principle can deal with stories. Even a story that is told can have a presentational logic, and a story that is shown a representational. Admittedly, the representational logic governs many popular books and movies, but this logic seems confidently at home in – not essential to – the medium-specific form of these particular media.

In terms of story, a Choose-Your-Own Adventure book operates differently than a traditional novel, just as a cinematic experiment as *Lady in the Lake* (Montgomery 1947) works differently than most classical Hollywood blockbusters. Moreover, the dominance of a representational logic does not exclude moments in which a presentational logic takes precedence. In fact, many of the special effects in popular cinema aspire to the effect of presence (Gumbrecht 2004, 140). The cinematic artform even finds its roots in experiments that try to place the audience in the mediated presence of spectacular or extraordinary scenes – like *Arrival of a Train at La Ciotat* (Lumière/Lumière 1896). Such examples are famously referred to as the 'cinema of attraction' by the noted film scholars Tom Gunning (1986) and André Gaudreault (with Gunning 1989; Strauven 2006).

I approach, then, the logics of representation and presentation epistemologically rather than ontologically. They do not explain the modus operandi of a medium's essential form, but describe differences in how media are creatively designed, publicly received and academically understood. Still, it does not surprise me that Abbott chooses to stick to the term representation, as the representational logic dominates the field of narrative media and arts. Most of the popular movies, books and plays indeed create the feeling that the story somehow pre-exists its expression. In game studies, this intangible yet familiar feeling has been brought into the discussion on game stories by ludologists to argue that the medium of games differs fundamentally from cinema, literature or theatre. Popular real-time avatar-based 3D-games such as first-person shooters or action adventures, evidently, do not evoke this particular feeling. In his pioneering article on game stories, Jesper Juul (2005, 222) writes:

> Although movies and theatre do not have a grammatical tense to indicate the temporal relations, they still carry a basic sense that even though the viewer is watching a movie, now, or even though the players are on stage performing, the events told are not happening now.

Though Juul's observation relates to a sensation many of us recognize, we should be aware that his observation only concerns movies and plays with a representational logic. In their search to distinguish games from narrative, ludologists borrow heavily from structuralist narratology, and in doing so, create a concept of narrative, which not necessarily applies to all narrative formats (Ryan 2006, 184). In recent decennia, many practices have arisen that explore new ways of storytelling.

These practices no longer belong solely to the artistic domain of the marginal or the avant-gardish, but have grown to become a widespread part of our popular entertainment culture. Not only a lot of the avatar-based 3D-games sold today, but also things such as LARP (Live Action Role Playing), PnP (Pen and Paper) role playing, war re-enactments and virtual or augmented reality belong to this category. To understand how these media and art practices deal with stories differently than conventional movies or plays, we need to further explore the narrative logic of presentation and the way it deviates from the representational one.

The Logics of Representation and Presentation

So, what is exactly the difference between a representational and presentational narrative logic? To get a clearer idea of how the two logics differ from each other, this article borrows from performance theory. In theatre studies, a clear distinction is made between representation and presentation, not to describe different ways of narrative transmission, but to describe different ways in which the performance of a story addresses the audience:

> There are two ways of relating to the audience during the performance of a story. The difference is clearest in theater. In a representational play, the actors all act as if there were a fourth wall between them and the audience. If they look in the direction of the audience, they give no sign of seeing that anyone is out there looking at them. Instead, they pretend that they're seeing only what would be there if the play were real – another wall of the drawing room, or the rest of the Forest of Arden. [...] Presentational theater, on the other hand, tears down that imaginary fourth wall. The actors don't just admit the audience is there, they make constant contact with the audience. (Card 1988, 134-135)

Following Card, I believe the essential difference between representation and presentation to lie in the way the audience is addressed in the performance of a story, and consequently the kind of spatiotemporal consciousness that arises from this difference. The audience is either addressed as physically present or physically absent in the world of the story. This essential difference, as emphasized by Card, not only holds true for theatre. Still, the difference is particularly clear in theatre, thus as example, theatre helps to further explore these two logics.

In a representational story performance, we often feel as if we are looking at events that belong to some other time and place, even though the performance happens in the here-and-now. The actions on stage 'stand for' or 're-present' actions that unfold in another spatial and temporal moment. Sceneries, actors, and props all portray places, people and objects belonging to this dimension of the there-and-then. Elam (1980, 88) thus describes the dramatic world in theatre as "a spatio-temporal *elsewhere* represented as though actually present for the audience."

We as the audience, consequently, have a strong feeling we do not belong to this other construct of space and time; we observe it hidden behind the fourth wall, but do not have our place within it. Even though we experience the story in the here-and-now, we still feel as if it happens somewhere else than the here-and-now of our own physical, lived existence. The representational performance of a story addresses the audience as if physically outside the story world, and thus, in a sense, as a ghostly presence: consciously present, but physically absent, able to travel through temporal and spatial barriers (Bordwell 1985, 10). In its goal to show the events that are relevant to the story, the performance often propels us forwards or backwards in space and time. In only a couple of hours, we are mentally transported through many different moments in time while visiting many different places.

To illustrate that not only plays, but also many other narrative expressions possess this particular representational logic, one only has to look at popular cinema. In their study on various forms of mediated presence, Schubert and Crusius (2002, 2) write:

With a few exceptions movies keep the viewer in the position of an invisible observer – characters in the movie do not look into the camera (i.e., do not look at the observer), and the viewer has no body in the filmed environment.

Much like the theatrical performance, most movies do not address the spectator as physically present within the world of the story. We should however be careful when using the word 'disembodied' when discussing the difference between presentation and representation. Though spoken to as a disembodied observer, the audience nevertheless becomes physically touched by the things happening on the screen. We identify with characters and their struggles, empathize with them, and thus go through all sorts of emotions and affects during a movie screening. Moreover, as convincingly argued by phenomenology-inspired media scholars (e.g. Sobchack 1991; States 1987), our understanding of what happens on the screen or on the stage always presupposes our physical presence. Without a mortal body, anchored in space and time, nothing in the story would make sense in the first place. In a sense, a phenomenon such as disembodiment does not exist, as we simply cannot escape our 'flesh.' The question therefore is not whether or not somebody feels physically touched in a performance, but whether or not the narrative *addresses* the audience as physically present within the story expressed, thereby *positioning* them either as disembodied observers or embodied participants.

Distinctive of narrative discourse when steered by a representational logic, is the feeling it creates in the audience as if they move away from the here-and-now of their physical existence towards the there-and-then of the story told. This feeling is commonly associated with the idea of narrative immersion, as Richard J. Gerrig (1993, 3) describes in *Experiencing Narrative Worlds*:

> Readers become 'lost in a book'; moviegoers are surprised when the lights come back up; television viewers care desperately about the fates of soap opera characters; museum visitors are captivated by the stories encoded in daubs of paint. In each case, a narrative serves to transport an experiencer away from the here and now.

As will be explained later, the exact opposite seems to happen when the discourse is steered by a presentational logic. While we move away from the here-and-now towards the there-and-then of the story in what I refer to as the represento*logical* mode, we seem to stay in the here-and-now and the there-and-then of the story moves towards us in the presento*logical* mode (think of reenactments, augmented reality or LARP). Notably, both modes alter our perception of the world around us. When following Janet Murray's (1997, 98) exemplary definition of immersion as "the sensation of being surrounded by a completely other reality, as different as water is from air, that takes over all of our attention, our whole perceptual apparatus", the feelings evoked in presentation and representation both fall within the definition of immersion, even though the former operates distinctively different than the latter.

In his ground-breaking thesis *Digital Games as Designed Experience*, Gordon Calleja (2007, 88) gives an insightful account of two forms of immersion in computer games that seems to align with my own distinction between representation and presentation.

> There is a distinction that needs to be made between holding mental images of a scene in mind while imagining being present within that scene, and occupying a location within a computer-generated environment that anchors users with regards to other agents and enables them to interact with the environment from that specific location. [...] When we identify with a character in a movie or a book, or imagine we are in the same room as the protagonist, we have no way of altering

the course of events; no way of exerting agency. Likewise, the environments and characters represented in these media have no way of reacting to our presence, no matter how strongly we identify with them.

I follow Calleja in the distinction he makes between a form of immersion in which one has the feeling of being in the presence of characters without them noticing your presence (representological mode), and a form of immersion in which one has the illusion of being physically grounded to one specific location in space and time, perceivable for those who share this spatial and temporal moment (presentological mode). I prefer however not to incorporate the idea of interaction in this distinction. The distinction between narrative presentation and representation is not essentially a distinction between interactive and non-interactive. Both forms can be either interactive or non-interactive. Interactivity, or 'ergodicity' in the context of storytelling, describes the condition of media objects where "nontrivial effort is required to allow the reader to traverse the text" (Aarseth 1997, 1-2). Admittedly, many presentational narratives possess this ergodic quality, but there are many examples of representational narratives which also need nontrivial effort to make the story unfold, think of interactive DVD's, games such as *Heavy Rain* or particular experiential forms of theatre. All these examples hand the audience some form of control over the story's direction, thereby giving them the power to (co-)decide the faith of the story's characters.

In the tentative article *Beyond Myth and Metaphor*, Marie-Laure Ryan (2001a; my emphasis) labels this form of narrative discourse 'External-ontological interactivity,' describing it as follows:

Here the user is like the omnipotent god of the system. Holding the strings of the characters, from a position *external* to both the time and space of the fictional world, he specifies their properties, makes decisions for them, throws obstacles in their way, and sends them toward different destinies lines by altering their environment.

Different from this form of interactivity, Ryan also proposes the categories of "Internal-ontological interactivity" and "Internal-exploratory interactivity," respectively referring to narrative discourse where "the user is cast as a character who determines his own fate *by acting within* the time and space of a fictional world" and narrative discourse where "the user takes a *virtual body* with her into the fictional world, but her role in this world is limited to actions that have no bearing on the narrative events" (ibid.; my emphasis). Although these two categories differ from each other in the way the player influences the unfolding story, they both belong to the presentational logic as both categories give players the feeling as if things are happening in the here-and-now of their physical existence.

In a presentational story performance, events seem to happen in the perceptual field of our direct, first-hand or lived experience, even when mediated through a screen or some other means of transmission. The moment the performers acknowledge our presence, make eye contact, and start interacting with us, we change from being an invisible observer to an active participant. We are made aware of our physical presence and through this contact are drawn back to the here-and-now of our own bodily existence: physically anchored to one location in space and time and in principle able to act. Contrary to the representational logic, we do not move away from the here-and-now towards the there-and-then of the story, but as already stated, seem to stay in the here-and-now while the there-and-then of the story moves towards us. In effect, we still feel as if existing in some other spatial-temporal moment, but one that aligns with our experience of being physically in the here-and-now. In theatre studies, many scholars have tried to explain how this presentational mode differs from the representational one.

Most importantly, performers make the audience aware of their own presence by inviting them into some form of interaction, thereby undoing the audience's spectorial and voyeuristic position. This is often accompanied by a focus on the execution of acts that are real in the here-and-now and find their fulfilment in the very moment they happen. What occurs in the interaction between audience and spectator could be, but is not necessarily, meaningful in comparison with what has happened in the past and is about to happen in the future (Lehmann 2006, 104-105). Also, the performers usually do not enact prescribed roles but carry out prescribed tasks. They can still assume fictional personalities, but no in the representational sense; their actions do not signify the actions of protagonists. Rather than representing others personas, performers try to alter their own self, typically by changing their appearance and behaviour (Kostelanetz 1981, 8). As a result, the audience recognizes the performer through the fictional disguise. Performers lose their conventional function as an actor portraying a role, and make their performativity an integral part of the theatrical experience, often introducing a strong element of role-playing and playfulness in general (Cremona et al. 2004, 4).

In his book on what he labels 'postdramatic theatre,' Lehmann (2006, 104) sums up rather precisely the various characteristics of presentological performances as discussed above:

> [These performances] work on the physical, affective and spatial relationship between actors and spectators and explore possibilities of participation and interaction, both highlight presence (the doing in the real) as opposed to re-presentation (the mimesis of the fictive), the act as opposed to the outcome.

These characteristics also apply to many story-driven games. In games such as *Half-Life*, *BioShock* (2K Boston 2007) or *Fallout 3* (Bethesda Game Studios 2008) the game characters, similar to the performers in the prior examples, make direct contact with players. They acknowledge our physical presence by looking into our eyes, and direct their speech towards us. The opening scene of *Half-Life 2* (Valve Corporation 2004) is particularly strong in making the player feel as if they are physically anchored in the story world. When the player steps of a train riding into a station, a flying robot moves in front of the player and takes a picture of him (fig. 1). In this very moment, the game explicitly addresses us as present and perceivable within the story world that unfolds around us.

Fig. 1: Half-Life 2

Not surprisingly, this does not happen in a representological game like *Heavy Rain*. Characters do not look into the camera directly. Their eyes focus on the avatar who the player is controlling, even in the case of a point of view-shot. As in conventional cinematography, the camera in these shots positions itself near, but not along, the avatar's line of sight (fig. 2). Rather than looking straight into our eyes, characters look slightly past us, thereby enhancing the sensation that these characters do not perceive us as being present.

Fig. 2: Heavy Rain

Also, in games like *Half-Life* 2 we hardly find as many temporal devices (ellipses, flashbacks and flash forwards) as in games like *Heavy Rain*. The extensive use of these editing techniques makes the existence of a narrator recounting a story apparent behind the seemingly 'presentness' of visual presentation (Branigan 1992, 146-147). Thus, *Half-Life* 2 avoids these techniques as they would disrupt our feeling of being, not only mentally, but also physically grounded in the story world. Like the theatrical performances discussed, the focus is not on the communication of events from the there-and-then, but on the execution of acts in the here-and-now, as Juul (2005, 223) also emphasizes: "Now, not just in the sense that the viewer witnesses events now, but in the sense that the events are happening now, and that what comes next is not yet determined."

Game characters play an important role in creating this focus. Like performers, they come equipped with a set of pre-scripted tasks. Their aim is not so much to represent certain events from a real or fictitious past, but rather to create new events through interaction within the confines of the narrative context. The freedom fighters the player encounters in *Half-Life* 2 for example assist the player in various ways, based upon the situation at hand and the decisions the player makes. Each encounter results in a different outcome, but stays meaningful within the story world.

As explained by Michael Nitsche (2008, 55) in his seminal book on *Video Game Spaces*, story events like these do not seem to pre-exist the discourse – they do not evoke the sensation of 'pastness' – but seems to come into existence the very moment they happen:

Narrating in video game spaces differs from that of fixed literary or cinematic pieces. It occurs at the same time as the generation of the interactive event and is influenced by it. While literary, cinematic, and many oral forms of narrating build on events past and retold, real-time virtual worlds – like live television or radio broadcasts – narrate the events at the moment of their manifestation.

A similar observation has been made by Henry Jenkins in his exploratory work on storytelling in computer games. In his often-cited article *Game Design as Narrative Architecture*, Jenkins discusses game stories as being essentially spatial. Although he does not really define the phenomenon of spatial stories or environmental storytelling, it seems that he understands them as being presentological in nature. Jenkins (2004, 122) characterizes spatial stories as follows: "In many cases, the characters – our guides through these richly-developed worlds – are stripped down to the bare bones, description displaces exposition, and plots fragment into a series of episodes and encounters."

Again, the same presentological characteristics I have discussed earlier seem to be foregrounded here: Events feel as if coming into existence in the very moment they are expressed as the discourse focuses on describing what happens in the here-and-now (description) rather than providing a lot of background information on the plot (exposition). Consequently, the discourse places events meaningfully besides each other rather than after each other. Unlike the representological mode, where events often structure themselves in tight strings of cause-and-effect, here events organize themselves in episodes and encounters. Spatial stories also portray the protagonist less as a distinctive other and more as an empty vessel for somebody to project one's own identity on. Because of this, they succeed in extending our physical presence and thus function effectively as guides through richly developed story worlds.

To conclude this paragraph, the aim of the presentational mode is to create a story event in the here-and-now, while the aim of the representational mode is to communicate a story event from the there-and-then, whether set in the past, the present or the future. The former creates a form of presence in which things seem to happen in a time and place aligned with the here-and-now of our own bodily existence, even though we are not always literally physically present. The latter creates a form of presence in which one feels consciously present when things happen to others in a time and place beyond the here-and-now of our own bodily existence.

(Re-)Presentological Game Design

So, what are the implications of the difference between narrative representation and presentation for the design of avatar-based 3D-games? I have tried to map the difference between narrative representation and narrative presentation by placing the representational and presentational logic besides the three commonly accepted constituents of narrative (Fig. 3): "Narrative representation consists of a world (setting) situated in time, populated by individuals (characters), who participate in actions and happenings (events, plot) and undergo change" (Ryan 2001a). On the left and upper side of the diagram, I have plotted three forms of presence. These forms of presence have been borrowed from an article of Heeter (1992) where she reduced the phenomenon of presence to three main categories:

A sense of presence in a virtual world derives from feeling like you exist within but as a separate entity from a virtual world that also exists. The differentiation and experience of self may be enhanced if other beings exist in the virtual world and if they appear to recognize that you exist. It may be enhanced if the virtual environment itself seems to acknowledge your existence.

Fig. 3: Two logics of narrative

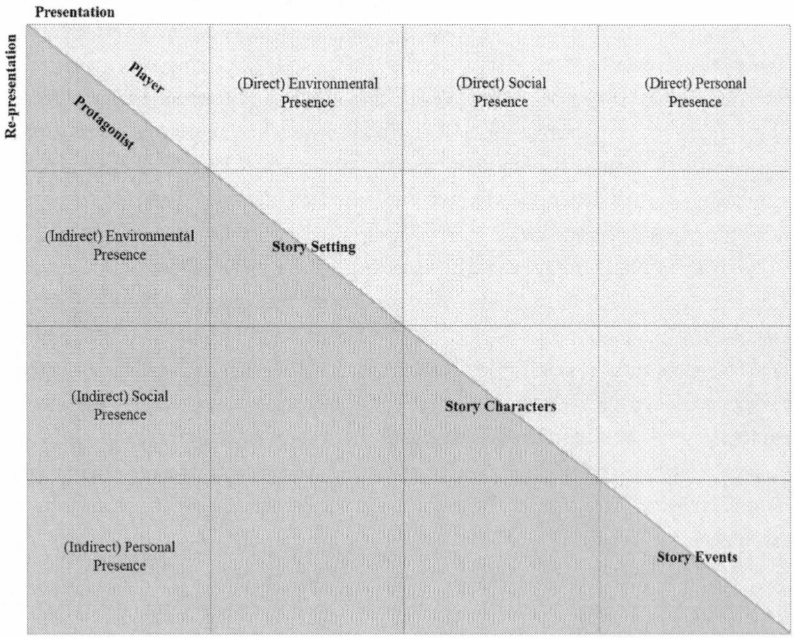

The three forms of presence discussed by Heeter (environmental, social, and personal presence) align with the three main constituents of narrative (story setting, characters, and events). On the presentological side of the diagram, I use the additive 'direct' to signal that in presentation the story setting, characters and events seem to exist in our direct physical presence. On the representological side of the diagram, I use the additive 'indirect' to signal that in representation, as the word 're' emphasizes, the story setting, characters and events seem to exist in another temporal and spatial moment, one that exists outside our direct physical presence. By positioning the three main constituents of narrative besides the various categories of direct and indirect presence, the diagram plots three primary points of friction: representational vs. presentational story settings, representational vs. presentational story characters and representational vs. presentational story events. What follows is an exploration of the implications of these points of friction for the development of avatar-based 3D-games, primarily from the perspective of presentological games.

Story Setting

When looking at the spatial design of 3D-games, the recurrence in sceneries is remarkable. Many games place the player in vast landscapes, from war-torn cities and stretched-out dungeons to grand canyons and endless forests. What is most striking about these locations is that, although they seem highly similar in their visual presentation, the way they are bodily experienced differs greatly. An endless forest can be experienced as a corridor, a maze, a branching path, even as a closed-off room, all depending on the way designers choose to structure them spatially. Everybody who plays 3D-games knows the awkward sensation of being blocked by an invisible wall when a forest visually stretches out for miles. Suddenly, the never-ending forest becomes ending, and thus, not an endless forest at all. (Often, designers use more elegant solutions than an invisible wall, for instance natural barriers such as a river or a mass of rocks.) This is where the difference and sometimes problematic relation between narrative presentation and representation in game design becomes visible.

The difference between representation and presentation concerning the story setting comes down to the idea of recounting once again. The story setting commonly refers to the where and when of the story expressed. Gerald Prince (1987, 86) in his *Dictionary of Narratology* defines it as the "spatiotemporal circumstances in which the events of a narrative occur". From a representational perspective, the setting recounts or re-presents the temporal and spatial circumstances in which the events pertinent to character(s) happened. To do this effectively, media rely on the ability of users to infer space and time from cues within the discourse, be it a description of a garden, an image of a city or the sound of a waterfall.

Cinema for example, calls upon our imagination to expand on that, which is actually seen, as Bordwell and Thompson (2001, 68; my emphasis) explain: "The narrative may ask us to *imagine* spaces and actions that are never shown." The setting when approached presentological on the other hand does not concern itself with communicating the spatiotemporal circumstances of events from the there-and-then. Space is not visually re-constructed through the imagination, but is constructed in real-time around the body of the user. Time is not represented, but develops in a progressing present. Thus, the spatiotemporal modus of presentation deals with environments addressing our bodily existence in the here-and-now, tied to one specific location in space and time, even when mediated by the screen-dependent technologies used in for example computer games or virtual reality.

The difference between representation and presentation leads to an interesting yet problematic tension in 3D-game design. As already discussed in the previous sections, avatar-based games do not position the player in an actual tangible environment. They need a screen-projected avatar to simulate the feeling of presence, which immediately invites a representational logic. As a result, their worlds always belong respectively to the avatar as protagonist and to the avatar as a disciplined extension of the player's body. When a 3D-game designs its setting solely as the world of the protagonist without taking into account that this setting also hands the player the feeling as if they themselves move through a world, aesthetic conflicts could arise. The body may disrupt the spaces developers want to trigger in the mind of the player. The way in which a story world is represented and consequently imagined can be drastically altered by the way this world, in its presentation, is experienced. Imagine a game in which we see an exciting cut scene of a character running through a forest chased by creatures unknown. This forest is shown to be vast and dense. It stretches out in all directions. The moment the game gives us control of this character, the forest that was first a maze, can suddenly become nothing more than a box with a clear exit. The moment at which the avatar changes from protagonist to the extension of the player's disciplined body, we suddenly, physically, feel the borders built into the game world. The vastness so convincingly portrayed visually, fades away when our bodies, confronted with the spatial borders of the game, remind us of the fact that we are simply running in a marked-off space.

Of course, this is not necessarily a bad thing. Some game genres, for instance Japanese Role Playing Games, design their spaces always in this fashion. Mainly because it is the representational quality of the story, expressed in elaborate cut scenes, that makes these games appealing. Whether the setting of the story changes from a canyon, to a mountain range or a forest, mostly it is, in experience, just a long pathway filled with enemies to beat before receiving another cut scene, which propels the story forward again. When we think about presentological avatar-based 3D-games on the other hand, especially action adventures, it becomes much more important to surpass this one-dimensionality in spatial design, as they are less concerned with representational storytelling.

When comparing the popular 3D-games sold today with those of previous decades, the development in setting is remarkable. Game developers have steadily become better at building rich, atmospheric sceneries, imbued with spectacular set pieces. The studio that developed the *BioShock* franchise for instance employed some of the best skilled artists to create this fibred underwater dystopia. However, in terms of presentation most 3D-games remain quite one-dimensional. To put it bluntly, the player still mainly moves through corridors, occasionally fighting off hordes of enemies. The next obvious step in 3D-game design will be the abandonment of this one dimensionality. Not only will the worlds of future games look even more atmospheric, they will also offer a richer, more meaningful palette of spatial experiences.

Story Characters

The relation between representation and presentation concerning story characters mirrors the previous paragraph on story setting. The same difference in logic applies. In presentational narratives beings exist in bodily presence to each other, and specifically to the player, within an environment, even when mediated through communication technologies. Story characters in representational narratives, on the other hand, come into existence through our imagination. They belong to the represented world of the main character and logically exist solely in his or her presence. Because representational narratives center on the trials and tribulations of the protagonist, our emotional investment in other characters is often channeled through empathic identification with this protagonist. Movies make us care for the main character so we feel moved when we see him or her struggling to reach a certain goal, as Torben Grodal (1997, 1; my emphasis) writes:

> The film experience is made up of many activities: our eyes and ears pick up and analyse image and sound, our minds apprehend the story, which resonates in our memory; furthermore, our stomach, heart, and skin are activated in empathy with the story situations and the protagonists' ability to cope.

Whether this protagonist is able to cope also depends on the characters surrounding him or her. That is why our emotional responses towards these characters depend largely on how they relate to the actions, feelings and desires of the main character. In short, we tend to feel sympathy for those who are loved or help-out. We dislike those who obstruct, endanger or deceive. The emotional reactions of the main character towards others, serve as cues for us to build our own emotional relationships. We closely observe facial expressions, body language and other signals to infer from them how we should relate to the other characters in the story. For example, when we see protagonists mourning the death of a friend, we tend to mourn with them. When we see them in pain, we tend to be deeply moved, which does not differ that much from watching a loved one in tears. Even if we have never actually seen the deceased friend in the movie, we care for his death, because the main character cares and we care for the main character. This empathy-driven investment in story characters does not work the same way in presentological avatar-based 3D-games.

Presentational narratives are less able to provide us with these sorts of emotional tie-ins. As already discussed in previous paragraphs, the game world does not solely belong to the protagonist, but also to the player, since the avatar functions as both the main character and the extension of the player's body. In presentational avatar-based 3D-games, the boundary between protagonist and player blurs, therefore we lose the empathic identification with the main character so typical for representational narratives. The emotional relationships we build in these games focus less on the main character and more on the characters surrounding him or her. Story characters do not longer only belong to the world of the protagonist, as they exist also within our simulated physical presence. Exactly this quality offers new possibilities for building emotional relationship with them.

When a presentological narrative confronts us with a deceased character, this often barely affects us emotionally when the meaning of this event is placed too much with the emotional state of the protagonist. It means something to him or her, but not necessarily to us. In presentational narratives, our empathic identification with the protagonist seems different from representational narratives. Because we are, in a sense, the main character, we barely see his or her emotional reactions to events, be it for the occasional cut scene. There is no camera registering every single facial expression or physical gesture. We see the world through the protagonist's eyes (first-person view) or from behind his shoulders (third-person view). In *Half-Life* for example, we almost never see or hear the protagonist Gordon Freeman. He remains for a large part a tabula rasa; an empty vessel for us to project our identity on. To really feel the loss of another character in a game, then, their continuous presence to us in the game world needs to be undone. To build an emotional relationship between players and characters, they must be placed in each other's physical presence in a meaningful way. To put it simply, they have to spend time together.

Presentological avatar-based 3D-games that succeed in building a meaningful bond between player and story characters mainly employ this approach. In its series on the best games of the last decade, the magazine *EDGE* pays homage to Valve's *Half-Life 2*, praising its character design with the following words: "Half-

Life 2's characters are engaging both dramatically and in action: they are a *tangible presence* in the world which help or hinder the player directly" (Anon. 2010, 70; my emphasis). In successful presentological games we often see that instead of the protagonist, the character(s) closest to the protagonist provide the player with emotional connections to other story characters. It is no coincidence that in *Half-Life 2* the most intense dramatic moments concern relatives not of Gordon Freeman, but of Alyx Vance, the girl who follows him throughout his adventures. For example, it is her father who gets killed in one of the episodes. Because the player spends a lot of time in the presence of Alyx instead of Gordon, we feel touched more easily when she rather than he suffers. Would it have been the death of Gordon's father, the effect probably would have been less as we play Gordon Freeman, and to empathize with the death of somebody else's father is in general emotionally more moving than to mourn the death of one's own imagined father.

Other successful games have asked players to visit their families regularly, like in *Fable II* (Lionhead Studios 2010), to escape a dungeon hand-in-hand with a little girl, like in *Ico* (Team ICO 2001) or to hang out with friends in bars, bowling alleys and clubs, like in *Grand Theft Auto 3* (Rockstar North 2001). As these games show, 3D-games can be emotional engaging when it comes to their characters. We humans have the peculiar ability to care for inanimate objects and anthropomorphic entities, think of the Tamagotchi or other robotic beings. Rather than re-presenting character relationships, the language of presentological games should further tune in on this particular human attribute. This is not only done by perfecting the way these digital beings act, look and talk to us. Also, their spatial position in relation to us is essential in how we relate to them emotionally. Space functions as a mediator. It can literally force us into someone's presence, or force us out of someone's presence. It can make a loved one reachable or condemn us to solitude. In simple ways, games have already been mapping emotional tensions on their spaces for decades. In *Super Mario Bros.* (Nintendo 1985), we have to cross a number of worlds in order to save the Princess. By expanding on these predecessors, future game designers will become more and more skilled in staging meaningful meetings between human and digital beings.

Story Events

The tension between representation and presentation in relation to story events also comes down to the difference between the player and the protagonist. From a representational perspective, story events are the events that happen to protagonists whereas from a presentational perspective they concern events that happen to players. Because in three-dimensional, avatar-based games the avatar is both player and protagonist, this tension is one of the most fundamental ones in 3D-game design. Are the things that happen to the protagonist still meaningful when they are experienced as if directed towards our personal presence? Marie-Laure Ryan (2001a) has written on this question:

> What kind of gratification will the experiencer receive from becoming a character in a story? It is important to remember at this point that even though the interactor is an agent, and in this sense a co-producer of the plot, he or she is above all the beneficiary of the performance.

One could indeed wonder if the majority of events that happen to characters in for example popular movies are still meaningful or pleasurable when they are staged as if happening to us. Ryan concludes they are not as "any attempt to turn empathy, which relies on mental simulation, into first-person, genuinely felt emotion would in the vast majority of cases trespass the fragile boundary that separates pleasure from pain" (ibid.). There seems to be a major difference in the sort of story events we like to experience ourselves and the sort of story events we like to be told about. A simple example will suffice to explain this. In games we enjoy running, jumping and shooting for hours on end, while most people would certainly not enjoy watching this for the same amount of time. Some events are worthwhile to be experienced in the here-and-now while others are worthwhile to be represented. It is not easy to say what characterizes the difference between these events. We need to study these differences in more depth which in the end will be of benefit to game designers. What sort of events are interesting to tell or to be told about (book), to show or to be shown (movie), to enact or to see being enacted (theatre), and what kind of events are interesting to stage in the here-and-now and to be experienced firsthand? When the answers to questions like these become clearer, the development of avatar-based 3D will equally mature.

It is important to emphasize the essential spatial quality of the presentational narrative mode at the end of this paper. When players are addressed as an embodied participant in the story world, the spatial design of the game world becomes important. Game designers indeed become, as Jenkins (2007) proposes in one of his articles, 'narrative architects.' Like architects, they trigger specific emotions in players just by structuring the spaces around their bodies in a particular way, thereby influencing the kind of stories players personally experience. Space thus can become much more than just the setting or background of the story, as explained by Mieke Bal (1997, 136) in her *Introduction to the Theory of Narrative*:

> Space functions in a story in different ways. One the one hand, they are 'only' a frame, a place of action. In this capacity a more or less detailed presentation will lead to a more or less concrete picture of that space. The space can also remain entirely in the background. In many cases, however, space is 'thematized:' it

becomes an object of presentation itself, for its own sake. Space thus becomes an 'acting place' rather than the place for action.

The spaces conjured up in narratives are not simply locations for events to take place. Narrative events often possess spatial structures that express profound meanings in themselves. One of Bal's well-known examples relates to the spatial tension between the house as a safe and the street as a dangerous place. Many movies deal with spatial transgression, with invaders who cross this threshold between the outside and the inside. These stories are powerful as they relate to broadly shared and deeply felt existential structures. In cognitive linguistics these structures or patterns are called image schema.

In *The Body in The Mind* Mark Johnson (1987) distinguishes some elemental ones, for example the container (inside/outside), the path or the blockade. In 3D-game design, too, these image schemata could be used as a language for staging arresting experiences. The beauty of 3D-games is that they seem to be able like no other medium to hand us the feeling as if we are physically present in the story world. Avatar-based 3D-games really excel in giving us sensations as if being inside or outside a building or as if being caught between two walls. The challenge for game designer, then, is to explore the various spatial experiences games can conjure up and embed them meaningfully in the context of a narrative. Besides running, jumping and shooting through corridors, computer games can stage many other worthwhile spatially grounded human emotions and experiences. When employed meaningfully within the context of thrilling story worlds, computer games move closer towards becoming that full-grown artistic medium we all long for.

Conclusion

In this paper, I have explored the logics behind two distinctive ways in which narrative media, particularly avatar-based 3D-games, deal with presence. I have argued that a basic distinction can be made between games in which players steer a hero through challenging trials and tribulations (e.g. *Heavy Rain*) and games in which players become the hero and have adventures of their own (e.g. *Half-Life*). Drawing on theories from structuralist narratology, the article has shown the former approach to be essentially representational in its logic. Subsequently, by bringing together alternative theories on storytelling from the fields of game-, film-, and theatre studies, the article has developed a new, additional concept of narrative, applicable to the latter approach. This presentological conceptualization explicates the narrative practice of creating story events in the present, while the representological concept describes the practice of communicating story events from the past, whether diegetically set in the past, the present or the future.

The former creates a form of presence in which things seem to happen in a time and place aligned with the here-and-now of our own physically anchored existence, even though we are not always literally present. The latter creates a form of presence in which one feels consciously present when things happen to others in a there-and-then; a time and place removed from the here-and-now of our own physically anchored existence.

The distinction between a presentational and a representational narrative logic proposed in this paper is broad and academically abstract. It only helps in making an elemental division in the broad range of narrative formats seen today, but does not suffice to describe the intricate differences between formats with the same logic. Popular avatar-based 3D-games for example share their narrative logic with experience theatre, but there still exist many differences between the two. For one, the former depends on the screen to stage its events, while the latter stages events in our material reality. It feels different when a real actor comes to you and shakes your hand than when a digital character does exactly the same, even when controlled by a real person. Future studies should elaborate on these difference forms of mediation, (dis)embodiment, participation and observation.

At the end of this paper, I like to mention that in principle not one of the two logics developed here is preferable over the other in future game design. It could well be that they originate from different basic human desires. Though more research is necessary to support this claim, it seems human beings on the one hand seem to enjoy listening to the adventures of others. We like to get an inside view on somebody else's experiences and thoughts, empathize with them and think how we would have done things differently. The affordances of real-time 3D computer technology enable people to have a say in how things turn out for story characters. We can steer heroes into specific situation and witness their reactions. This is one of the novel narrative pleasures 3D-games offer us.

On the other hand, human beings also want adventures of their own. We love to venture out into the unknown. In our contemporary experience society, the advent of previously marginal practices such as extreme sports, experience theatre, free running, land art, survival tours and interactive architecture testify to a culture evermore captivated by this direct exposure to intense experiences, from the subtle and the gentle to the extreme and the spectacular. Computer games take center stage in this development. Their affordances enable people to visit places non-existent in real life. Build like no other medium, games elaborate fantasy worlds for us to dwell in. This is another revolutionary pleasure offered to us by the story-driven games of today.

In the end, both logics make use of the affordances of game technology in their own particular ways. If designers and critics proceed on the paths they have now taken, these logics will steer the future design of game stories into two promising yet alternative directions.

References

2K Boston (2007): *BioShock*, Xbox 360: 2K Games.

Aarseth, Espen (1997): *Cybertext: Perspectives on Ergodic Literature*, Baltimore, MD: Johns Hopkins UP.

Abbott, H. Porter (^{2}2008): *The Cambridge Introduction to Narrative*, Cambridge, MA: Cambridge UP.

Anon. (2010): Popular Science, *EGDE* (April), 68-75.

Bal, Mieke (1997): *Narratology: Introduction to the Theory of Narrative*, Toronto: University of Toronto Press.

Bethesda Game Studios (2008): *Fallout 3*, Xbox 360: Bethesda Softworks.

Bolter, Jay D./Grusin, Robert (1999): *Remediation: Understanding New Media*, Cambridge: MIT Press.

Bordwell, David (1985): *Narration in the Fiction Film*, London/New York, NY: Routledge.

Bordwell, David/Thompson, Kristin (^{6}2001): *Film Art: An Introduction*, New York, NY: McGraw-Hill [1979].

Branigan, Edward (1992): *Narrative Comprehension and Film*, London and New York, NY: Routledge.

Calleja, Gordon (2007): *Digital Games as Designed Experience: Reframing the Concept of Immersion*, PhD. Diss, Victoria University of Wellington.

Card, Orson Scott (1988): *Characters and Viewpoint*, Cincinnati, OH: Writers Digest.

Carr, Diane (2006): Space, Navigation and Affect, in: *Computer Games: Text, Narrative and Play*, edited by Diane Carr et al., Cambridge, MA: Polity Press, 59-71.

Chatman, Seymour B. (1978): *Story and Discourse: Narrative Structure in Fiction and Film*, New York, NY: Cornell UP.

Cremona, Vicki A. et al. (2004): *Theatrical Events: Borders. Dynamics, Frames*, New York, NY/Amsterdam: Rodopi.

Dickens, Charles (1843): *A Christmas Carol*, Cambridge, MA: UP Welch, Bigelow and Co.

Elam, Keir (^{2}1980): *The Semiotics of Theatre and Drama*, London: Routledge.

Gaudrealt, André/Gunning, Tom (1989): Le cinéma des premiers temps: un défi à l'histoire du cinéma?, In: *Histoire du cinema: Nouvelles approaches*, ed. by Jacques Aumont, André Gaudreault and Michel Marie, Paris: Sorbonne/Colloque de Cerisy, 49-63.

Gerrig, Richard J. (1993): *Experiencing Narrative Worlds: On the Psychological Activities of Reading*, New Haven: Yale UP.

Grodal, Torben (1997): *Moving Pictures: A New Theory of Film Genres, Feelings, and Cognition*, Oxford: Clarendon Press.

Gumbrecht, Hans. U. (2004): *The Production of Presence: What Meaning Cannot Convey*, Stanford, CA: Stanford UP.

Gunning, Tom (1986): The Cinema of Attraction(s): Early Film, Its Spectator and the Avant-Garde, in: *Wide Angle* 8/3-4, 63-70.

Heeter, Carrie (1992): Being There: The Subjective Experience of Presence, in: *Presence: Teleoperators and Virtual Environments* 1/2, 262-271.

Jahn, Manfred (2005): *Narratology: A Guide to the Theory of Narrative*, uni-koeln. de/~ameo2/pppn.htm.

Jenkins, Henry (2004): Game Design as Narrative Architecture, in: *First Person: New Media as Story, Performance, and Game*, ed. by Noah Wardrip-Fruin and Pat Harrigan, Cambridge, MA: MIT Press, 118-130.

———— (2007): Narrative Spaces, in: *Space Time Play: Computer Games, Architecture and Urbanism – The Next Level*, ed. by Friedrich von Borries, Steffen P. Walz and Matthias Böttger, Basel/Boston, MA/Berlin: Birkhäuser, 56-60.

Johnson, Mark (1987): *The Body in the Mind: The Bodily Basis of Meaning, Imagination, and Reason*, Chicago, IL/London: University of Chicago Press.

Juul, Jesper (2005): Games Telling Stories?": in: *Handbook of Computer Game Studies*, ed. by Joost Raessens and Jeffrey Goldstein, Cambridge, MA: MIT Press, 219-226.

Klevjer, Rune (2006): *What is the Avatar? Fiction and Embodiment in Avatar-Based Singleplayer Computer Games*, PhD. Diss., University of Bergen.

Kostelanetz, Richard (1981): *Theatre of Mixed-Means*, Ridgewood, NJ: Archae Editions.

Lehmann, Hans-Thies (2006): *Postdramatic Theatre*, London/New York, NY: Routledge [1999].

Lionhead Studios (2010) *Fable II*, Xbox 360: Microsoft Game Studios.

Lumière, Auguste/Lumière, Louis (1896): L'Arrivée d'un train en gare de La Ciotat, Film: France.

McMahan, Alison (2003): Immersion, Engagement, and Presence: A Method for Analyzing 3-D Videogames, in: *The Video Game Theory Reader*, ed. by Mark J.P. Wolf and Bernard Perron, London/New York, NY: Routledge, 67-86.

Metz, Christian (1974): *Film Language: A Semiotics of the Cinema*, New York, NY: Oxford UP.

Montgomery, Robert (1947): *Lady in the Lake*, Film: USA.

Murray, Janet H. (1997): *Hamlet on the Holodeck: The Future of Narrative in Cyberspace*, New York, NY et al.: Free Press.

Nintendo (1985): *Super Mario Bros.*, NES: Nintendo.

Nitsche, Michael (2008): *Video Game Spaces: Image, Play, and Structure in 3D Worlds*, Cambridge, MA: MIT Press.

Prince, Gerald (1987): *A Dictionary of Narratology*, Lincoln, NE/London: University of Nebraska Press.

Quantic Dream (2005): *Fahrenheit*, Xbox: Atari SA.

———— (2010): *Heavy Rain*, PS3: Sony Computer Entertainment.

Rimmon-Kenan, Shlomith ([2]1983): *Narrative Fiction: Contemporary Poetics*, London/ New York, NY: Routledge.

Rockstar North (2001): *Grand Theft Auto III*, PS2: Rockstar Games

———— (2008): *Grand Theft Auto IV*, Xbox 360: Rockstar Games.

Ryan, Marie-Laure (2001): *Narrative as Virtual Reality: Immersion and Interactivity in Literature and Electronic Media*, Baltimore, MD: Johns Hopkins UP.

———— (2001a): Beyond Myth and Metaphor: The Case of Narrative in Digital Media, in: *Game Studies. The International Journal of Computer Game Research* 1/1, game-studies.org/0101/ryan.

———— [Ed.] (2004): *Narrative across Media: The Languages of Storytelling*, Lincoln, MN: University of Nebraska Press.

———— (2006): *Avatars of Story*, Minneapolis, MN/London: University of Minnesota Press.

Schubert, Thomas/Crusius, Jan (2002): Five Theses on the Book Problem: Presence in Books, Film and VR, igroup.org/projects/porto2002/SchubertCrusius-Porto2002.pdf.

Sobchack, Vivian (1991): *The Address of the Eye: A Phenomenology of Film Experience*, Princeton, NJ: Princeton UP.

States, Bert (1987): *Great Reckonings in Little Rooms: On the Phenomenology of Theater*, Berkeley, CA: University of California Press.

Stout Games (2010): *Dinner Date*, PC: Stout Games.

Strauven, Wanda (2006) [Ed.]: *The Cinema of Attractions Reloaded*, Amsterdam: Amsterdam UP.

Tamborini, Ron/Skalski, Paul (2006): The Role of Presence in the Experience of Electronic Games, in: *Playing Video Games: Motives, Responses, and Consequences*, ed. by Peter Vorderer and Jennings Bryant, Mahwah, NJ/London: Lawrence Erlbaum Associates, 225-240.

Team ICO (2001): *Ico*, PS2: Sony Interactive Entertainment.

Todorov, Tzvetan (1969): *Grammaire du Décaméron*, The Hague: Mouton.

Valve Corporation (1998): *Half-Life*, PC: Sierra Entertainment.

———— (2004): *Half-Life 2*, PC: Valve Corporation.

Space and Narrative in Computer Games

Sebastian Domsch

> Some impasses in critical approaches to vid-
> eogames might be resolved by taking a spatial
> turn.
> (Huber 2009, 383.)

This essay wants to look at the relation between freely navigable space and narrative potential in computer games. Computer games, especially recent ones, have
put more and more effort into their narrative potential (creating individualized
and believable characters, original storylines, meaningful actions). However,
where in most narrative media like written text or film narrative works primarily
as a sequence of events in time, one of the unique features of games is the player's
free movement through space. Thus, another trend in computer games is towards
the creation of open-world, or 'sandbox' games that do not restrict the player's
movement, and that do not impose a (chronological) order in which different
spaces are to be visited – as many first-person-shooters did and still do. The challenge for the game designer who wants to combine open worlds with narrative
potential is therefore to find new forms to 'narrativise' space; to provide it with
high narrativity, without linearizing it back into a sequence in time.

   A few introductory remarks might be necessary in order to situate this essay
and its specific focus within debates about the proper place of narratology in
game studies, not least since much, if not all, of the controversy hinges on mis-
understood or poorly expressed definitions. The most simplified (and seemingly
incompatible) arguments run like that: Narratologists claim that videogames *are*
narratives, ludologists claim that videogames are *not* narratives. In order to see
that both standpoints are not mutually exclusive, one needs to specify what they
actually relate to. When ludologists claim that videogames are *not* narratives, they
are giving a partial answer to the question: what is the *essence* of a videogame?
Their answer to this is, correctly, that the essence of a videogame, its *differentia
specifica*, is not captured by cataloguing them as just another form of narrative.
Or, to put it another way: what differentiates them from other narratives is not
the fact that they are narratives. When, on the other hand, narratologists make

the claim that videogames *are* narratives, they are (or they should be) talking about the properties that videogames have/contain. In this sense, videogames *are* narratives because they *contain* narratives (just like a picture might be a narrative because it contains one, without losing its *differentia specifica* as a visual image).

Now, a strict ludologist perspective goes even further, claiming that not only is the element of narrative in a videogame not sufficient (saying that it is a narrative does not sufficiently describe what it *really is*), but it is also not necessary: a videogame can be a videogame without containing any narrative. As Markku Eskelinen (2001) polemically puts it: "If I throw a ball at you I don't expect you to drop it and wait until it starts telling stories." This means that the narratologist claim has to be further qualified: *some* videogames contain narrative (which makes them also 'a' narrative). The legitimization for the narratological perspective lies in the statistic relevance of the 'some.' Because an empirical overview of the existing videogames, and even more when considering the trends of videogame development, will clearly show that 'some' means 'most.' Narrative elements are almost as ubiquitous in videogames as visual elements (about which one could make the same claims of non-sufficiency and necessity), and their importance and complexity increases steadily, which has led Marie-Laure Ryan (2009, 183) to talk about an "elective affinity (rather than necessary union) between computer games and narrative."

But not only the quantity of narrative elements (many of which could be deemed as external to gameplay proper and therefore not part of what game studies are interested in) makes narratological approaches to computer games productive – even more so does the mode through which so many games are choosing to convey their gaming experience to the player: as the experience of navigating through space. Though these spaces can be presented as pure abstractions devoid of any meaning but their spatial properties, such a presentation will run counter to human cognition's tendency to semanticise spaces – to give space a meaning. As we experience spaces, whether they be real or created by computers, we read them for their meaning and the stories they contain, and as we perform these spaces through movement and interaction, we inscribe our own narrative into them. We do this all the time, and computer games reward our interest in the narrative potential of space by providing extremely dense spaces, "charged with meaning to the utmost degree," as Ezra Pound has said about great literature.

It is clear that this progressive investment with meaning is nothing that is necessary to the playing of a game. It is unimportant to successful gameplay whether we refer to the chess piece as 'the king' or 'the-piece-that-is-allowed-to-move-for-one-field-in-each-direction.' It is unimportant, and yet it constantly happens when we play, and it happens with no games more thoroughly than with videogames. Videogames are the epitome of this tendency to invest the activity of playing with a fictional frame of reference, to imagine our decisions within a rule-bound system as narratively relevant events in a fictional world and to understand the performance of a game as the gradual development of a narrative story. Videogames are the triumph of fiction in gaming, or as Jesper Juul (2005, 162) has put it, "the emphasis on fictional worlds may be the strongest innovation of the videogame."

Game spaces, therefore, have a very high narrative potential, as they have "the ability [...] to evoke the mental representation that we call story" (Ryan 2008, 412). They do so as an integral part of the gaming experience, rather than an external element like a cut scene. This is maybe the most important reminder or qualifier when talking about narrative and games: *narrative is what happens in the minds of those who experience*. As humans, we experience life – our presence and agency within it – and we make sense of it by casting it in the form of narratives. Now, it is the magic of fiction to make us experience something that is *not* us, an experience that is again cast as narrative. While classic narrative media like prose or cinema tend to de-emphasize our presence and to substitute it with the presence of the other, interactive media like computer games or role-playing stress our presence, but they still retain the element of (fictional) otherness: the player experiences her presence within the navigable space of a computer game, but it is not identical to her own space, as her avatar is not identical to her. The difference between the two is narratively relevant fiction. Game spaces are spaces that we can experience through our presence within them as *other* spaces. And this otherness is conveyed by giving this space a story of its own, a story that the player will come to understand through experience and influence through agency. In videogames, spaces tell their own stories, that is, they provoke the player to construct these stories within her mind. This provocation is achieved by different methods, which will be sketched in the following, under the general term spatial narrative.

Spatial narrative as a term is suggested as the opposite of *sequence narrative*, i.e. narrative that happens primarily as a sequence of events in time, and that is presented as a recounting of these events through sequentially arranged signs, such as words on a page. Sequence narratives are conveyed through concrete narrative artefacts that usually name states and chronicle state changes. Spatial narratives do not necessarily do so, this is why they do not look the same, though their effect in the perceiver is similar. Spatial narratives are especially dominant in computer games that use navigable space. Henry Jenkins (2004, 124) has argued for the fundamental difference between sequence and spatial narratives:

> Spatial stories are not badly constructed stories; rather, they are stories which respond to alternative aesthetic principles, privileging spatial exploration over plot development. Spatial stories are held together by broadly defined goals and conflicts and pushed forward by the character's movement across the map.

Another currently used term for spatial narrative is *environmental storytelling*, a term suggested by Don Carson and further theorized by Henry Jenkins. Carson (2000) started out from his experiences as a designer of amusement park rides, stating that

> it is my objective to tell a story through the experience of travelling through a real, or imagined physical space. Unlike a linear movie, my audience will have choices along their journey. They will have to make decisions based on their relationship to the virtual world I have created, as well as their everyday knowledge of the physical world. Most important of all, their experience is going to be a 'spatial' one.

In a very similar sense, Jenkins talks about "games less as stories than as spaces ripe with narrative possibility" and sees "game designers less as storytellers and more as narrative architects." He then enumerates four ways in which

> [e]nvironmental storytelling creates the preconditions for an immersive narrative experience: spatial stories can evoke pre-existing narrative associations; they can provide a staging ground where narrative events are enacted; they may embed narrative information within their mise-en-scene; or they provide resources for emergent narratives (Jenkins 2004, 123).

Two of Jenkins' ways are of direct relevance to this analysis of spatial narrative and will therefore be discussed here; one is discussed under a slightly different approach, while the fourth (emergent narratives) seems to rather lead away from the purely spatial focus.

Evocative Spaces

Evocative spaces, according to Jenkins, are spaces that refer to or evoke previously existing conceptions of spaces, for example by relating to certain genres like the haunted house stories, or to fictional franchises like *Star Wars*. These spaces contain narrativity because they remind the player of narratives she has already encountered:

> In such a system, what games do best will almost certainly center around their ability to give concrete shape to our memories and imaginings of the storyworld, creating an immersive environment we can wander through and interact with (ibid., 124).

While spaces, or rather: the specific look and design of spaces, trigger narrative content, this content is all derived from memory, consisting of pre-existent scripts that the player recalls and incorporates into her experience of space.

One example might be the genre of the 'foot soldier re-enactment'-computer game, where well-known large-scale fictional combats can be re-experienced by the player not through the character of one of the protagonists, but through that of a common soldier, like the *Star Wars Battlefront*-series or *Lord of the Rings: Conquest* (Pandemic Studios 2009). While not experiencing the original story events, and possibly never meeting any of the well-known characters, the players nevertheless immediately recognize the spaces they are navigating/conquering/defending as part of the larger narrative of the fictional franchise. When looking at *Lord of the Rings: Conquest*, it is obvious that the main evocative element is visual, as the spaces are carefully constructed to resemble those of the movie version rather than being faithful to the book descriptions (fig. 1).

Fig. 1: Fight against the 'Olifants' as enacted in Lord of the Rings: Conquest

Another very intriguing example is the level design of *Brütal Legend* (Double Fine Productions 2009) that is heavily inspired by the artwork of heavy metal covers (Alexander 2009). Thus, even though the settings are not directly recognizable references to narrative franchises as in the *Lord of the Rings*-game, they are still highly allusive and rich in evoking narrative potential. In this case, it is exactly their lack of a concrete and unambiguously recognizable reference that makes them so successful in evoking narrative. The setting called 'Screaming Wall,' for example, a wall consisting purely of loudspeakers, and reminiscent of heavy metal stage design (fig. 2), has won the *Escapist*'s award for 'Most Ingenious Location.' The task of the player is to go to this wall and retrieve a number of speakers as 'acoustic weapons' in the ensuing fights. It is an interesting example of how a visual scenery that is familiar to fans of heavy metal concerts (and that has always been a merely visual symbol of acoustic power, since the actual speakers on the stage never were functional/plugged in) and therefore part of the myth of that music and the stories it tells (e.g. of sound as aggression and power) is being further enhanced and mythologized through integration into the narrative structure of the game's storyworld.

Fig. 2: A 3x6-stack of Marshall-guitar cabinets on the Tuska Open Air Metal Festival-main stage in 2008, setup of Jeff Hanneman from Slayer

Visual Clues

Another way to make spaces narratively evocative is by placing visual clues that point to narratives. In order to understand the visual clues left in game spaces, players often need to 'read the space,' that is, put elements/signs in a spatial relationship that then reveals a temporal/causal relationship, and therefore a *sequence* narrative. Visual clues are here defined as any kind of visually detectable signs within a videogame's navigable space that has narrative potential. Visual clues can relate directly to the main storyline or simply broaden and deepen the back story. In their presentation for the GDC 2010, Matthias Worch and Harvey Smith (2010, 16), while employing the general term 'environmental storytelling,' concentrated mainly on visual clues within material space (which they call 'player-space'): "Environmental Storytelling is the act of 'staging player-space with environmental properties that can be interpreted as a meaningful whole, furthering the narrative of the game.'"

Visual clues are everywhere in modern computer games. The game spaces of the *Fallout* (Interplay Productions 1997) or *BioShock* (2K Boston/Australia 2007) games convey almost all of their back story through carefully distributed and elaborate visual clues, as do many others. Most visual clues are structured after the basic model of detective fiction, where a detective minutely searches a crime scene for clues as to the exact narrative of the crime that has happened there. According to Worch and Smith (2010, 18),

> [e]nvironmental storytelling relies on the player to associate disparate elements and interpret as a meaningful whole [and] fundamentally integrates player perception and active problem solving, which builds investment.

Thus, visual signs are distributed spatially for the player to encounter. This encounter is non-linear, since there is no (necessary) predetermined chronology in which the player perceives the different signs. But by implying that they are the traces of past events, these signs prompt the player to perform an indexical operation, concluding the past events and their correct sequence out of them.

The main premise of detective fiction that follows the archetypical model of Arthur Conan Doyle's *Sherlock Holmes*-stories is that events inscribe themselves as observable traces in space. It is the task of the detective (and the reader as well) to correctly read these spaces for the relevant signs. As these spaces are *created*, they are intentionally filled with such narratively relevant signs. Creating spaces in written text or games alike means giving them meaning. That elements within material space mean something, that they are part of the general game's narrative, is one of the main expectations that gamers bring towards their encounter with these spaces. One just needs to think of the earliest adaptations of visual forensic clues into computer games, the so-called point-and-click adventures. Their whole point was the expectation that the presented spaces were not merely abstract surfaces with geometrical properties. A recent example of the use of forensic clues that nicely shows their roots in detective fiction comes from the game *Heavy Rain* (Quantic Dream 2010), where the player has to search a crime scene (in the aptly titled chapter "Crime Scene") for clues using a futuristic enhanced reality device called 'Added Reality Interface (ARI)' (fig. 3).

Fig. 3: 'Added Reality Interface' in Heavy Rain

She can review these clues at a later stage in the form of a (non-linear) database and make further research on them in order to better construct the (linear) narrative of the crime (fig. 4).

Fig. 4: Clues-review in Heavy Rain

The *Heavy Rain* example shows how next-generation games make use of the enhanced graphics to align the investigative process with other visual media like motion pictures, while commenting on what is possibly the next step in games' narrativization of space: augmented reality games take the concept of charging spaces with additional (and narratively relevant) meaning and use it on real spaces.

Not all visual clues are isolated elements/signs that are placed within perceptible space – sometimes it is the whole ensemble of visual elements that forms this perceptible space or a part of it (the landscape) that serves as a clue to narrative meaning. In a pre-scripted way, this is the way that Henry Jenkins' evocative spaces work: landscapes that, by their design, set a mood or atmosphere that contains narrative potential. More interestingly, landscapes in computer games can also reflect, directly or indirectly, the player's actions and tell of their consequences. The most common form of visual landscape clue – one that usually contributes more to back story – is the phenomenon that is comparable to the one known to literary scholars as 'Seelenlandschaft (*soul-landscape*),' that is, landscapes that reflect the mood of a protagonist, a scene, or a whole narrative (e.g. the fact that it is raining at a funeral). Jenkins (2004, 127) has made the connection to this literary device very clear:

> Game designers might study melodrama for a better understanding of how artifacts or spaces can contain affective potential or communicate significant narrative information. Melodrama depends on the external projection of internal states, often through costume design, art direction, or lighting choices. As we enter spaces, we may become overwhelmed with powerful feelings of loss or nostalgia, especially in those instances where the space has been transformed by narrative events.

But game designers not only already use this method, they can also use it either in the static way of printed literature (the landscape represents a mood that has been predetermined by the author), but also in a dynamic way, that is whenever a landscape's visual look is representative of the emotional or ethical significance of past player choices. One example that Jenkins himself cites is the game *Black and White* (Lionhead Studios 2001), where

> the player's ethical choices within the game leave traces on the landscape or reconfigure the physical appearances of their characters. Here, we might read narrative consequences off mise-en-scene the same way we read Dorian Gray's debauchery off of his portrait (Jenkins 2004, 127).

Another, more recent example is the game *Prototype* (Radical Entertainment 2009): Manhattan Island is one of five boroughs of New York and the setting of *Prototype*. Over the course of the game, Manhattan goes from being (relatively) safe and well-guarded to being overrun by infected creatures and hives. While the military is initially successful with containing the first hives and keeping the populous calm, the situation rapidly deteriorates until the only 'safe' zones are at the very edges of the map. This deterioration of the city can be seen as the mundane advertisements are slowly replaced with quarantine posters and graffiti-ed propaganda along the walls and billboards within the city, while the military starts to take a more proactive role.

These examples are all representative of a player's *indirect* influence on the game world. As games grow ever more complex, the level of interaction with the game world (still mostly in the form of destruction) is increasing, making game spaces submit to the player's physical 'narration.' One example for this is what Carson (2000) has called 'Cause and Effect'-elements:

> 'Cause and effect' elements can also depict the passage of time. A game charac-ter may return to a place that they had become familiar with earlier in the game, only to find it completely altered. This may be due to a cataclysmic event, or the disappearance of elements remembered from a previous visit. 'Cause and effect' elements could also be triggered directly by the actions of the game player.

This can for example be found in *Dragon Age: Origins* (BioWare 2009), when, after playing the mage's origin story, one returns to the magicians' tower to find the place utterly altered. Many other fantasy role-playing games like *Fable* feature this effect. In these cases, the change of the game space happens in the player's absence and only as a result of the general story, and not the player's direct inter-action. The same is true for the world-changing events that are introduced into the online-world of *World of Warcraft* (Blizzard Entertainment 2004) through the add-on "Cataclysm." But it can also happen in the presence of the player and more closely linked to his actions, as in the *Fallout 3* (Bethesda Game Studios 2008) add-on "Point Lookout." Part of the main mission of this add-on happens in a large villa that is being besieged by a group of 'tribesmen.' The owner of the villa gives the player a mission to oppose his main enemy. After returning from the mission, the villa is being blown up just as the player approaches it.

Though the influences on the game's space mentioned in these examples are direct, they are still, in a sense, static, as they still follow pre-scripted rules. Con-cerning the use of space in computer games, Espen Aarseth (2001, 159) has distin-guished along

> player's level of influence on the gameworld, where some simulation games, such as *SimCity* or *Warcraft*, let the player change the world, whereas in other types, such as the adventure games or most 3D action games, the player has no construc-tive influence and the world is completely static.

This is changing rapidly, though, with the rise of game physics. By making the spa-tial form of the game world depend, instead of the pre-scripted decisions of the designer, on the dynamic computation of the laws of physics (however simplified) in response to the actions of the player, the whole of the navigable space becomes a plastic element into which the player can inscribe her narratives. The deforma-tion of space becomes the (narrative) trace of the events that have happened as a result of the player's choices, just like the heart and initials cut into a tree might be a reminder of a romantic encounter below that tree. Game physics dynamize the landscape/navigable space and make it part not only of the pre-scripted, but also of the emergent spatial narrative. So far, and with the exception of games focusing exclusively on construction like *SimCity* (Maxis 1989), the player's interaction with her environment has albeit been mainly destructive. Many recent games use the high 'destructibility' of their environment as a marketing factor, like *Just Cause 2* (Avalanche Studios 2010), *Battlefield: Bad Company 2 (DICE 2010)*, or *Red Faction: Guerrilla* (Volition 2009).

Embedded Narratives

The second method of environmental storytelling that Jenkins (2004, 126) cites is the use of embedded narratives:

> Read in this light, a story is less a temporal structure than a body of information. The author of a film or a book has a high degree of control over when and if we receive specific bits of information, but a game designer can somewhat control the narrational process by distributing the information across the game space. Within an open-ended and exploratory narrative structure like a game, essential narrative information must be redundantly presented across a range of spaces and artifacts, since one cannot assume the player will necessarily locate or recognize the significance of any given element. [...] The game world becomes a kind of information space, a memory palace.

Under embedded narrative is understood all kinds of explicit narrative content that a player encounters while navigating the world of a videogame. These narratives can be either included in the conversations that the player has with non-player characters (NPC), or in artefacts that the player discovers, such as diaries, audio- and video logs, answering-machine messages, letters, scrolls, books, etc. Such textual, visual, or auditory narratives embedded into the game-world can heighten the non-linearity of the game's storytelling. Though these mini-narratives are usually all part of the storyworld and its meta-narrative (e.g. personal stories of in-game characters, news reports about the general development of the storyworld, myths that explain the storyworld's structure), the player can choose to read them whenever she wants, and the order of their encountering is often not pre-determined. Sometimes it is, as in the narrative that forms the background myth of *Brütal Legend*. Though the player encounters parts of this story in different specified places in the game-world in an order that he chooses himself, he will always find the parts in the right chronological order. Frequently, piecing the fragments of the embedded narratives together to form a coherent whole is an important task that the player is given ("Ask around the village for more information on X"). Sometimes they trigger new quests of their own, as when the player discovers a note left by an NPC asking for help. In their non-linear form, embedded narratives are an example of *narrative as archaeology* that is one of the main principles of alternate reality games.

Depending on the type of narratives that the player encounters, gathers, and mentally orders, the result could be a very linear narrative, with only the process of gathering being non-linear, or it could remain non-linear. In the first case, the embedded narratives are just pieces of a single larger narrative, e.g. the single scattered pages that form the account of a sea voyage and shipwreck. In the second case, the player simply gathers encyclopaedic information, all of which is in itself narrative and contributes to fleshing out the storyworld, without having to fall into a necessary sequence, or having to be complete. Fantasy-themed computer role-playing games like *Dragon Age* that can rely on their players' high interest in the storyworld make heavy use of the latter form. In *Dragon Age*, the player gathers together an encyclopaedia, called the Codex, that consists of over 300 different parts. Similarly, after experiencing certain events or encountering certain enemies in *Brütal Legend*, the 'tour book' of the protagonist is updated with readable text. An interesting case can be found in the game *Alan Wake* (Remedy Entertainment 2010): during the game, Alan the protagonist discovers pages of a manuscript the he does not remember writing. The player can read these pages, and they actually foreshadow events later in the game, thus serving as important gameplay clues as well as part of the narrative and its mystery.

The use of embedded narratives can also be a way to make an engagement with the storyworld more optional. This is the case, for example, with *Dungeon Siege 3* (Obsidian Entertainment 2011), a game that emphasizes 'hack&slash'-combat gameplay. By conveying most of the narrative information about the storyworld through embedded narratives, players have the option to learn or ignore this information, in contrast to games that rely more on cut scenes. There is often (from the viewpoint of design) a limited control about the order in which embedded narratives are encountered by the player, depending on the degree of linearity that the level design provides. Therefore, in order to be enjoyable, the individual elements need to be more self-contained and not rely too strictly on a causal sequence. An example of this are the 'web of intrigue'-sequences in *Prototype*.

Enacting Stories/Event Triggers

Jenkins' (2004, 125) concept of 'enacting stories' and 'micronarratives' is somewhat fuzzy:

> Micronarratives may be cut scenes, but they don't have to be. One can imagine a simple sequence of preprogrammed actions through which an opposing player responds to your successful touchdown in a football game as a micronarrative.

A possibly better way to deal with these phenomena is by using the concept of the 'event trigger.' An event trigger is an action performed by a player that triggers a narratively relevant event that would not have occurred or started without this action. The important distinction to other player actions lies in her (usually unwitting) temporal control over the triggering. Within a combat situation, for example, the player also performs actions that trigger responses, but her actions are themselves already responses to a previously triggered event (e.g. the encounter of an enemy), and she has no options to delay her own actions without being penalized by the game – if she stops fighting, she will be killed, but if she does not walk through a door behind which an enemy is waiting, this enemy will keep on waiting indefinitely (Egenfeldt-Nielsen et al. 2008, 121). In most cases, event triggers are spatial choices, that is, the event is triggered by the player moving to a certain point in space.

In all different media, narratives happen in time and space. Videogames give the player apparently the option to control space, but not time (the exception being the pause button, but that is a complete disruption of the narrative). Navigable/material space is usually fixed in computer games (it does not shift or stretch while the player walks through it), but if time were equally fixed, the player would miss most of the narrative content that a game world provides, because she would simply not be at the right place at the right time to experience it. Therefore, most narrative games are constructed in a way that makes time variable, and ties it to the player's actions via event triggers.

This variability applies only to the extradiegetic level, though, the way the game is constructed, since the very point of the event trigger is to narratively motivate the event on the intradiegetic level. This motivation works best (most immersively) when the event trigger is not noticed as such. Most games therefore try to hide event triggers, thereby exchanging the player's perception of a pre-scripted (and therefore completely linear) event to one with a high level of contingency, while retaining the high narrativity that lies in a pre-scripted scene's perfect timing. This is done almost to perfection in big-budget 'cinematic' games like *Call of Duty: Modern Warfare 2* (Infinity Ward 2009) or *Uncharted 2: Among Thieves* (Naughty Dog 2009). In *Brütal Legend*, for example, the player in one scene has to drive her vehicle across a collapsing bridge (fig. 5). Though in her experience it might feel like she barely just makes it through, most of the collapsing is triggered according to her current spatial position: the bridge will always collapse at just the right moment.

Fig. 5: Brütal Legend

While so far interest and research has been concentrated exclusively on space in computer games as an aspect of the *player's* perception and cognition, some of the more recent games make it worthwhile to consider the spatial perception of in-game characters as an interesting extension and dynamization of the concept of event triggers. Especially through the heightened emphasis on tactics of stealth in games like *Metal Gear Solid 4: Guns of Patriots* (Kojima Productions 2008) or *Assassins Creed II* (Ubisoft Montreal 2009), it becomes more and more important for the player to consider what NPCs can see, adding an interesting (and narratively relevant) dimension to his cognitive construction of the game space.

Many stealth games visually incorporate the information whether the player character (PC) is visible to other characters or not. In *Assassin's Creed II*, for example, there are signs above hostile NPCs indicating how 'interested' the NPC is in the player character (depending, among other things, on whether the PC is in the NPC's line of sight) and a colour coding on the mini-map indicating when the PC is not visible to any NPC. The 2010 game *Tom Clancy's Splinter Cell: Conviction* (Ubisoft Montreal 2010) has a feature called "the 'Last Known Position,' which occurs when the player breaks the line of sight of an alerted guard. This creates a visual silhouette of where the guard thinks Sam is, allowing the player to strategically flank his enemies" (Wikipedia 2010). This development mainly relies on the heightened efficiency of the NPCs' artificial intelligence, and it is to be expected that this feature will become more and more important in future games, dynamizing space and the player's conception of it. For example, it will most likely dynamize the concept of the event trigger: instead of patiently waiting while the PC approaches close enough to an NPC to start a conversation and trigger an event, that NPC might start to react on his own as soon as he sees the PC, for example by waving and calling (or running away screaming).

Doubling of (Player's) Spatial Perception

One area that is not explicitly considered in Jenkins concept, but that needs to be looked at closer in order to better understand the narrativization of space and linearity, is the doubling of the player's perception of space through an experiential (first- or third-person) and a cartographic view. As Espen Aarseth (2001, 157) has noted, the fact that almost all 3D-games double the player's perception of space with a 2D-representational perspective "stands in striking contrast with the prophesies of certain virtual reality proponents who believe that the 3D interface will render all other perspectives obsolete." Representational spaces are still important for the player's understanding of material spaces, and both perspectives can contain (non-linear) narrative markers or (linearizing) directional suggestions. While narrative markers are all elements with narrative potential that refer to the intradiegetic level of the storyworld (stories that have their significance in being part of the storyworld) and that are encountered by the player's character, the directional suggestions' ultimate target are the extradiegetic, gameplay-related decisions of the player herself, e.g. narrowing her possibilities of movement by pointing towards the best direction to take.

Material space and narrative markers: Everything that appears as part of the material space must be intradiegetically motivated, and narrative markers in material space are identical to what has been discussed earlier as visual clues.

Material space and directional suggestions: Sometimes, visual clues within material space can serve as directional suggestions. The easiest form of this are road signs that the player might encounter (fig. 6 and 7), but also traces or hints left by NPCs that the player is following. Carson (2000) has called the latter form 'Following Saknussemm':

> Derived from the story *Journey to the Center of the Earth* by Jules Verne. In Verne's story the main characters follow a trail of symbols scratched into subterranean walls by their adventuring predecessor, a sixteenth century Icelandic scientist, Arne Saknussemm. In this way, the game player is pulled through the story by following 'bread crumbs' left behind by a fictitious proceeding game character. Whether you create notes scattered throughout your environments, or have the

game player follow the destructive path of some dangerous creature, 'cause and effect' elements will only heighten the drama of the story you are trying to tell.

Fig. 6: An interior in Fallout 3 *with signs leading into different directions*

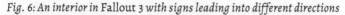

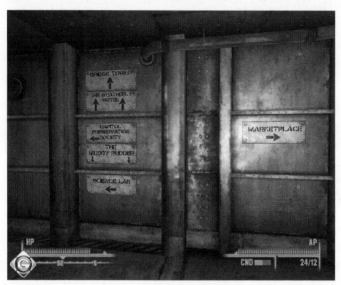

Fig. 7: In Batman: Arkham Asylum *(Rocksteady Studios 2009), the player can see the environment through a 'detective mode' that enables her to follow traces, e.g. of tobacco, to find a person*

These directional suggestions linearize space, but in a less mechanic way than those that are positioned in representational space. Part of the reason for this is that diegetically they are positioned on a lower level, and have therefore less authority (the road sign could be simply wrong, or misleading), while at the same time not breaking the narrative immersion.

A borderline case, but very important as a tool for the narrativization of space are the suggestive camera movements that effectively constitute in-game mini-narratives that 'explain' certain spaces, as with certain spatial riddles in *God of War* (SCE Santa Monica Studio 2005). These are a special form of the establishing shot known from film theory (or rather, a further evolution of it) that are used to explain and narrativize the game's navigable space. Formally, the main difference to the mostly static establishing shot from film is that it involves a camera *movement* that effectively temporalizes space by continually showing parts of it in a certain order in time. The goal of these shots is usually to acquaint the player not only with the dimensions of the space she will from then on navigate, but also with the special obstacles that this room provides for her navigation, as well as possible solutions for these obstacles. These establishing shots serve as implicit directional suggestions while at the same time helping the player read the space and the story it contains (e.g. the riddle of how to cross it).

Representational spaces and narrative markers: Maps can tell stories. This is by no means restricted to maps in computer games. Topographical details can tell stories about the terrain and its possible navigation through forests, mountains, glaciers, deserts, streets, etc., the positioning of cities and villages can tell stories about how a land has been colonized etc. One thing that is rather specific to computer games is that maps are not static in what they present, but respond dynamically to the actions of the player, especially her spatial exploration. This is usually seen in the gradual filling of a previously empty or black map with markers for those spaces that the player has already explored, implying the story of that exploration. Marked places on the map are often even hyperlinked to the questlog, chronicling either done deeds, or future tasks. Moving over the symbols for side missions in this map for *Brütal Legend* will reveal information about the type of mission.

Fig. 8: Narrative markers within representational spaces are highly non-linear, as their ordering principles cannot be chronological

Representational spaces and directional suggestions: The main use of maps and other representational spaces is usually orientation, and that means: enabling the player to know in which direction she wants to go next. That is why they not only consist of iconic signs, but also of indexical signs that tend towards hierarchization and therefore linearization. While the spatial distribution of side and main missions on an in-game map is non-linear, their semantic differentiation into 'main' and 'side' already prioritizes the main missions; and since the main quest chain is usually progressive (different parts need to be solved in a pre-set order), the player, while looking at such a map, gets a number of possibilities where she *could* go (the side missions) and one markedly different suggestion where she *should* go (the next part of the main quest).

The main linearization happens in the (functional) doubling of the perspective. The view of the map only gives the player her long-term destination, but only in combination with her view of the material space does it actually tell her *where to turn/go next.* This becomes most obvious when material and representational space are combined on the screen. Below is the third-person view in *Assassins Creed II.* It contains a fragment of the map view in the lower right corner that indicates both the direction that a desired destination is at as well as the distance to it (fig. 9).

Fig. 9: Assassins Creed II

A borderline case is the compass display in Fallout 3 (fig. 10).

Fig. 10: This is the map view in Fallout 3, *where different quests will make directional markings appear on the map*

Below is the first person-view in *Fallout 3* (fig. 11). Note the compass in the lower left corner that gives directions to a point that has been marked on the map. Thus, while the information given through the compass about the cardinal direction that the player is facing can still be explained as part of the character's perception of the material space (the compass might be part of his display), the directional marking is clearly part of representational space.

Fig. 11: Fallout 3

Still, true to the game's overall structure, this linearization in *Fallout 3* is not very strong, as, additionally to the main destination (the reaching of which will trigger an event that will further the story), the compass will among other things also show the direction of areas that have not yet been discovered by the player, thus inviting for non-linear spatial exploration.

Conclusion

As this essay has hopefully shown in a first sketch, to analyse the narrative potential of computer games by considering their narratives to be 'spatial' uncovers a multitude of highly interesting narrative structures and elements that are largely unique to these games. As game development progresses and games grow in complexity, these structures will only become more, as well as more differentiated. Space is one of the dominating aspects of today's computer games, and it is those narratives that are tied to space, that are told *in* and *through* space, that mark computer games' major contribution towards the enlargement of narrative, and not just structural borrowings from other media.

References

2K Boston/Australia (2007): *BioShock*, PC: 2K Games.

Aarseth, Espen (2001): Allegories of Space: The Question of Spatiality in Computer Games, in: *Cybertext Yearbook 2000*, ed. by Markku Eskelinen and Raine Koskimaa, Jyväskylä: Research Centre for Contemporary Culture, 152-171.

Alexander, Leigh (2009): GDC: The Art of *Brutal Legend*, in: *Gamasutra. The Art & Business of Making Games*, March, 27th, gamasutra.com/php-bin/news_index. php?story=22954.

Avalanche Studios (2010): *Just Cause 2*, PC: Eidos Interactive.

Bethesda Game Studios (2008): *Fallout 3*, PC: Bethesda Softworks.

BioWare (2009) *Dragon Age: Origins*, PC: Electronic Arts.

Blizzard Entertainment (2004): *World of Warcraft*, PC: Vivendi.

Carson, Don (2000): Environmental Storytelling: Creating Immersive 3D Worlds Using Lessons Learned from the Theme Park Industry, gamasutra.com/view/ feature/3186/environmental_storytelling_.php.

DICE (2010): *Battlefield: Bad Company 2*, PC: Electronic Arts.

Double Fine Productions (2009): *Brütal Legend*, PC: Electronic Arts.

Egenfeldt-Nielsen, Simon/Smith, Jonas Heide/Tosca, Susana Pajares (2008): *Understanding Video Games: The Essential Introduction*, New York, NY/London: Routledge.

Eskelinen, Markku (2001): The Gaming Situation, in: *Game Studies* 1/1, gamestud ies.org/0101/eskelinen.

Huber, William H. (2009): Epic Spatialities: The Production of Space in *Final Fantasy* Games, in: *Third Person. Authoring and Exploring Vast Narratives*, ed. by Pat Harrigan and Noah Wardrip-Fruin, Cambridge, MA/London: MIT Press, 373-384.

Infinity Ward (2009): *Call of Duty: Modern Warfare 2*, PC: Activision.

Interplay Productions (1997): *Fallout: A Post Nuclear Role Playing Game*, PC: Interplay Productions.

Jenkins, Henry (2004): Game Design as Narrative Architecture, in: *First Person: New Media as Story, Performance, and Game*, ed. by Noah Wardrip-Fruin and Pat Harrigan, Cambridge, MA: MIT Press, 118-130.

Juul, Jesper (2005): *Half-Real: Video Games between Real Rules and Fictional Worlds*, Cambridge, MA/London: MIT Press.

Kojima Productions (2008): *Metal Gear Solid 4: Guns of Patriots*, PS3: Konami.

Lionhead Studios (2001): *Black and White*, PC: Electronic Arts.

Maxis (2013): *SimCity*, PC: Maxis.

Naughty Dog (2009): *Uncharted 2: Among Thieves*, PS3: SCE.

Obsidian Entertainment (2011): *Dungeon Siege 3*, PC: Square Enix.

Pandemic Studios (2009): *Lord of the Rings: Conquest*, PC: Electronic Arts.

Quantic Dream (2010): *Heavy Rain*, PS3: Sony Computer Entertainment.

Radical Entertainment (2009): *Prototype*, PC: Activision.

Remedy Entertainment (2010): *Alan Wake*, Xbox 360: Microsoft Game Studios.

Rocksteady Studios (2009): *Batman: Arkham Asylum*, PC: Eidos Interactive.

Ryan, Marie-Laure (2008): Transfictionality across Media, in: *Theorizing Narrativity*, ed. by John Pier and José Ángel García Landa, Berlin: de Gruyter, 385-417.

–––– (2009): *Avatars of Story*, Minneapolis, MN/London: University of Minnesota Press.

SCE Santa Monica Studio (2005): *God of War*, PS2: SCE.

Ubisoft Montreal (2009): *Assassins Creed II*, PS3/Xbox 360: Ubisoft.

–––– (2010): *Tom Clancy's Splinter Cell: Conviction*, PC: Ubisoft.

Volition (2009): *Red Faction: Guerrilla*, PS3/Xbox 360: THQ.

Wikipedia (2010): *Tom Clancy's Splinter Cell: Conviction*, en.wikipedia.org/wiki/ Tom_Clancy%27s_Splinter_Cell:_Conviction.

Worch, Matthias/Smith, Harvey (2010): 'What Happened Here?' Environmental Storytelling, worch.com/files/gdc/What_Happened_Here_Web_Notes.pdf.

II. Places

Ludoforming
Changing Actual, Historical or Fictional Topographies into Ludic Topologies

Espen Aarseth

How are non-ludic geographies used in games? What happens in the process of changing a real or fictional space into a virtual arena for gameplay? Most ludic spaces are invented more or less from scratch, usually inspired from real, historical or fictional spaces but without any claim to absolute or approximate fidelity. Like Metropolis or Gotham City, they are not representing a particular place in our world, but generic ideas of the possible or the fictional. Adams (2003, 6) even makes the claim that "ludic architecture is disanalogous from real-world architecture." But sometimes, real, fictional or historic landscapes are found in games, and that situation is the focus here. What operations are performed in the ludification of a geography?

This paper addresses the process and significance of *ludoforming*, that is, turning a contemporary, historical or fictional landscape into a gameworld. Ludic landscapes consist of two layers that are superimposed, but independent: The topographical, which is presented by the game engine to the player, and the topological, which is the actual room-for-movement through which the player's tokens navigate. This distinction is inspired by Andreas Gregersen's (2008, 182) doctoral dissertation where he distinguishes between the physical simulation of a game object and its graphical representation (fig. 1a-b). Why we would want to make this distinction becomes clear when we consider familiar game situations where parts of bodies are seemingly impossibly overlapping with walls or floors.

Fig. 1a-b: Combine soldier from Half-Life 2: *physical model and fully textured character model*

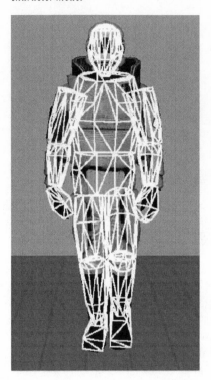 

This is yet another aspect of the fundamental duality between code and appearance or between mechanics and semiotics, that I pointed out in *Cybertext* (Aarseth 1997), and which was first theorized as 'intrinsic' vs. 'extrinsic fantasy' by Malone (1980). Information about the hidden layer is fed us through the representation layer, but we usually have no problem seeing through the representation and discern the ludic reality of the situation. When parts of our avatar appear temporarily lodged in the landscape, we don't panic but simply dismiss the tableau as a graphical 'artefact' without ludic significance (fig. 2a-b). In a fiction, on the other hand, we would assume that body parts submerged in walls would have special significance and possibly even fatal consequences. But games are not fictions, although *videogames* may contain both.

Fig. 2a-b: The Quake Arena *tower (right) also consists of (collision) boxes, not human-shaped avatars*

Ludoforming is not a new trend in games, but can be found in the very first extensive landscape game, Crowther and Woods' (1976) *Colossal Cave Adventure* where William Crowther faithfully mapped parts of the Mammoth Cave-system in Kentucky to serve as the world simulation. Crowther was an avid spelunker, and created the cave simulation as a hobby project for his daughters (Jerz 2007).

If we zoom out and look at game landscapes in general this way, we can make the same distinction between topography and topology. In *Myst* (Cyan 1993), we are bound to very narrow points of navigation, within a topology that resembles a hypertext novel or a bidirectional graph, while the visual representation of the landscape appears much more accessible, promising a lot more than the player can access. In *Half-Life 2* (Valve Corporation 2004), we are marching along a unicursal corridor that is cleverly masked by being embedded in a seemingly open world. Even in fairly open worlds, such as the 50 km² world of *Far Cry 2* (Ubisoft Montreal 2008), the hills and mountains form a labyrinth very similar in shape to that of *Pac-Man* (Namco 1980) (Fig. 3a-b).

Fig. 3a-b: Pac-Man *and* Far Cry 2 *with the same labyrinthine topology (including teleportation between certain points on the edges of the map), but different topography; bad guys inhabit the center*

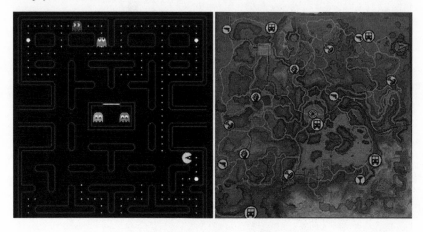

This is all well and good. Players understand and accept the game makers' need to shape the game world in order to achieve their ludic design goals. But what about game worlds explicitly modelled on real or fictional locations? One of my biggest ludic disappointments was playing *Project Gotham Racing* (Bizarre Creations 2001), which promised racing tracks from cities like San Francisco. Unfortunately, the very narrow view from the track could have been from anywhere, and lacked any kind of resemblance to the real city.

We can assume a number of different motivations for using well-known landscapes as game worlds: 1. *sheer recognition value*: Having a famous location generates curiosity and an interest in exploration; 2. *nostalgia*: In a model of a real place the players may revisit a favorite spot; 3. *authentic simulation*: Geographical fidelity is a must for historical games and simulators of all kinds. The careful mapping of known landscapes provides players with not just added value, but possibly also the best reason to pick one game over another. Ludoforming provides multiple pleasures but also the risk of player dissatisfaction and rejection if its promise is not made good.

Topology vs. Topography in Ludic Environments

Ludic landscapes consist of two layers that are conceptually superimposed, but independent: The topographical, which is the sign-stream presented by the game engine to the player, and the topological, which is the actual room-for-movement through which the player's tokens navigate. In these projects, where real or fictional space is modelled and virtualized for ludic purposes, or *ludoformed*, the latent conflict between topology and topography becomes apparent. Doors that should have been openable aren't, and fences that ought to be climbable are impassable. The topography, inasmuch as it pretends to represent real space, fails to do that as well as support the gameplay. The worlds have borders where none should be, and painted-on doors where functional and openable ones should be. Topology rules the ludic world. Gameplay is topological, and the fidelity of the topography therefore yields to the ludic topology.

S.T.A.L.K.E.R.: Ludoforming as Cut-Up Technique

S.T.A.L.K.E.R.: Call of Pripyat (GSC Game World 2009) is a case in point. The game takes place in the vicinity of the real Chernobyl site, to the extent that the game map is clearly borrowed from the real, abandoned town of Pripyat. However, the topographies are not identical. Areas in the game world are pieced together from the real locations in a most eclectic fashion. In this case, Ludoforming appears to be taking the interesting bits of a landscape, cut them up, and put them together in a new map, a bit like reconstructive surgery. The face of the landscape has been changed, but we recognize certain areas (fig. 4a-b).

Fig. 4a-b: Pripyat, left: Google Earth, right: ludic landscape – notice the different width of buildings

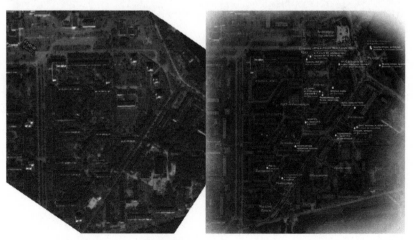

The *S.T.A.L.K.E.R.*-series is a special case of ludoforming, given the extraordinary heterogeneous origins of the landscape. The initial work in this heteroglossic, transmedia amalgam is the Strugatsky brothers' novel *Piknik na obotschinje*

from 1971, first adapted into a film as *Stalker* (Tarkovsky 1979) and then the game series in 2007 to 2009. In the novel, an alien, space traveling race has visited earth briefly and left behind certain mystical and powerful artefacts, like leftover trash from a picnic by the roadside, thereby creating hostile and unpredictable 'zones.' In the novel and film, guns are not the way to solve problems, but will only create worse ones, whereas in the games, weapons are a commonplace necessity. In the book and games, however, there is a focus on the artefacts and their effects which are completely missing from the movie. Finally, today real 'stalkers,' documented on YouTube, are entering the zone around Chernobyl/Pripyat and bringing back artefacts from the abandoned houses, as a parallel to the novel (fig. 5a-d).

Fig. 5a-d: Pripyat on the left, ludo-Pripyat on the right

TLOTRO: From Fictional to Virtual Map

The MMORPG-adaptation of J.R.R. Tolkien's *The Lord of the Rings* from 1954 is perhaps the best example of the ludoforming of a fictional world, since the fictional map in the novel is the most recognized and detailed of its kind. The virtual world of the game is dramatically different from the fictional, even though it topologically resembles it to a certain degree. As can be seen from the below illustrations (fig. 6a-b), however, the areas which are ludoformed represent a selection of the novel's core landscape rather than the whole sub-continent. Furthermore, the distances are shrunk to such a degree that the 200-mile road from Bree to Rivendell can be traversed on horse in ten minutes in the game. In the words of one anonymous player of *The Lord of the Rings Online* (Turbine 2007) complaining on a game forum: "Why can't I go where I want? Why are there invisible walls, why are the trees in Old Forest more like a wall than like trees? Why the hell does it take 10 minutes to ride from Bree to Rivendell?"

Fig. 6a-b: Map of Middel-Earth in Tolkien's printed novel (left) and in TLOTRO (right)

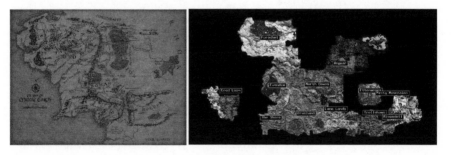

Ludo-Compression in 'Red Dead Redemption 2'

We see this same mismatch in most large-scale open game worlds that are ludoformed; a recent example can be found in *Red Dead Redemption 2* (Rockstar Studios 2018), where the player/protagonist, Arthur Morgan, must ride from the snowy Rocky Mountains to the fictionalized New Orleans, 'St. Dennis.' This can be done in minutes, not weeks, and as we study the map, we see ludo-compression at work; the whole of the American Southwest, an area that should span at least a quarter of the lower 48 states, is reduced to a few dozen square miles (fig. 7). Notice how much relative space is taken up by the city itself. Railroads carve through the landscape, from the low-land lakes by the city to the mountains in the North, but as I rode the train for a good hour or so, and as can be seen below, it looped around to the same place I boarded it, circling the map like a typical but expensive model railroad display cabinet.

Fig. 7: Red Dead Redemption 2 – *the wildish west in a nutshell*

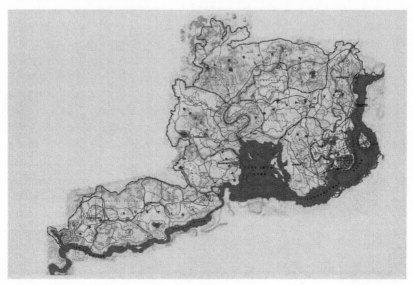

'Fallout 3': Washington, D.C., as an Incomplete Wasteland

Fallout 3 (Bethesda Game Studios 2008) has an interesting, dual map structure; primarily a vast, open landscape littered with various places to the west and north, and a labyrinthine set of ground-zero-like ruins in what used to be Washington, D.C., to the southeast (fig. 8). In the ruined city, the player must navigate by subway tunnels to make their way, while in the open wilderness most areas can be reached by straight-forward trajectories. The game is a spectacular form of ludoforming, which retro-anticipates a post-holocaust land, using nuclear devastation as a form of estrangement that has transformed the familiar urban and suburban areas into a wilderness that retains place-names and ruins from the players' present and future.

Fig. 8: Fast-travel locations in Fallout 3

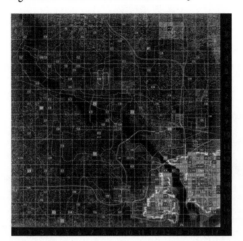

Ludic Space Deludified

The inverse of ludoforming occurs when an indigenous ludic space reaches a status that transcends its ludic purpose. This opposite movement might be termed deludification, whereby an original game landscape is transformed by social experience into an ontologically non-fictional, merely physically virtual space of social importance. Typical examples hereof is central meeting places in massive multiplayer games like *World of Warcraft* (Blizzard Entertainment 2004), where virtual cities like Ogrimar or Stormwind become non-physical but socially real alternatives to our places of living and doing business.

This may happen when players attach meaning to the place independent on the intended gameplay the place was designed for. One example is the lake in Winterspring in *World of Warcraft* where the infamous 'funeral raid' took place, in which members of the enemy faction crashed a commemorative moment for a deceased guild member; it used to be the mourned guild member's favourite fishing spot, but is now remembered as the site of one of the most contested episodes in the history of MMO gaming (Goguen 2009).

Deludification of this nature is most typical in social, multiplayer games, where of course many non-ludic activities tend to transpire as part of the players' use of the virtual world for non-ludic socializing. However, one might also imagine *deludified* space in other kinds of games. A classic example was made by the artist Jim Munroe (2004), when he was documenting his experience as a tourist in Liberty City, by simply walking around and observing the city as though it were a real place and not a gameworld (fig. 9). Munroe ironically also points out the positive difference between a ludoformed city versus its source.

Fig. 9: "It's the place where the game Grand Theft Auto III is set..."

Aesthetic Parallels to Ludoforming in Painting and Fiction

Although ludoforming is by eponymous necessity restricted to games, it might be worthwhile to contemplate parallels from the other arts. In literature, the phenomenon of fictionalizing real space by adapting it to narrative needs is common but also a bit hard to pinpoint, since the comparison may not be very clear. In painting, it is easier to spot transformations, as the differences show up visually, just like in ludoforming. For instance, in James Holland's *Venice* from 1850 we have a scene that absolutely resembles Venice, except that it does not "correspond to any real view but is a pastiche of known and imaginary features" as the wall text in the Manchester Art Museum reads (fig. 10).

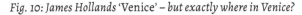

Fig. 10: James Hollands 'Venice' – but exactly where in Venice?

In theatrical plays and in movies, likewise, it is far from unusual to use real places that represent themselves or stage sets that faithfully mimic the real location in which the action is taking place. But here also, the mixing of faithful or real and invented elements will often be the preferred technique, serving the needs of the dramatic presentation rather than expectations of historical accuracy.

What is Ludoforming?

Perhaps my construction of *ludo*forming might be a form of ludo-essentialism (the insistence that games are essentially different from all other kinds of human expression); or, does it perhaps belong to a more general phenomenon? If so, which one? Are there aspects of ludoforming that cannot be found in non-ludic spatial transformations, or can it simply be subsumed under a more general label? Here we might consider a number of possible candidates:

Simulation: Simulations typically work by reducing a phenomenon to its essential features (with the essential thus defined by the context and purpose of the simulation), thereby avoiding the full and indiscriminate representation of everything present in a situation. Therefore, ludoforming could be seen as a form of simulation, where only game-relevant aspects are included, but with most ludoformed landscapes this is not truly the case. Instead, we see that the landscape is altered from the original (tweaked, pinched, and otherwise enhanced to afford better gameplay), and this is not congruent with simulation.

Remediation: Bolter and Gruisin's (1999) concept is not very clearly defined, but has to do with the media-channel transfer of content. As such, it is clear that a real or historical landscape cannot be said to be remediated, only mediated, since it is not mediated originally. A fictional landscape, on the other hand, can be said to be remediated when it appears in a game, but this does not mean that it has been ludoformed, since no special care need have been made for its ludification. So ludoforming and remediation are not necessarily overlapping, nor, when they do overlap, sufficiently overlapping concepts.

Adaptation: Ludoforming could be seen as simply a form of adaptation, that is, aesthetic code-switching from one medium to another, eg., from novel to film, or from videogame to board game. However, while some cases of ludoforming are clearly adaptations, such as the LOTRO example above, most are not. And even when they to some extent are, such as the early instalments of the *Call of Duty* series, they present the player with so much new material that 'adaptation' is not a fitting term. 'Allusion' might be a better term here.

Theming: Theming, or "the use of an overarching theme, such as western, to create a holistic and integrated spatial organization of a consumer venue" (Lucas 2007: 1) can also be connected to ludoforming, but it does not have to be; instead, they appear to be orthogonal: one can theme without ludoforming and one can ludo-form without theming, but they can also be combined. An extreme example of such a combination would be the Parker Brothers' board game *Monopoly* from 1935, which not only is themed with the street names from a capital or important city in its localized versions, but also can be said to be a ludoformed version of same. The main difference, however, is that theming involves modifying the representational aspects of the *target* alone (and functional), while ludoforming does the opposite: it tries to reproduce the representational aspects of the *source* while modifying its structural aspects.

As should now be clear, ludoforming is not really reducible to these somewhat similar representational processes. This does not mean that it could not in principle be reduced to some other, overarching concept, but let's assume, for now, that such a concept does not (yet) exist. Might there be other terms that provide parallels to ludoforming? I have already coined 'picturaforming' in the case of James Holland's *Venice*, but there are much more well-established notions at hand. For instance, fictionalization, and also dramatization, are clear parallels which contain some but not all of the operational qualities of ludoforming. In both cases key representational aspects are typically sought preserved, which structural aspects are modified to meet the target purpose. But neither these purposes, their structural aspects, nor the operations needed to modify them are the same.

Ludoforming's more general category is *ludification*. To ludify is to turn something into a game (as opposed to gamification, which does not change the main purpose of the endeavour, but only tries to stimulate the operators' motivation), by changing communicational, structural and material aspects in such a way that the original purpose is secondary or abandoned altogether. Ludoforming, then, is that part of ludification which has to do with the landscape. Ludoforming works by editing an existing topography to fit the ludic topology. It often but not necessarily involves a restriction, reduction or distillation of the source landscape, or simply a reshaping that meets the ludic demands, for instance in terms of balancing the game or making it more (and sometimes less) challenging.

The actual world is not a good playground, so when it is used unchanged, like the last area in *S.T.A.L.K.E.R.*, it is the least successful in the game. Another example is the highly documentary WWII-shooter *Brothers in Arms: Road to Hill 30* (Gearbox Software 2005), where the landscape from historical battles were faithfully modelled down to the shape of the window sills (fig. 11). While the title deserves praise for successfully recreating the tedious and repetitive tactics of authentic warfare, it did not, at least for this player, give the same satisfactory feeling of play as the more cinematically derived, ludoformed titles.

Fig. 11: Brothers in Arms: Road to Hill 30

References

Aarseth, Espen (1997): *Cybertext: Perspectives on Ergodic Literature*, Baltimore, MA/ London: Johns Hopkins UP.

Adams, Ernest (2003): The Construction of Ludic Space, in: *Proceedings of the 2003 DiGRA International Conference: Level Up*, digra.org:8080/Plone/dl/db/ 05150.52280.pdf.

Bethesda Game Studios (2008): *Fallout 3*, PC: Bethesda Softworks.

Bizarre Creations (2001): *Project Gotham Racing*, Xbox: MS Game Studios.

Blizzard Entertainment (2004): *World of Warcraft*, PC: Vivendi.

Bolter, Jay David/Grusin, Richard (1999): *Remediation: Understanding New Media*, Cambridge, MA/London: MIT Press.

Crowther, William/Woods, Don (1976): *Colossal Cave Adventure*, PDP-10: Crowther/ Woods.

Cyan (1993): *Myst*, PC: Brøderbund.

Gearbox Software (2005): *Brothers in Arms: Road to Hill 30*, PC: Ubisoft.

Gregersen, Andreas Lindegaard (2008): *Core Cognition and Embodied Agency in Gaming: Towards a Framework for Analysing Structure and Function of Computer Games*, PhD thesis, University of Copenhagen.

Goguen, Stacey (2009): Dual Wielding Morality: World of Warcraft and the Ethics of Ganking, in: *Proceedings of The Philosophy of Computer Games Conference 2009*, proceedings2009.gamephilosophy.org.

GSC Game World (2009): *S.T.A.L.K.E.R.: Call of Pripyat*, PC: bitComposer Games.

Jerz, Dennis G. (2007): Somewhere nearby Is Colossal Cave: Examining Will Crowther's Original 'Adventure' in Code and in Kentucky, in: *Digital Humanities Quarterly* 1/2, digitalhumanities.org/dhq/vol/1/2/000009/000009.html.

Lukas, Scott A. [Ed.] (2007): *The Themed Space: Locating Culture, Nation, and Self*, Lanham, MD/Plymouth: Lexington Books.

Malone, Thomas W. (1980): *What Makes Things Fun to Learn? A Study of Intrinsically Motivating Computer Games*, Palo Alto, CA: Xerox.

Munroe, Jim (2004): My Trip to Liberty City, youtube.com/watch?v=fxpDHiH5PKk.

Namco (1980): *Pac-Man*, Arcade: Midway Games.

Rockstar Studios (2018): *Red Dead Redemption 2*, PS4/Xbox One: Rockstar Games.

Tarkovsky, Andrei (1979): Stalker, Film: USSR.

Turbine (2007): *The Lord of the Rings Online*, PC: Turbine.

Ubisoft Montreal (2008): *Far Cry 2*, PC: Ubisoft.

Valve Corporation (2004): *Half-Life 2*, PC: Valve Corporation.

There's No Place Like Home
Dwelling and Being at Home in Digital Games

Daniel Vella

More than four decades after the text adventure game *Adventure* (Crowther/ Woods 1976) began with the player "standing at the end of a road before a small brick building," the adventure game *Everybody's Gone to the Rapture* (The Chinese Room 2015) opens with the player still standing at the end of a road before a small brick building, at the start of a wandering journey around the landscape of an English country town to which she does not belong. Again and again, whenever the player is granted an embodied standpoint in the virtual environments of digital games, the standpoint is outside the place of habitation, looking in. We take our first steps as strangers in a strange land, filling the shoes of a rogue's gallery of exiles, amnesiacs, castaways, escaped prisoners, explorers and conquerors, all of whom have, in their various ways, been uprooted and taken out of place. We are visitors in a place that is not ours (Murray 1997, 107) – we orient ourselves, explore, roam and, having found our way, journey towards our goals.

Based on this observation, the very idea of dwelling in the gameworld and of being 'at home' in a videogame might appear strange. Nevertheless, we find ourselves lingering on a bench in *Life Is Strange* (Dontnod Entertainment 2015), resting at a bonfire in *Dark Souls* (From Software 2011), returning to the decks of the *Normandy* between missions in *Mass Effect* (BioWare 2007) or to our bombed-out shelter in *This War of Mine* (11 Bit Studios 2014), gathering materials to build a stronghold in *Minecraft* (Mojang 2009) or decorating and furnishing our rooms in *Animal Crossing: New Leaf* (Nintendo EAD 2012 [hereinafter *AC:NL*]). Such examples suggest that, running parallel to the (literal) setting-into-motion of the existential form of the journey, a less foregrounded but complementary mode of spatial practice is brought into play in our experiential engagement with the virtual worlds of videogames.

The approach I shall follow to the understanding of space is phenomenological, drawing in particular on discussions of spatiality by Martin Heidegger, Gaston Bachelard, Yi-Fu Tuan, Christian Norberg-Schulz and Edward S. Casey. On the basis of Heidegger's (2004b) argument that dwelling is the basic condition of human being-in-the-world, I will introduce Casey's (1993, 133) distinction between two modes of dwelling, which he terms the *hestial* and the *hermetic*. Hestial dwelling refers to the centered, inward-gathering dwelling of the domestic sphere, focused upon the image of the home (Rybczynski 2001, 62), while hermetic dwelling accounts for the outward-looking, decentered mode of spatial being defined by movement and wandering. I shall make the argument that, to date, critical engagement with the experience of game space has tended to focus on the hermetic dimension of dwelling, understanding gameworlds primarily in terms of paths of traversal, and predicating the player's spatial practice on the presupposition of constant movement (Aarseth 1997; 2001; Nitsche 2008; Wolf 2011; Calleja 2011; Gazzard 2012).

Through a focus on *AC:NL* and *Minecraft* as case studies, I shall make the case that the player's spatial being-in-the-gameworld has room for the practices of hestial dwelling, including the lingering pause that halts the onward journey and the activity of *building* in place. This shall then lead me to a consideration of the home as the locus of hestial dwelling, and to the ways in which the notion of home is brought to bear upon the player's being-in-the-gameworld. I shall highlight a set of salient features of the image of the home, in its intertwined architectural and existential dimensions: namely, the setting-down of a *center;* the demarcation of the binary opposition of *inside* and *outside,* together with the significance that comes to be attributed to each; the idea of the home as *continuity* and as a site of *repetition;* and the idea of the home as a *private* sphere, a cradle of identity and selfhood.

Implicit in the argument is the idea, suggested by Eugen Fink (2016, 21), that play stands over and above the other existential phenomena of human being-in-the-world and brings them into view – a point Sebastian Möring (2013, 118) has rendered even more explicit, saying that "play is a specific way of engaging with Being or with one's existence, since it makes some essential laws and structures of Being experienceable."

Elsewhere, I have made the case that this is due to the double phenomenology of ludic engagement (Vella 2015, 55-72). When playing, we take on a subjective standpoint internal to the gameworld, as a ludic subject, and retain a simultaneous standpoint as players at a remove from the gameworld. This double perspectival structure establishes the formal conditions for a ludic aesthetics founded on the bringing-into-presentation of the existential practices that constitute the player's being-in-the-gameworld (Vella 2016, 82). The claim I wish to make, then, is that when games invite us to pause, linger and dwell in the places they present to us, what is happening is not simply a repetition in the gameworld of the spatial practices of emplacement by which we engage with the world. It is a bringing-into-presentation of these practices in the aesthetic mode, allowing us, as players, to experience, engage with and interpret our own practices of dwelling.

Two Modes of Dwelling

For Heidegger (2008, 26), human being – as *Dasein*, literally 'being-there' – is emplaced being; it is being-in-the-world. And to be in the world, according to Heidegger (2004b, 349), is to *dwell*: "the way in which you are and I am, the manner in which we humans *are* on the earth, is *buan*, dwelling. To be a human being [...] means to dwell." Dwelling, then, is "a basic condition of humanity" (Norberg-Schulz 1985, 12). It is a two-way process – by dwelling, not only do we demarcate and internalize a particular locus, rendering it visible as a *place* and granting it a particular meaning in experience. At the same time, a place gives shape to our dwelling within it, and to our being: "when we identify with a place, we dedicate ourselves to a way of being in the world" (ibid.).

We are never so thoroughly *in place* as when we are at home. Witold Rybczynski (2001, 62) notes that the notion of 'home' "connotes a physical 'place' but also has the more abstract sense of a 'state of being.'" A home is not just a location – for which the word 'house' would suffice – but the existence we have in that place, a 'being-at-home.' Anchored as it is in the home, however, dwelling is not a unitary phenomenon. There are as many ways to dwell as there are places, or, to trace the process in the other direction, there are as many existentially significant places are there are ways to dwell. Every home sets in stone its particular way of dwelling. Nor do we always dwell at home. At times, the call of the road must be heeded, and we inhabit temporary dwellings along the way as we map out a transitory being in unfamiliar spaces. If we can be *at home*, it is only because we can be, at other times, *not at home* – which, of course, entails not the absence of an existential engagement with the place we are in, but, rather, a different way of being emplaced.

With this in mind, Casey (1993, 133) makes a phenomenological argument for the existence of two distinct modes of dwelling. Drawing on Greek mythology to anchor the terms in the roots of the Western imagination, Casey calls these the *hestial* (after Hestia, goddess of the hearth) and the *hermetic* (after Hermes, the fleet-footed messenger of the gods). The hestial and the hermetic "call upon two ways of being bodily in the world (stationary and mobile)" (ibid., 140-141). Hestial dwelling is inward-looking, centralized and enclosed. It represents a gathering-in, a lingering, a staying. Its model is the domestic enclosure of the home – "the centered, long-suffering, and measured movements of Hestia at the hearth epitomize the habitual body motions and memories that are part and parcel of domestic life" (ibid., 140). Hermetic dwelling is the opposite – "if the hestial mainly gathers in [...] the hermetic moves out resolutely" (ibid., 137-138). It is dynamic and decentred, implying outward movement, openness and divergent lines: "the mercurial movements of Hermes, god of thieves, are suited to the nonhabitual, de-centered actions of traversing open spaces rapidly," being characterized by "mobile actions that proceed swiftly and in decidedly linear fashion" (ibid., 140). Where hestial dwelling is gathered up in the figure of the home, hermetic dwelling is defined through its absence, through being *"somewhere else* than home, not 'settled in'" (ibid., 121).

For an aesthetic representation of this opposition between the hestial and the hermetic, being-at-home and being-not-at-home, we need look no further than the narrative of the journey. As a chronotopic form (Bakhtin 1981, 84) the journey strings the events of its story along a geographical vector, resulting in a simultaneous temporal and spatial progression – "a narrative of *events in place*" (Casey 1993, 277). Its archetypal form is the "arduous journey" of the epic hero (Moseley 2009, 64). When Gilgamesh, in the ancient Mesopotamian text that bears his name – and that lies at the root of the written epic tradition – announces his intention to travel to the distant Cedar Forest to kill Humbaba, its divine guardian, he states that, "I must travel on a road that I do not know" (Kovacs 1989, 25-26).

It is the journey itself, as much as any foe to be faced at the end of it, that constitutes the epic hero's trial, and its first step represents the crossing of a fundamental boundary. The boundary enshrines the binary opposition of *home* and *not-home*, around which is structured a dense layering of symbolic oppositions – between inside and outside, center and periphery, the familiar and the unfamiliar, the safe and the perilous, order and disorder, society and the wilderness. So strong is this opposition that each of the two terms appears to gain its meaning purely as a negation of the other: the wilderness is a wilderness because it is not home, and home is that which is shored up to stand against the wilderness outside.

Across the threshold, being-at-home and being-not-at-home, hestial and hermetic dwelling, frame, and reflect upon, each other. These are not mutually exclusive dispositions. Instead, "the two basic modes of dwelling act to enhance each other's presence" (Casey 1993, 143). The traveler carries her home with her along the journey – the hardships of the wilderness are sharpened by the memory of the home that has been left behind, and mitigated by the hope of either returning or of settling down in a new home at the journey's end. Tuan (1993, 149) has noted that "home is of course necessary to the adventurer as a secure base and point of departure," and, as Casey (1993, 274) notes, "it is also where one returns to in a journey of homecoming."

This theme is foregrounded most forcefully in the *nostos* (Ancient Greek νόστος, meaning 'homecoming') narrative, which, as an element of "the archetypal Greek foundation story" (Purves 2010, 165), has cast a long shadow on Western culture. The *nostos* narrative inverts the outward impulse of the hero's journey on the quest for glory or *kleos* (κλέος) impulse motivating the epic hero's departure from home), presenting us with a situation in which "a voyage out is only incidentally a journey of discovery and victory. Primarily it is an ardent quest to return home" (Reed 2006, 153). The *Odyssey* is the most famous, though far from the only, example of this trope, and its enduring resonance is evident – the journey away from home and the subsequent return home is a particularly recurrent pattern, for instance, in children's narratives: In the film adaptation of *The Wizard of Oz* (Fleming 1939), Dorothy Gale is whisked away from her habitual *topos* by a tornado, and her initial reaction to the magical land of Oz in which she inexplicably finds herself is precisely to note that she has been, very literally, *displaced* – that she is "not in Kansas anymore." In her subsequent adventures in the land of Oz, Dorothy is driven by the quest to return home, motivated by the realization that, "there's no place like home."

If home is ineluctably present on the journey's path, the inverse is also true: the lure of the journey reaches its tendrils into the stationary being of the home-dweller. In Charlotte Brontë's (1994, 87) *Jane Eyre*, we encounter a scene every bit as familiar and resonant as that of the traveler pining for home – that of the home-dweller dreaming of the adventure of the journey. Jane, having spent eight years at Lowood Institution, first as a pupil, then as a teacher, finds herself one evening looking out of the window of her attic, past the wings of the building, to the distant horizon: "I traced the white road winding round the base of one mountain, and vanishing in a gorge between two. How I wished to follow it further!" It is not only her physical surroundings she has grown weary of, but her being within the place: "school rules, school duties, school habits and notions, and voices, and faces, and phrases, and costumes, and preferences, and antipathies [...] I tired of the routine of eight years" (ibid.).

Lost in an unfamiliar landscape, the familiar safety of the homeplace, as it is for Odysseus and Dorothy Gale, is a refuge to which we retreat in spirit. In Tuan's (1977, 3) words, "place is security, space is freedom: we are attached to the one and long for the other." Nestled in the gathering of the hearth, we yearn, like Jane Eyre, for unknown open spaces and the undetermined, unfettered being for which they can serve, to borrow a term from Heidegger, as *Spielraum*, room to unfold and play out (2008, 419). The hestial and the hermetic, inside and outside, mapped place and unmapped space, are equally essential components of our dwelling in the world.

Games and the Hermetic Mode of Dwelling

Given how fundamental this dual-sided structure appears to be to our spatial practice of being-in-the-world, it would appear safe to assume that videogames, so invested in spatial themes, would similarly reflect this duality in the existence they grant the player in the gameworld. However, a survey of the existing theorizations of game space reveals a more one-sided understanding of the player's spatial practice. With some notable exceptions, an all but exclusive emphasis is placed on practices that enact a hermetic mode of dwelling, sidelining, virtually to the point of erasure, the complete category of experiences and practices relating to hestial dwelling – the pause, the rest, the return, the home.

This is already evident in Espen Aarseth's (1997, 1) theorization of the ergodic as the mode of textuality that applies to videogame form. In fact, the term *ergodic*, derived from the combination of the Greek terms *ergon* and *hodos*, 'work' and 'path,' is itself inscribed with the assumption of a hermetic mode of dwelling. The concept of the ergodic text as that which requires the user to actively work out a path implies the presupposition that it is in fact experienced precisely as a path of traversal – in other words, as a journey, with a beginning, end and constant forward motion between the two. It is unsurprising that the spatial metaphors Aarseth reaches for in order to convey the aesthetic experience of the ergodic text describe a hermetic spatial practice: "it is possible to explore, get lost, and discover secret paths" (ibid., 4).

This is only reinforced by the image of the labyrinth or maze which proves central to the conceptualization of the ergodic text. In terms of the spatial practices it invites, a labyrinth is a complex place, requiring multiple modes of engagement as we move around it. And yet, *move around* is what we inevitably do. One does not feel at home in a maze; one wanders, one moves towards the center. One tends not to pause at all, except perhaps momentarily, in order to determine the best way to proceed: First, we are likely to meander, making a trial of the routes the maze suggests, trying to find our way – it is with this in mind that Aarseth notes that the "spatially oriented themes" which are brought to the fore by the adventure game, as a specific form of the ergodic text that has been particularly central to the development of videogames, are those of "travel and discovery" (ibid., 100).

Once we have, or believe ourselves to have, found our way, we proceed, in linear fashion, along the path that will take us to the center. Ariadne's thread traces a line through Minos' labyrinth, bringing into view one path of traversal and turning the complex network of routes into background to this path. As Alison Gazzard (2012, 20) points out, the mode of spatial being we engage in when venturing into a labyrinth is that of "traveling across a landscape," a highly determined, convoluted, but ultimately linear journey from point A to point B – which, in turn, suggests (and here again the link to the notion of ergodicity comes to the surface) that the topological structure that describes the existential engagement with the maze is the path. In videogames, she argues, "the maze (even with its choices and multiple routes) is seen as directing the player to one goal with a "single solution"" (ibid., 14). The movement, moreover, is inherently teleological: "the game-maze is a *pathway to*, a device for *completing* the multiple objectives of the game" (ibid., 40).

The image of the maze, then, reveals the phenomenological assumptions underlying game studies' grasp of the player's spatial involvement with the game-world. These are the assumptions at work when Mark Wolf (2011, 21) theorizes game space as "navigable space," which he defines as "a space in which way-finding is necessary" – a procedure he links specifically to movement (ibid., 23). The necessity of finding one's way – of working out one's path – implies an understanding of oneself as being *on the way* towards a final destination, which marks one's spatial practice as being focused on movement, and one's dwelling as hermetic. In the same vein, Stephan Günzel's (2007, 174) comment that "the ego has to wander through game space in order to apprehend the spatial setting" assumes a rootless, peripatetic existence for the player in the gameworld.

On the basis of these assumptions, typologies of game space are often, in effect, typologies of "path structures" (Gazzard 2012, 12). Whichever spatial organization a particular game adopts, it can be understood, in the experience of play, as a path. The most direct forms this takes are the tracks of racing games and the "invisible tracks" the player is led along in rail-shooters, and it is only a small leap to the rigidly drawn corridors of the unicursal pathways of games like the first-person shooter *Medal of Honor* (DreamWorks Interactive 1999), which Nitsche (2008, 172-175) goes so far as to call "invisible rails."

Even in the case of multicursal or open game spaces, the structure of the quest as a determiner for the vector of the player's movement (Tosca 2003; Aarseth 2004) "presents a unicursal path overlaid onto the maze" (Nitsche 2008, 178). As a result, "the virtual journeys of players criss-crossing the available space can be interpreted as the creation process of a labyrinth of experienced locations. Their movements form a spatial practice, and this practice leads to labyrinthine spaces" (ibid., 183). In other words, even an open world is experienced as a linear journey, with everything that implies for the player's spatial being.

The same purely hermetic understanding of the player's mode of dwelling in the gameworld is in evidence in Gordon Calleja's development of Nitsche's typology of game spaces. Calleja (2011, 73) emphasizes "exploration" as the macro-level driving force for the player's moment-to-moment navigation of the game space. The player is cast as a wanderer, traveling in an unfamiliar landscape, and this basic assumption carries across Calleja's discussion of the various spatial structures, whether this is the unicursal corridor in which "traversing the scenarios is a strictly linear affair" (ibid., 78), multicursal mazes which "offer multiple routes through their domains" (ibid., 80), or an open landscape structure "in which one can freely roam" (ibid., 84).

By pointing out that game studies have overwhelmingly discussed the player's experience of game space in terms of a hermetic mode of dwelling, I do not wish to suggest that game scholars have distorted their object of study. In the tradition that spans the four decades between the aforementioned examples from *Adventure* and *Everybody's Gone to the Rapture*, genres as diverse as the adventure game, the role-playing game, the first-person shooter and the platform game have overwhelmingly foregrounded practices of exploration, navigation, pathfinding, travel and movement. Game studies' emphasis on such themes in its engagement with the spatiality of games appears to be, by and large, an accurate descriptive analysis.

This, perhaps, should not be too surprising. For most of their history, videogames and the act of videogame play have been firmly ensconced in hestial dwelling-places: bars, video arcades and, eventually, the home itself, in the private domain of the bedroom and around the television set, the heart(h) at the center of the contemporary home. Taking their place in the midst of our repose in habitual, hestial dwelling, videogames came to represent a new way of escaping the routines of familiar dwelling in familiar places into a reverie of hermetic adventure. The screen becomes a virtual window, offering a prospect onto a virtual hermetic space that highlights its promise of exploration, discovery and, most fundamentally, spatial freedom; And yet, once we venture through this window – once, through a cognitive mechanism of "incorporation," we find ourselves occupying an embodied subjective standpoint within the gameworld (ibid., 169), once, in other words, we have made that *there* our *here*, must our being remain rootless and uncentred?

Speaking of the aesthetics of landscape in *The Elder Scrolls IV: Oblivion* (Bethesda Softworks 2006), Paul Martin (2011) argues that the player's engagement with the virtual word of Tamriel shifts from the sublime to the pastoral as it becomes familiar and 'domesticated' – in other words, as the player's being in this place becomes habitual. The aesthetic movement from the sublime to the pastoral describes a shift between an experience of the landscape as unbounded, formless, extending beyond the limits of perception and knowledge, and a markedly divergent experience of the same landscape rendered familiar, mapped out according to the existential practices of action within it. The window of the screen no longer opens onto a path leading out into the unknown, but onto a placescape shaped by a network of habitual practices.

Martin's aesthetic analysis of the experience of landscape in *Oblivion* thereby suggests that processes of familiarization and emplacement are as intrinsic to our engagement with game space as they are to our negotiation of physical space, and that, as players, we do, in an important sense, arrive at a form of settled habitation of the gameworld. The instances of spatial dwelling I have already mentioned in *Life is Strange, Dark Souls, Mass Effect, This War of Mine* and *AC: NL* demonstrate the forms that such a habitation might take. All enact ways of being-in-the-gameworld defined by a hestial orientation, and by the emergence of figures of home.

On this evidence, an understanding of dwelling in gameworlds that subscribes to a purely hermetic understanding is a reductive one that fails to account for the richness of the player's spatial engagement with the gameworld. In order to address this markedly undertheorized presence of hestial dwelling-in-the-gameworld, it is necessary to pay attention to the phenomenological mechanisms, and the related existential practices, by which the hermetic practices of exploration, traversal and movement give way to settlement, stasis and domesticity – in other words, by which the path through the gameworld finds its terminus in the home in the gameworld.

Minecraft and *AC:NL* can serve as useful case studies on which to ground the investigation. Both are examples of games in which hestial dwelling is primary, with the player's movements around the gameworld centering on a figure of home rather than following the linear advance represented by the path. In the sandbox construction game *Minecraft*, the home that the player builds in the gameworld – as an activity of building and as an architectural form – both motivates and anchors the player's hermetic explorations of the landscape, thematizing the interweaving of hestial and hermetic practices. In the community simulation game *AC:NL*, on the other hand, the gameworld as a whole constitutes an elaborate homeplace, a concentric organization of spheres of dwelling, the home proper contained within the hometown, resulting in a focused enactment of the multiple, mutually supportive practices of hestial dwelling. Thanks to these divergent approaches, *Minecraft* and *AC:NL*, taken together, can demonstrate the range of hestial practices through which the player can come to feel at home in the gameworld.

Pausing and Lingering

The first step between the hermetic and the hestial mode of dwelling is the interruption of movement. Tuan (1977, 138) gives the moment of pause a great importance, suggesting it represents the experiential move from space to place: "place is a pause in movement [...] the pause makes it possible for a locality to become a center of felt value". Very rarely in games do we have the time, or the motivation, to stand and stare. 'Pausing' generally refers to an interruption of play, rather than an act or disposition within it. In fact, the idea of 'play' as an existential concept has been linked explicitly to movement, both in philosophy (Gadamer 1989, 104) and in game studies (Salen/Zimmerman 2004, 304). In this regard, the fact that the general term for a guide to playing a videogame is a 'walkthrough' is hardly surprising.

In this context, one of the most mundane icons of pausing along a journey – the pathside bench – becomes practically a subversive gesture. The very idea that, while playing a videogame, we might wish to stop and sit along the way, rather than moving forward at all costs, almost strikes us as absurd, and yet, now and again, we do come across benches in our wanderings through various gameworlds. In the adventure game *Ico* (Team ICO 2001), for example, benches serve as a checkpoint, allowing the player to save their progress. Upon choosing to 'use' one of the stone-benches the player encounters in the game's ruined milieu, the eponymous player-character and his companion, Yorda, take a break from their journey to rest on the bench. However, this pausing is not a part of the player's spatial being-in-the-gameworld, but an interruption of it: upon performing this action, the scene fades away and the player is taken to a menu in order to save their game. There is no meaningful lingering here.

Compare this to the park benches in *AC: NL*, which give the player the opportunity to linger as long as she wishes. When the player sits on the park-bench she constructed on a cliff overlooking the beach in her *AC:NL* town, the camera angles downwards from the usual top-down point-of-view to grant a more panoramic perspective, bringing together earth and sky to frame the avatar peacefully seated on the bench. This sitting serves no functional purpose – it does not advance the player's progress in any way, except for time continuing to pass. It can go on for as long as the player likes – the avatar will only get up once the player gives the command to do so. It is, in other words, a pure lingering, a pause in the teleology of the player's spatial practice.

It is revealing to note the way in which the phenomenological implications of this deliberate choice to linger in a particular place – through the act of sitting on the bench – are represented through the language of the game's visual presentation. The avatar's sitting results in a picturesque visual framing which brings the *genius loci* of the surrounding scene – its placeness in all its sensual richness – into view. Tuan's observation regarding the phenomenology of the pause, and its bringing of a place into view, holds true. However, there is an added dimension to what is being presented. When I choose to sit on the bench overlooking the sea in my hometown, *AC:NL* does not present me with the view over the ocean that my avatar is presumably enjoying; instead, my avatar himself remains the point of visual focus, with the scene composed around him. True to Fink's (2016, 21) depiction of play as the representation of existential practices, this is not only the experience of lingering, but the *presentation* of the experience of lingering.

Minecraft, conversely, provides no formalized enactment of the experience of lingering. In fact, the instrumental mode into which the player's being-in-the-gameworld is enframed brings the things of its world into consciousness, in Heideggerian terms, as ready-to-hand (2008, 98), visible only insofar as they figure towards the player's purposes and are incorporated into the player's practices (Vella 2013) – a teleological, forward-looking (and forward-moving) orientation which runs counter to the unassuming gaze of the settled pause, which reveals things as present-at-hand for their own sake. Nonetheless, this does not mean the player cannot choose to pause during her explorations of the game's landscape – say, to disinterestedly, with no instrumental purpose in mind, take in the view after climbing to the summit of a hill. Even more than this, the player can choose to set this possibility for lingering in stone while building her home in the gameworld – for instance, by constructing a tower with a west-facing window in its highest room, intended for the primary purpose of serving as a lookout from which to take in the sun setting on the horizon at the end of the day. However, this observation takes us beyond the momentary pause and into the more settled practice of building in place (and building *a* place), which – as a more advanced step in the enshrining of hestial dwelling – I shall consider next.

Building

I have already referred to Tuan's (1977, 13) claim that the point at which we interrupt our wandering to linger in a particular locus is the point at which that location is revealed to us as a place within which we can dwell. Keeping in mind that "to dwell implies the establishment of a meaningful relationship between man and a given environment," what is revealed, primarily, is a way of being-in-the-world, which "comprises a *how* as well as a *where*" (Norberg-Schulz 1985, 15).

For Christian Norberg-Schulz, the determination of this *how* occurs in a twofold manner. First – relating back to the pause and the lingering, the bringing-into-view of place – we employ "the faculty of understanding the given things," a receptive dimension or openness to the possibilities a place holds for the determination of our dwelling. Second, once we have understood the particular way of being-in that a place *is* for us, dwelling involves "the making of works which keep and "explain" what has been understood" (ibid., 17). In other words, *building*, in phenomenological terms, is the setting-in-stone of a revealed mode of being. As we have already seen – in the case of the bench looking out onto the sea in *AC:NL* and the window at the top of the tower in *Minecraft* – the built work allows for the "gathering" (Heidegger 2004b, 355) of a landscape into a meaningful place.

Norberg-Schulz's architectonics of dwelling are founded upon Heidegger's conceptual intertwining of *building* and *dwelling*. Heidegger traces the etymological root of *dwelling* in the Old High German *buan*, which, inseparably from the sense of *to build*, also "signifies to remain, to stay in a place" (ibid., 348). *Building* is essential to *dwelling* – not in the sense that "the latter, building, has the former, dwelling, as its goal" (ibid., 347). It is not the case that first we build, then we dwell in the place we have built – rather, "building is really dwelling" (ibid., 350). To pause is to settle is to build is to dwell – all form one continuous existential movement of being-in-place.

In one of the few studies to engage explicitly with the question of dwelling in games, Bjarke Liboriussen documented the building practices of a community of players of *Second Life* (Linden Lab 2003) who identified themselves as 'builders,' and who had embarked on an ambitious collective project to build a castle. What his ethnographic account reveals is that it is the activity of building itself, rather than the final result of the process, that motivates players intrinsically. As a result, "the building understood as *activity* is never over" (Liboriussen 2012, 39), and it is this activity which gave shape to these players' dwelling in *Second Life*. For Heidegger (2004b, 349), building, in this existential sense, takes two forms: First, there is "building as cultivating," which manifests in the preservation of, and the caring for, that which grows of its own accord; in practices such as agriculture and gardening. Second, there is "building as the raising of edifices," which involves the construction of works within a place.

Both *AC:NL* and *Minecraft* foreground the two forms of building – in this way, they are typical of games that locate the player in a fixed place which she inhabits as 'home' for the duration of the game. In almost all such cases, the player is directly or indirectly tasked with improving this home, a task which brings the existential practices of building-as-dwelling into view. To wit, in *AC:NL*, being vested with the role of town mayor, the player is tasked with developing her village. Building-as-cultivation is present here, in the planting of trees and flower-beds, the patient waiting for trees to grow and bear fruit, and the watering of plants to maintain them in (literal) sparkling good health. However, this village development primarily takes the form of public works projects – constructions such as bridges, benches, fairy-tale clocks and Zen-gardens that the player can undertake in order to improve the town.

Having decided what project she wishes to undertake, the player must then accompany Isabelle, her mayoral assistant, to choose a location for it. When the player suggests a spot, the game provides a representation of how the location will look with the completed project in place – the span of a bridge across the river, the aforementioned bench looking out over a cliff, a totem pole framed against the sky. Before the player confirms her decision and sets the project underway, then, she is given a glimpse of the place that the building work will set in stone.

Few games, however, enact the existential practices of building as richly, and as significantly, as *Minecraft*. At the start of a new game, the player is situated in a complete wilderness, a natural landscape with no mark of human activity. She is shown no path and handed no goal or quest. Instead, what motivates her engagement with the landscape is the existential drive to build, and, through building, to make of the landscape a place of habitation (Vella 2013). Initially, this building answers the need for survival. The player is unlikely to live through her first night if she is not able to build herself a shelter from the hostile creatures that emerge under cover of darkness. Accordingly, the first building the player will work on out of necessity will likely take the form of a single room, or perhaps a walled-off cave – either of which would perform the basic function of keeping out night-time threats.

From these humble beginnings, the player can expand her home in order to structure the various practices of her dwelling. She is likely to build more rooms in order to house crafting tables, chests for storing raw materials and a bed that serves as a respawn point. She might choose to expand her home downwards, by digging tunnels connecting her home to underground caverns which can be 'domesticated' – made part of 'home' – through the placing of torches for light and the construction of stairways and passages for easy access. She can build upwards, erecting towers and battlements from which the surrounding landscape is gathered into the unity of a prospect. Finally, she can build outwards, enclosing trees and fields within the bounds of the built place of her home.

Two points are important to note here. The first is that this process of building occurs in dialogue with the topological character of the place within which it stakes its claim: "Architecture serves to reveal and emphasize qualities that are already present" (Norberg-Schulz 1984, 31). Thus, a battlement built upon a hill to act as a vantage-point for the player calls attention to the verticality of the hill; a bridge spanning a gorge accentuates its breadth and vertiginous depth; a shaft dug into a cavern underlines its claustrophobic subterranean character and its distance from the surface. All these building-acts respond to the *genius loci*, and shape a way of being-in-the-world which brings it to the fore of the player-dweller's experience. The second thing to note is that, in *Minecraft*, this revealing takes a very particular form. It can be characterized as a technological one, in the sense in which Heidegger (2004a, 320) understands technology as a *Gestell*, an 'enframing' of the world which enshrines a particular way in which the world is revealed to perception. For Heidegger, the essence of the technological way of being lies in the impulse to frame the world in the mode of *standing-reserve*: in his words, "everywhere everything is ordered to stand by, to be immediately on hand, indeed to stand there just so that it may be on call for a further ordering" (ibid., 322).

The amassing of stockpiles of resources standing in reserve is, indeed, both what makes the player's project of building in *Minecraft* possible, and the primary function of the project of building. Tunnels are dug into the rock and caverns are connected to, and incorporated into, the player's home in order to give the player access to underground seams of coal, iron, gold, diamonds, redstone and obsidian, all of which she can mine. Fields are enclosed and saplings planted so that the player is ensured a supply of wood to chop down. All of this – coal, wood, stone, iron, gold, and so on – is accumulated, through the player's efforts, in the form of stockpiles of resources stored in chests in the player's house, ready to be put to use towards further building. One does not, in *Minecraft*, build to survive; rather, one survives to build.

Centre, Inside, Walls and Outside

Having lingered, in turn, on the phenomenology of the pause along the path, the temporary dwelling along the journey and the existential practice of build-ing-as-dwelling, it is now time to focus on the formal structures of place that are revealed through building – in other words, on the architectural figure of the home itself, as the locus of hestial dwelling. This does not entail a shift away from the discourse of the phenomenology of space towards that of architectural form; rather, it highlights the common ground shared by the two. As Norberg-Schulz (1985, 19) writes, "works of architecture [...] *embody* existential meanings," and it is with a view to their existential meanings – to the way they shape our dwelling in place – that I shall consider architectural forms in this section. In order to focus my analysis, I shall concentrate on two fundamental architectural gestures inher-ent in the idea of the home, which serve to give shape and form to human dwelling. These two gestures, which I shall expand upon in turn, are the setting-down of a center and the delineation of inside and outside.

Home as the marking of a center: Home acts as the center and point of orientation for the human being's engagement with the world, and thereby organizes around itself the entirety of her spatial existence in the world. Norberg-Schulz writes that "the goal or *center* is the basic constituent of existential space" (ibid., 20). Centre and periphery, near and far, local and remote are set forth deictically, in relation to the home as *origo* or point of origin for the individual's spatial being, as that which is taken up as 'her' place. "The center," Norberg-Schulz argues, "represents what is *known*, in contrast to the unknown and perhaps frightening world around" (ibid., 21); it thus enshrines a distinction between the home place which lies at the center and the "alien space" outside its boundaries (Tuan 1993, 140).

Thus, in *Minecraft*, the compass always points back to the player's bed – it is home which serves as the point of orientation in the player's exploration of the wil-derness, structuring a relative rather than absolute mode for the player to experi-entially position herself in the gameworld. Not only direction but also proximity and distance is measured in terms of whether one is near or far from the home as the center. The necessity of finding shelter come nightfall makes the player conscious of how far she has wandered from her home during the course of her daytime explorations, and of how much ground she has to cover to get back to the familiar territory and safety of the home. The vertiginous sense of the enormity of open space in *Minecraft* is felt most keenly when that space spans a too-far dis-tance home. The sense of being out of place, or, in the worst case, of being lost and not knowing the way back home, is possible only because there is a home to be away from and a center to be far from.

The existential domain of being-in-the-world is thus organized, according to the principles of hestial dwelling, around the home as a central point of orientation. Tuan characterized this organization as "a succession of concentric circles, at the center of which is home narrowly defined, or homeplace" (ibid., 139), beyond which we encounter "broadening, increasingly abstract, rings of 'home space,'" to each of which pertains its respective degree of familiarity and intimacy (ibid., 140) – the hometown, the home country, and so on until, at the furthest extent, we find ourselves not-at-home. Norberg-Schulz (1985, 13) maps out these nested circles from the outside in, locating as the outermost circle of 'home' the settlement within the landscape; within the settlement, the urban space; next, the institution; arriving, finally, at the home itself.

AC:NL deploys this concentric structure of dwelling-places, allowing the player to move between her home proper, the private space she makes her own, and the "*collective dwelling*" (ibid.) of the town, where she can interact with her neighbors. She is no less at home while strolling about the familiar paths of her town than she is while sitting inside her house, with the collection of furniture, decorations and sundry items she has accumulated and arranged in its rooms. She is at home in a different way, in a manner which befits the sphere of urban space, "the place where *meeting* takes place" (ibid., 51): she is taken up into the gathering of the community, greeting her familiar neighbors as they go about the activities that determine the shape of the town as a lifeworld, and which she can also partake in. Within this place of collective dwelling, the player engages in the tasks that determine the role she identifies with as being 'hers' in the community – that of mayor, a role which ties her into an identification with "the totality to which the role belongs" (ibid., 53).

Home as the demarcation of inside and outside: For Tuan (1993, 140), the primary characteristic of the home place is its "enclosure," its being "everywhere a protected – at least partly enclosed – space." Accordingly, the second architectural gesture of home, intimately tied to the first, is the raising of walls to delimit the homeplace and mark out its enclosure of the center. Bachelard (1994, 5) writes that "the sheltered being gives perceptible limits to his shelter": by setting physical boundaries on both geometrical and experiential dimensions, the act of building sets both a space and a place in stone.

The raising of walls renders the space they enclose a shelter, protecting its inhabitants from the elements, from enemies, wild beasts and every other manner of threat. "Come what may the house allows us to say: I will be an inhabitant of the world, in spite of the world" (ibid., 46-47). This clearly applies to *Minecraft*, where every home the player will build – from the simple shelter of the first night to the most extensive and architecturally elaborate palace that weeks of work can muster – will have this as its basic function: before any other consideration, it must shelter the player from the creepers, zombies, skeletons and assorted other hostile mobs that come out at night, and answer her need for survival.

At the same time as the walls define their enclosure as 'inside,' they give everything beyond their enclosure the status of outside. As a result of the architectural delineation of the circle of home, "outside and inside form a dialectic of division" (ibid., 211), thereby establishing the basic experiential opposition of inside and outside to which the distinction between hestial and hermetic dwelling is intimately tied. If the inside is shelter, the outside is that which we require shelter from; if the inside is the center, the outside is the periphery. In its depiction of an extended sphere of hestial dwelling in the form of the town community, *AC:NL* places less emphasis on the distinction between inside and outside. Having said that, the player can take trips outside the town – either by catching a train from the train station to visit another player's town, or by taking the Kapp'n's boat to Tortimer Island, a linked set of resort-themed areas housing a number of mini-games.

In a gameworld that is pointedly free of threats, the opposition between safety and danger that the inside/outside distinction upholds in *Minecraft* does not exist. Instead, the opposition that is structured is that between the habitual and the novel. Taking an excursion to another player's town provides an intriguing glimpse of a home that is not one's own, and whose organization represents the outcome of a different activity of building, resulting in a homeplace that – in perhaps small but significant ways – structures a different way of dwelling. Likewise, a trip to Tortimer Island is explicitly coded as an exotic vacation, with the island's various locales replete with the instantly recognizable iconography of the idyllic tropical getaway. In both cases, returning to one's own town – whether from another player's town or from Tortimer Island – bears the distinct sense of coming back home.

Familiarity

The establishment of a center and the delineation of inside and outside therefore constitute the fundamental architectural qualities of home, setting in stone the conditions for hestial dwelling. However, dwelling is not an architectural feature, or even a spatial one, though it takes its character from the place in which it is situated. Our relation to the home, our dwelling within it, is a happening – it unfolds over time as well as across space, and it is in its temporal dimension that the character of dwelling is shaped. The home is the familiar domain: Norberg-Schulz (1985, 89) writes that "the house is the place where *daily life* takes place. Daily life represents what is continuous in our existence, and therefore supports us like a familiar ground." The home shelters the familiar. It gives rise, through the repetition of the quotidian routine, to the familiarity of habit, to the way of life in which we are so invested we come to identify it as an intrinsic part of our being.

Both *Minecraft* and *AC:NL* encourage – even demand – the formation of such habitual practices around the player's in-game home. In *Minecraft*, this generally takes the form of a pattern of departure and return, as the player must venture outside her home to gather food and resources for crafting and further building. The paths she treads around the home (between the storage chests where she keeps her resources and the crafting table, or between both and the door to the outside) will be worn into familiarity as the player follows them again and again.

Arguably, this is even more the case in *AC:NL*, which establishes a set of habitual practices organized according to an interlocking system of temporal cycles – not only day and night, but also the days of the week and the changing of the seasons. The player will tend to settle into a routine of daily and weekly tasks which take her along habitual paths around her hometown – the way from her house to the grove of orange trees where she picks fruit every third day, the route between the orange trees and the Re-Tail store where she sells the fruit, her daily hunt for the three fossils which spawn every morning and the subsequent walk to the museum to have the fossils assessed by Blathers, the museum director, her Sunday morning visit to Old Sow Joan to purchase turnips to trade on the turnip market, and so on.

As these examples show, the familiarity of the domestic sphere is mapped out according to the practices that constitute our habitual being within the homeplace. The things we encounter around the home, that are given meaning through their incorporation into this routine – the tools and appliances we use every day, the keepsakes that turn the home into a tissue of memory – concentrate, and come to stand for, these practices: "in the home we find the things we know and cherish," the things to which we form an intense attachment because they "represent 'our world'" (ibid., 91).

For Tuan, the phenomenological playing-out of this familiar attachment to the house and its things takes on a seemingly paradoxical duality. On the one hand, our engagement with the things of the house become so habitual that we barely pay any conscious attention to these "ordinary objects" – instead, "we know them through use [...] they are almost a part of ourselves, too close to be seen" (Tuan 1977, 144). The distinct echo here of Maurice Merleau-Ponty's (2002, 121) observation regarding the intuitive, almost unconscious engagement of the craftsperson with his tools and the practices of his craft is no accident. What is foregrounded in this philosophical echo is the extent to which we identify with the practices of our homely dwelling – so much so that, in becoming an intrinsic part of our being, they slip below the level of our conscious perception. However, Tuan (1993, 139-140) also argues that, through the leisure we experience in the home, it also opens itself up to us in an aesthetic mode, unfolding in a sensual richness: "homeplace is also a variegated world of shapes and colors, sounds and odors," offering "a complex mix of sensory stimuli" which we come to know thoroughly and intimately, and to which we can develop strong emotional associations.

The instances of dwelling in game homes I have presented so far provide us with examples of both kinds of familiarity. No matter how extensive and convoluted a network of rooms, corridors, stairways and tunnels she has built in *Minecraft*, the player is likely to not even need to consciously consider its traversal. Having integrated the home as a whole into the body-schema of her embodied being-in-the-gameworld, she can ascend from the subterranean coal mine, having excavated as much coal as she can carry, through the bridge over the lava fall, up the stairwell to the third door on the left, down the corridor, taking a left past the glass-roofed room and up a narrower staircase to deposit the coal in a chest in the storeroom – all without paying the slightest intentional attention to what she is doing or where she is going.

Conversely, while residing in her home in *AC:NL*, the player is provided with little in the way of active engagement. This occurs largely in the communal dwelling of the town outside, and there is little for the player to 'do' in the house apart from play their choice of music, lie down on the bed or sit on a sofa or chair, and use the freely rotatable camera to take in the surrounding room and the collection of furniture, wallpaper, *objets d'art*, knick-knacks and decorations she has arranged within it. Divorced of any lived practicality which would allow the things of the home to be engaged with in terms of their readiness-to-hand for the purposes of this or the other task, the player's relation to them becomes entirely aesthetic. She might consider their arrangement and decide to move the furniture around for a more harmonious effect; she might simply sit on the sofa and admire the way light falls through the window onto the carpeted floor. It is the player's intimate familiarity with her in-game home that clears out the space within which thingness of the objects in her game home can be brought forth.

The Home and the Individual

So far, I have discussed the home insofar as its form gathers together the images and existential structures of a generalized sense of dwelling that, as Heidegger argues, is intrinsic to human being-in-the-world. However, one's home is not only a figure that stands for dwelling *in general* – on the contrary, it is a domain whose defining characteristic is its particularity, which rests on the fact that each home, while embodying the overarching phenomenological qualities of hestial dwelling, does so in its own way, and is marked by the specificities which distinguish it from other homes.

The familiarity that is an intrinsic component of the sense of dwelling is nurtured with respect to the specific configuration of things and structures that makes up one's proper home. As such, it is that which sets one house apart from all others which allows me to identify (and identify with) a particular house as my home. My home is experienced proprioceptively: it is precisely *mine* and no-one else's, an intimate place within which my own particular being takes place. So ingrained is this idea of the home that it might be surprising to note that it is by no means a universal dimension of homeliness – rather, it is tied to a specific historical conception of selfhood. Rybczinski (2001, 36) positions the origin of "the appreciation of the house as a setting for an emerging interior life" in the cultural shift between the Middle Ages and early modernity in Europe, inextricably associating the idea of home as the private sphere with the emergence of the idea of the private self as a cornerstone of bourgeois culture. The home, then, is the cradle of the self – this is what Virginia Woolf (1991, 110) had in mind when she wrote that "a lock on the door means the power to think for oneself." The interior life of consciousness and the private domestic sphere of the home are so closely related as to be inseparable.

In its intimate familiarity, the home in its objective qualities – as an architectural form and as an arrangement of things – becomes an animated structure of being, embodying the practices of a dwelling that is determined equally by the place and by the individual within it. For Jean Baudrillard (1996, 14), "human beings and objects are indeed bound together in a collusion in which the objects have a certain density, an emotional value – what might be called a 'presence.'" As a result, the homeplace comes to represent a "complex structure of interiority, and the objects within it serve for us as boundary markers of the symbolic configuration known as home" (ibid.).

The first sense in which one's home is tied to one's self emerges in the wake of the activities of building or home-making, upkeep and repair – actions that inscribe themselves into the figure of the home. In their ethnographic study of Chicago homeowners, for instance, Mihaly Csikszentmihalyi and Eugene Rochberg-Halton (1981, 131) found that, particularly for men – in view of the cultural notion of the male as the breadwinner and head of the nuclear household – "the house represents the accomplishments of the owner's self," the tangible reward for their hard work, standing not only, to neighbour's eyes, as a marker of hard-earned social status, but, more personally, granting the homeowner "a sense of achievement and control." In this case, the identification of the home as 'mine' includes within its remit not only the home itself, or the things within it, but also the practices through which the home was constructed and maintained in good condition – the building work, the diligent maintenance on weekends, the career which brought in the money to pay off the mortgage, and so on.

This is no less true, on a smaller scale, with respect to games, specifically in cases where the building of the player's home-in-the-gameworld demands active effort and a considerable investment of time and energy. The *Second Life* "builders" studied by Liboriussen (2012, 39) had a strong attachment to the castle they had built due to the extent to which, in their words, it embodied "the long time and hard but successful work" that went into its construction. A similar feeling of prideful ownership can be felt by the *Minecraft* player standing back to take in the fruits of her labor once she decides that a building project is 'done' – at least, since building is never truly over, for the moment, until the idea for the next addition comes along. Building a home in *Minecraft* demands time, thought and active effort: a completed construction stands for the exploration in search of the necessary resources, the quarrying of stone, the chopping of timber, the transportation of raw materials back to the construction site, the crafting of these materials into building-blocks, the meticulous planning for the building layout, the gradual placing of block on block, and so on. The player's identification with her *Minecraft* home, then, represents not only an attachment to the form of the structure in itself, or to her existence as centered within it, but to the practices that went into the building of it, by which she has defined herself as, for instance, a hard worker, or a creative visionary.

Things in the home can also gain in personal significance thanks to their propensity for accumulating a veneer of associated memories. In the E.M. Forster (2012, 156) novel *Howards End*, as the Schlegel siblings prepare to move out of the London home they had lived in most of their lives, they note that every item in the house bore the weight of associations, bringing to mind past events and departed family members – "round every knob and cushion in the house sentiment gathered." On a more modest scale, our in-game homes speak to us about our existence in the gameworld, keeping a record of our achievements, experiences and attachments just as our homes embody the past they recollect through keepsakes and mementos. In *AC:NL*, the pachira plant the player keeps in the corner might make her recall the friend who gifted it to her, while the trophy on the mantelpiece commemorates her triumph in the town fishing tournament.

Finally, a home can also represent a conscious attempt at self-construction on the part of the individual. Within the network of socio-cultural conventions and practical considerations the dwelling inhabits, the functional and aesthetic choices one makes in the design of one's homes provide, both to oneself and to others, an externalized construction of the dweller's self (Halttunen 1989, 186-189) – "homes are full of hints and clues that should be meticulously coded and interpreted as describing their inhabitant's personality" (Paasonen 2009, 345).

When – as in *Minecraft* and, even more so, *AC:NL* – a game allows the player to make choices regarding the layout, organization and appearance of their in-game home, a similar kind of identification can develop. In *AC:NL*, for instance, the player is invited to seek out and purchase furniture, wallpaper patterns, ornaments and the various other accoutrements of the comfortable bourgeois home. She chooses their arrangement about the house, which ornaments go on the mantelpiece, where each item of furniture should go, what music to fill the space with, and so on. When she invites other players to visit her home through the Nintendo

3DS console's online connectivity, the sense of pride she might feel has as its object her home as a conscious externalization, within the limited choices the game offers her in decorating her home, of her tastes and sensibility. In this regard, it is telling that one of the scripted compliments visiting neighbor NPCs most commonly pay while taking a tour of the player's home is, "This room is so you!" – a statement which effortlessly reinforces the idea of the home as a reflection of the self, and which reinforces the idea that our home in the gameworld serves as the cradle within which an in-game self can be nurtured and represented.

Conclusions

This cursory examination of the experience of dwelling in the gameworld could only hope to serve as an antechamber for a more far-reaching study, from which a number of routes for further investigation could open up for mapping out a more fully-developed poetics of dwelling in games.

I have not, for instance, paused to consider the temporary home-along-the-way represented by examples such as the campsite in *Dragon Age: Origins* (BioWare 2009) or the bonfires in *Dark Souls*, whose kindling tangles together the hestial and the hermetic in complex patterns. Nor have I tackled the theme of the house that is not (or is no longer) a home, in which – as in *Gone Home* (The Fulbright Company 2012), or in the player's later return to their early-game homeplace in *The Legend of Zelda: Ocarina of Time* (Nintendo EAD 1998) or *Baldur's Gate* (BioWare 1998) – the dissociation of a physical locus from the situation of dwelling it once supported results in a powerful sense of the uncanny. Likewise, I have not addressed the tendency for games to furnish their virtual worlds with the icons of dwelling without structuring a corresponding existential praxis of dwelling for the player (Liboriussen 2012, 40). Also largely left unexplored is the social dimension of dwelling with others in multiplayer gameworlds (Hayot/Wesp 2009; Klastrup 2009). Perhaps most crucially, the phenomenological approach according to which the investigation has proceeded has largely sidelined the socio-cultural and political charges inherent in the notion of home and in the constitution of the homeplace as a Lefebvrean (1991, 39) "representational space" that cannot but bear the mark of ideology.

Instead, it has been my aim with this investigation to clear the ground and set down the foundations for an understanding of dwelling and being-at-home in gameworlds. By identifying, in *Minecraft* and *AC:NL*, the phenomenological qualities and existential practices that relate to dwelling as defined by Heidegger, Tuan and Norberg-Schulz – and, even more specifically, to the idea of hestial dwelling developed by Casey – I have shown that games have the capacity to enact, and play with, this basic dimension of embodied being in space and place. In doing so, I have not only tried to shed light on aspects of the player's spatial engagement with gameworlds that have, for the most part, not been well accounted for. More fundamentally, by demonstrating that finding our feet in the gameworld is only the beginning (that settled, hestial dwelling can await at the end of our hermetic, exploratory wandering) games can not only re-enact our practices of being at home, but, in doing so, can represent to us these practices and senses of 'home,' and lead us to reflect on – and, perhaps, to engage critically with – what is entailed in the idea of being at home.

References

11 Bit Studios (2014): *This War of Mine*, PC: Deep Silver.

Aarseth, Espen J. (1997): *Cybertext: Perspectives on Ergodic Literature*, Baltimore, MN: Johns Hopkins UP.

–––– (2001): Allegories of Space: The Question of Spatiality in Computer Games, in: *Cybertext Yearbook 2000*, ed. by Markku Eskelinen and Raine Koskimaa, Jyväskylä: Research Centre for Contemporary Culture, 152-171.

–––– (2004): Beyond Myth and Metaphor: Quest Games as Post-Narrative Discourse, in: *Narrative Across Media: The Languages of Storytelling*, ed. by Marie-Laure Ryan, Lincoln, NE: Nebraska UP, 361-376.

Bachelard, Gaston (1994): *The Poetics of Space*, Boston, MA: Beacon Press [1958].

Baudrillard, Jean (1996): *The System of Objects*, New York, NY: Verso [1968].

BioWare (1998): *Baldur's Gate*, PC: Interplay Entertainment.

–––– (2007): *Mass Effect*, Xbox 360: Microsoft Game Studios.

–––– (2009): *Dragon Age: Origins*, PC: Electronic Arts.

Brontë, Charlotte (1994): *Jane Eyre*, London: Penguin [1847].

Calleja, Gordon (2011): *In-Game: From Immersion to Incorporation*, Cambridge, MA/London: MIT Press.

Casey, Edward S. (1993): *Getting Back into Place: Towards a Renewed Understanding of the Place-World*, Bloomington, IN: Indiana UP.

Crowther, William/Woods, Don (1976): *Collosal Cave Adventure*, PDP-10: Crowther/Woods.

Csikszentmihalyi, Mihaly/Rochberg-Halton, Eugene (1981): *The Meaning of Things: Domestic Symbols and the Self*, Cambridge/New York, NY/Melbourne: Cambridge UP.

Dontnod Entertainment (2015): *Life Is Strange*, PC: Square Enix.

Fink, Eugen (2016): Oasis of Happiness: Thoughts toward an Ontology of Play, in: id.: *Play as Symbol of the World and Other Writings*, Bloomington, IN: Indiana UP, 14-31 [1957].

Fleming, Victor (1939): *The Wizard of Oz*, Film: USA.

Forster, Edward M. (2012): *Howards End*, London: Penguin [1910].

From Software (2011): *Dark Souls*, PS3/Xbox 360: Bandai Namco.

Gadamer, Hans-Georg (²1989): *Truth and Method*, New York, NY: Continuum [1960].

Gazzard, Alison (2013): *Mazes in Videogames: Meaning, Metaphor and Design*, Jefferson, NC: McFarland & Co.

Günzel, Stephan (2008): The Space-Image: Interactivity and Spatiality of Computer Games, in: *Conference Proceedings of the Philosophy of Computer Games 2008*, ed. by id., Michael Liebe and Dieter Mersch, Potsdam: Potsdam UP, 170-188.

Halttunen, Karen (1989): From Parlor to Living Room: Domestic Space, Interior Decoration and the Culture of Personality, in: *Consuming Visions: Accumulation and Display of Goods in America, 1880-1920*, ed. by Simon J. Bronner, New York, NY: Norton, 157-189.

Hayot, Eric/Wesp, Edward (2009): Towards a Critical Aesthetic of Virtual World Geographies, in: *Game Studies* 9/1, gamestudies.org/0901/articles/hayot_wesp_space.

Heidegger, Martin (2004a): The Question Concerning Technology", in: id.: *Basic Writings*, London/New York, NY: Routledge, 311-341 [1953].

–––– (2004b): Building Dwelling Thinking, in: id.: *Basic Writings*, 347-363 [1951].

–––– (2008): *Being and Time*, New York, NY: Harper [1927].

Klastrup, Lisbeth (2009): The Worldness of *Everquest*: Exploring a 21st Century Fiction, in: *Game Studies* 9/1, gamestudies.org/0901/articles/klastrup.

Kovacs, Maureen Gallery (1989) [Ed.]: *The Epic of Gilgamesh*, Palo Alto, CA: Stanford UP.

Lefebvre, Henri (1991): *The Production of Space*, Hoboken, NY: Wiley-Blackwell [1974].

Liboriussen, Bjarke (2012): Collective Building Projects in *Second Life*: User Motives and Strategies Explained from an Architectural and Ethnographic Perspective, in: *Virtual Worlds and Metaverse Platforms: New Communication and Identity Paradigms*, ed. by Nelson Zagalo, Leonel Morgalo and Ana Boa-Ventura, Hershey, PA: Information Science Reference, 33-46.

Martin, Paul (2011): The Pastoral and the Sublime in *Elder Scrolls IV: Oblivion*, in: *Game Studies* 11/3, gamestudies.org/1103/articles/martin.

Merleau-Ponty, Maurice (2002): *Phenomenology of Perception*, London: Routledge [1945].

Möring, Sebastian (2013): *Games and Metaphor: A Critical Analysis of the Metaphor Discourse In Game Studies*, PhD-Dissertation: ITU Copenhagen.

Mojang (2009): *Minecraft*, PC: Mojang.

Moseley, Merritt (2009): The Epic of Gilgamesh and the Hero's Journey, in: *The Hero's Journey*, ed. by Harold Bloom, New York, NY: Infobase Publishing, 63-74.

Murray, Janet H. (1997): *Hamlet on the Holodeck: The Future of Narrative in Cyberspace*, New York, NY et al.: Free Press.

Nintendo EAD (1998): *The Legend of Zelda: Ocarina of Time*, Nintendo 64: Nintendo.

———— (2012): *Animal Crossing: New Leaf*, Nintendo 3DS: Nintendo.

Nitsche, Michael (2008): *Video Game Spaces: Image, Play, and Structure in 3D Worlds*, Cambridge, MA: MIT Press.

Norberg-Schulz, Christian (1985): *The Concept of Dwelling: On the Way to Figurative Architecture*, New York, NY: Rizzoli.

Paasonen, Susann (2009): Immaterial Homes, Personal Spaces and the Internet as Rhetorical Terrain", in: *Homes in Transformation: Dwelling, Moving, Belonging*, ed. by Hanna Johansson and Kirsi Saarikangas, Helsinki: Suomalaisen Kirjallisuuden Seura, 338-357.

Purves, Alex C. (2010): *Space and Time in Ancient Greek Narrative*, Cambridge, NY et al.: Cambridge UP.

Reed, Brian H. (2006): *Hart Crane: After His Lights*, Tuscaloosa, AL: University of Alabama Press.

Rybczynski, Witold (2001): *Home: A Short History of an Idea*, London: Pocket Books.

Salen, Katie/Zimmerman, Eric (2004): *Rules of Play: Game Design Fundamentals*, Cambridge, MA: MIT Press.

Team ICO (2001): *Ico*, PS2: Sony Interactive Entertainment.

The Chinese Room (2015): *Everybody's Gone to the Rapture*, PS4: SCE.

The Fulbright Company (2012): *Gone Home*, PC: The Fulbright Company.

Tosca, Susana Pajares (2003): The Quest Problem in Computer Games, in: *Technologies for Interactive Digital Storytelling: TIDSE 03 Proceedings*, Darmstadt: Fraunhofer, 69-81.

Tuan, Yi-Fu (1977): *Space and Place: The Perspective of Experience*, Minneapolis, MN: University of Minnesota Press.

———— (1979): *Landscapes of Fear*, Minneapolis, MN: University of Minnesota Press.

———— (1993): Desert and Ice: Ambivalent Aesthetics, in: *Landscape, Natural Beauty and the Arts*, ed. by Salim Kemal and Ivan Gaskell, Cambridge, NY: Cambridge University Press, 139-157.

Vella, Daniel (2013): The Wanderer in the Wilderness: *Minecraft*, *Proteus* and Being in the Virtual Landscape, in: *The Philosophy of Computer Games Conference – Computer Game Space: Concept, Form and Experience*, Bergen, gamephilosophy2013.w.uib.no/files/2013/09/daniel-vella-the-wanderer-in-the-wilderness.pdf.

———— (2015): *The Ludic Subject and the Ludic Self: Analyzing the 'I-in-the-Gameworld'*, PhD-Dissertation: ITU Copenhagen, en.itu.dk/~/media/en/research/phd-programme/phd-defences/2015/daniel-vella---the-ludic-subject-and-the-ludic-self-final-print-pdf.pdf.

———— (2016): The Ludic Muse: The Form of Games as Art, in: *Countertext* 2/1, 66-84.

Wolf, Mark J.P. (2011): Theorizing Navigable Space in Videogames, in *DIGAREC Keynote Lectures 2009/10*, ed. by Stephan Günzel, Michael Liebe and Dieter Mersch, Potsdam: Potsdam UP, 18-49.

Woolf, Virginia (1991): *A Room of One's Own*, New York, NY: Harcourt Brace [1929].

Videogame Wastelands as (Non-)Places and 'Any-Space-Whatevers'

Souvik Mukherjee

On reflecting upon the hundred-plus hours that the average gamer spends in playing games like *Fallout 3* (Bethesda Game Studios 2008), it seems strange that one would like to spend so much time roaming a virtual post-apocalyptic wasteland. Given the recent popularity of the wasteland setting in videogames, such as *Fallout 3*, *S.T.A.L.K.E.R.: Shadow of Chernobyl* (GSC Game World 2007) and *Borderlands* (Gearbox Software 2009), it might be worth asking what makes wastelands so interesting to the gaming community. Post-apocalyptic wastelands are a popular trope in Science Fiction on which all of the above games as well as others such as *Half-Life* (Valve Corporation 1998) and *BioShock* (2K Boston 2007), with their dystopian environments, heavily draw on. However, that is not the only reason: even a game like *Far Cry 2* (Ubisoft Montreal 2008), where the player drives through seventy miles of African bush, offers an experience similar to the wanderings of *Fallout 3's* protagonist. This is the experience of travelling in a world fraught with danger and uncertainty through wide expanses of game space interspersed with nodes of activity.

The Post-Apocalyptic Wasteland: A Metaphor for Videogame Spaces?

The environment of *Far Cry 2*, although contextually very disparate and having brighter-coloured African bush-vegetation, still resembles *S.T.A.L.K.E.R.*'s backdrop of the irradiated forests of the Chernobyl area in the Ukraine. Even if the environments vary significantly, the experience of videogame wastelands can be seen to have marked similarities in the games and, arguably, is also perceptible to a degree in other kinds of game spaces whether they are cities, buildings or battlefields. This paper, therefore, explores the experience of wasteland spaces with a view to commenting on their appeal to gamers and also on how the wasteland experience links to the experience of game spaces in general. In the main, the analysis here concerns itself with the above-mentioned examples and the first-person shooter (FPS) and role-playing game genres into which all of them can be roughly categorised.

Located on the opposite extreme of the utopic Garden of Eden or the Land of Cockaigne with their symbolism of progress and plenty, the conception of the wasteland has been that of a space without fixed meanings. Post-apocalyptic wastelands are especially characterised by a lack of the sense of place and are vast, cold expanses of ruined landscape as seen in films like *The Road* (Hillcoat 2009) or in stories like Ray Bradbury's *There Will Come Soft Rains* from 1950. Bradbury takes his title from Sara Teasdale's eponymous poem *Flame and Shadow* from 1920 which imagines nature reclaiming the earth after humanity has been wiped out by war – in Bradbury's story this meaning collapses into irony and in *Fallout 3*, if the player happens to encounter the poetry-reading 'Mr Gutsy' inside the McClellan Town Home, the robot reads out Teasdale's poem, which amid the ruined landscape seems almost meaningless. The game of course can possibly avoid Bradbury's conclusion of the permanent loss of meaning (the result of the permanent destruction of life) if the player is able to fulfil the quest for restoring fertility to the wasteland but even then, the ending is fraught with uncertainty where stability and meaning still remain elusive.

For the most part the environment of *Fallout 3*, however, closely resembles that of the film *The Road* with its destroyed landscape where objects and cultures have lost their meaning. The lack of fixed meaning is of course characteristic of the wasteland in general: a most notable example is T.S. Eliot's poem, *The Waste Land* from 1922. As Lawrence Rainey (2007, 49) comments, "*The Waste Land* doesn't have a narrative; instead, it has the scent of a narrative, hovering in the air like a perfume after someone has left the room". As Eliot says, describing his urban wasteland (and perhaps the wasteland of his psyche): "On Margate Sands / I can connect / Nothing with nothing".

Models of Videogame Spatiality:
Space, Place, Non-place and Further Possibilities

Videogames have earlier been described as "*space of possibility*" (Salen/Zimmerman 2004, 390) and it can be argued that like Eliot's wasteland they leave the behind the 'scent of a narrative'. Many, though not all, games tell stories and whether in the monorail narratives of earlier games or in the increasingly open-world environments of recent games, the game creates a space for the player to play out different iterations of a story. Videogames are, therefore, story-spaces. Or even better, story-spaces of possibility. As spaces of possibility, videogame spaces are multiple. They do not lend themselves to linear structures. Instead, one can keep repeating one's game and the space configures and reconfigures itself with each temporal iteration and creates multiple planes of spatiality and also multiple choices for the player. Instead of the beginning, middle and end, stories in games end up having structures that are difficult to even visualise, and are often described by abstract poststructuralist concepts, such as Gilles Deleuze and Felix Guattari's (1987, 3-25) rhizome.

Instead of analysing the spatial structure per se, the key interest here is to approach the fuller spatial experience in videogames through the wasteland metaphor. Previous attempts to describe such complex and multiple story-spaces of possibility have involved models from Michel de Certeau's differentiation of space and place as well as Marc Augé's concept of 'non-places.' These models, while appropriate entry points for the discussion are, however, a more detailed analysis exposes some limitations in the way in which they describe game spaces. An alternative model, based on Gilles Deleuze's idea of non-homogenous and multiple spaces, is examined as being possibly a more applicable description. This is then seen in context together with the wasteland metaphor.

Enroute to the Deleuzian model, the earlier positions provide some key insights that need consideration. de Certeau famously differentiates 'space' [espace] from 'place' [lieu] on the premise that place is stable and 'proper' whereas 'space' is mobile, always in development and is in effect place that is being 'practised.' According to de Certeau's (2002, 117) definition,

> A place is the order (of whatever kind) in accord with which elements are distributed in relationships of coexistence. It thus excludes the possibility of two things being in the same location (place). The law of the 'proper' rules in the place: the elements taken into consideration are beside one another, each situated in its own 'proper' and distinct location, a location it defines. A place is thus an instantaneous configuration of positions. It implies an indication of stability.

A 'place' for de Certeau can be inhabited or not but for it to become 'space,' it needs movement and, therefore, needs to be peopled. The lack of fixed meanings and connections in the wasteland allow it to be viewed as a multiplicity. The many interpretations of Eliot's poem are illustrative of this because the stories in The Waste Land are too many by far. According to de Certeau, "Stories thus carry out a labour that constantly transforms places into spaces or spaces into places. They also organize the play of changing relationships between places and spaces" (ibid., 118). The multiplicity and the implicit constant movement that characterise wastelands make them categorizable as spaces in de Certeau's model. However, although they might be actualised into multiple narrative instances, wastelands do not have identity, relations and history.

Augé, however, modifies this concept significantly in his definition of 'space'; his understanding of 'place' includes movement, possibilities and is a more inclusive conception. For Augé (1995, 87) 'place' has the anthropological connotation characterised by "identity, relations and history":

> Place as defined here is not quite the place that Certeau opposes to space [...] it is place in the established and symbolised sense, anthropological place. [...] There is nothing to forbid the use of the word space to describe this movement. But that is not what we are saying here: we include in the notion of the anthropological place the possibility of journeys made in it (ibid., 81).

For Augé, such spaces are classified as 'non-places.' Sans identity and definition, they are zones that are throbbing with a multiplicity of possible meanings.

The Relevance of the Non-Place Model to Videogame Wastelands: Summarising Earlier Positions

Returning to the story(ies) of *Fallout 3*, the player encounters ruins of monuments in Washington that have all but ceased to have any meaning in the wasteland. There are, of course, small groups of people who cling to distorted history and myth: for example, the renegade ex-slave called Hannibal Hamlin has saved the stone head of Lincoln's statue as an icon of freedom but most of his speeches about Lincoln are inaccurate. This is similar to Russell Hoban's post-apocalyptic novel *Riddley Walker* from 1980, where the whole of human history has been distorted and summarised into a brief incantation. According to Augé (1995, 95),

> certain places exist only through the words that evoke them, and in this sense they are non-places, or rather, imaginary places: banal utopias, cliches. [...] Here the word does not create a gap between everyday functionality and lost myth: it creates the image, produces the myth and at the same stroke makes it work.

The identity and bearings being lost, the myth becomes a superficial token and almost a fabrication of the words which surround it. The 'wish-granter' myth in the *S.T.A.L.K.E.R.* game, about a fabled place where one's wishes come true, is one such fabrication. The wish-granter is supposedly a room whose history has been distorted into legend in the wasteland expanses of the game's setting.

All the games mentioned so far have the common element of travelling across vast stretches of wasteland. The player is essentially a traveller and, as Sybille Lammes points out, a cartographer as well. Lammes illustrates how de Certeau's differentiation of the 'map' and the 'tour', where one is based on 'seeing' and the other on 'going,' collapses in videogame spaces where the two functions get conflated. In a similar vein, Stephan Günzel (2007) observes how GPS-systems, where cartography is highly subordinated to the user's individual needs, find a parallel in the videogame maps (players in both *S.T.A.L.K.E.R.* and *Fallout 3* have GPS-like maps on their in-game PDA's) which he calls 'augmented virtuality.' Furthering expanding on the role of the player in videogame spaces, Lammes (2008, 95) states that

> As cartographers on tour, players are engaged in a process that is targeted towards a personal rather than a global or homogenous conception of spatiality. Such games do more than just ask a certain degree of spatial attentiveness from players to win the game. In addition, they invite them to create and transform maps and landscapes according to their individual choices. Gamers are thus actively exploring and transforming territories and maps in a highly personal, precise and even reflexive way.

In *Fallout 3*, one of the perks that players can attain at an advanced level is to view all locations that they haven't explored or discovered as yet. Personally speaking, the experience can be really rewarding. Deviating slightly from the game's intended course, it is possible to play a game-within-the-game wherein one is a tourist as well as a cartographer in the Capital Wasteland. The map on the PDA (called 'pip boy' in the game) reveals all the locations as nodes on the map but the player still has to figure out the paths connecting the various nodes.

Lev Manovich (2001, 273) compares the user navigating a virtual space to nineteenth century explorers. One can easily visualise explorers such as Mungo Park, Humboldt or Tavernier as cartographer-tourists. The player who tours the Capital Wasteland travelling from node to node is both an explorer as well as a *flaneur* who is truly at home only when displaced amongst a crowd. The latter is Manovich's metaphor for the internet surfer. Because of the *flaneur*-figure's identityless wandering, Lammes (2007) compares the internet to Augé's concept of 'non-place.' Manovich also explores similarities between zones of navigation and what he calls the 'mega-non-place.'

Taking the example of Centre Euralille, the train terminal complex near the entrance to the Chunnel (the underground tunnel that connects the Continent to the UK), Manovich (2001, 280) points out that "[l]ike the network players of Doom, Euralille users emerge from trains and cars to temporarily inhabit a zone defined through their trajectories, an environment to 'to just wander around inside of'." The comparison is of further interest because it makes a direct link between videogames and non-places. *Doom* (id Software 1993) is indeed one of the earliest FPS ancestors of games like *Fallout 3* or *Borderlands*: the lone space-marine in the wasteland of an alien planet is a classic FPS game story. Before, moving further into the description of videogame wastelands as 'non-places,' it will be instructive to return to Augé's original concept and the examples to which he applies them.

This will help in understanding how far the concept applies to the experience of videogame players and to comment on earlier critical positions related to videogame space.

Augé (1995) describes spaces such as train and air terminals, supermarkets, theme parks and leisure centres as 'non-places.' As products of a 'supermodern' situation, they are devoid of meaning themselves and are the liminal or threshold spaces, where the individual moves from the social to the solitary in terms of his or her sense of identity. These spaces are characterised by movement as in de Certeau's formulation; however, they do not translate into 'places' but rather into zones that are drained of any immediate meaning once the movement stops – think about an airport where the staff are on strike. For Augé (1995, 94),

> Non-place' designates two complementary but distinct realities: spaces formed in relation to certain ends (transport, commerce, leisure) and the relations that individuals have with these spaces. Although the two sets of relations overlap, they are not confused with each other; for non-places mediate a whole mass of relations, with the self and with others, which are only indirectly connected to their purposes. An anthropological space creates the organically social, so non-places create solitary contractuality.

Instead of 'passing through,' as one would do in a city with its distinctive history and culture, one would 'pass by' a non-place. Augé points to the experience of the driver on the bypasses who sees the city as it is constructed for him through images and words on billboards and signs. As discussed in relation to the perception of identity and culture through the distorted myths in the wasteland, there is meaning-making going on in the non-places through the fragmentary symbolism of the billboards.

This brings up immediate parallels with *Far Cry 2* – and even *Grand Theft Auto: San Andreas* (Rockstar North 2004); although that comparison will be made in a later section. The protagonist in *Far Cry 2* drives for miles together on the highways, paths and bypasses and the only way of construing the significance of his surroundings from randomly scattered cues around him such as signposts, enemy outposts, arms dealers' shops and bus stations. Even when he does get into the heavily barricaded towns, such as Pala and Mosale Seto, he is just a passer-by. He rarely encounters civilians and visits only for missions, medicine or money: there is no scope or even need to explore the history of the place and the culture of the people.

The same is true of *Fallout 3*, where settlements have started in random places, but they still remind the player of being in an airport or a train station. Rivet City, the game's largest civilian human settlement, is a case in point. It is a settlement within a partly destroyed aircraft carrier and its denizens live in cabins and interact with each other in certain community areas. There is an attempt at reconstructing fragments of history (there is a church, a market and even a museum) but the identity of the place seems to be much the same as that of the Euralille terminal complex described by Manovich. Rivet City is a 'non-place' that tries to differentiate itself from the rest of the wasteland and to become an anthropological place. Sometimes, indeed, the player might even feel that he is passing through rather than just passing-by but in general, Rivet City is just another place to trade or to sojourn in (hence comparable to Augé's non-place examples like the supermarket and the terminals).

According to Augé, the "person entering the space of non-place is relieved of usual determinants. He becomes no more than what he does or experiences in the role of passenger, driver, customer; passive joys of identity-loss, and the more active pleasure of role-playing" (1995, 103). From a videogame perspective, it is important to note how Augé links identity-loss and the active pleasure of role-playing. From the very outset, videogame studies has linked this to notions of immersion and involvement. It is easy to see why early game research such as Janet Murray (1997) saw structuring participation as a visit as one of the ways to produce immersion.

The players as visitors (or cartographer-tourists) would then be seen as losing their identity-markers and seamlessly entering the non-place. Augé's position, arguably, does not allow for such seamlessness. Within the non-place, the spectator is simultaneously the spectacle – and this makes seamless immersion impossible as it constantly raises questions about the construction of identities within the non-place. The protagonist's in-game name in *Fallout 3* provides a good example. Although the player is given the choice to input his or her preferred names, the game narrative keeps referring to the player as the 'Lone Wanderer.' In effect, although the player has customised preferences (name, hair colour, gender, ethnicity) in the game, he or she is still the Lone Wanderer and the first-person narrative keeps slipping into the third-person.

To return to the discussion of videogame non-spaces, the name 'Lone Wanderer' adds another layer of significance to the role cartographer-tourist. This name suggests two things: the player is a solitary character and a nomad. The nomadic existence is characteristic of the wastelander and the Lone Wanderer's visits to the different settlements do not serve to give him or her a sense of place. The Lone Wanderer can get materials from other settlements and even a house in Megaton or a bunk in Vault 101 but he or she is always alone (even though there is the option to team up with some characters) and the relationship with characters in most part is that solitary contractuality.

The main driving force in the creation of the non-places with their identity-less existence and communities of solitary contractuality is what Augé describes as 'supermodernity.' Supermodernity "stems simultaneously from overabundance of events, spatial overabundance and individualisation of references" (Augé 1995, 109), all of which are characteristics of the wasteland scenario. The lack of fixed meanings creates a plurality of narratives that, following de Certeau, create multiple spaces and related events. As described using the example of the Lone Wanderer figure, these overabundant spatial and temporal possibilities in the wasteland (as non-place) are traversed by solitary characters. Finally, according to Augé, this implies that there are no remembered places as "everything proceeds as if space had been trapped by time, as if there were no history other than the last 48 hours of news; as if each individual history were drawing its motives, words and images from the inexhaustible stock of an unending history in the present" (1995, 109). Memory has little to do with non-places.

Videogame Non-places beyond the Wasteland: Applying the Theory to Other Scenarios

Going by the above comparisons between videogame spaces and Augé's outline of the concept, it is not surprising that the non-place has been a popular concept for describing videogame spatiality. Manovich (as quoted above), Torill Mortensen, Jay Bolter and Richard Grusin among others have variously applied the concept to describing videogames or similar entities. Mortensen (2003) even observes that "the airport [is] more similar to a play-space than the public spheres of the net," which in turn have already been described as non-places earlier in this analysis. So far, this paper has been focusing on wasteland scenarios in videogames and analysing their similarities to non-places. Judging from the similarities, the appeal of the wasteland story for videogames seems to be related to the way both wastelands and videogame spaces function in the player's/traveller's experience of them as non-places. Before we can proceed further, one question comes to mind: does the wasteland's status as a non-place have any significance for videogame spaces in general and across genres?

While the wasteland-scenario is a popular one, there are many successful titles that use other settings for their game environments. Common examples would be city locations, such as San Andreas (modelled on sections of California and Nevada) or battlefields, such as Omaha Beach in *Medal of Honour: Allied Assault* (2015, Inc. 2002). As far as the exploration of or survival in an alien planet, the similarity of the experience of playing *Doom* to that of passing by non-places has already been pointed to. Although the landscape is vastly different, the experience of the city is not all that different from walking in Capital Wasteland or driving in the Savannah. There are certainly more cars (sometimes one can even steal them) but the buildings are usually inaccessible and those that let you step in are fast-food joints, gyms, police stations or hospitals. The player is still the lone wanderer and even though he or she might perch atop the tallest tower in Jerusalem, as in *Assassin's Creed* (Ubisoft Montreal 2007), exploring and charting the rooftops and streets with intense detail, the player is always the solitary cartographer-tourist. One might make a comparison with Augé's (1995, 91) comments on Chateaubriand's visit to Jerusalem where he claims that "the abundance of verbiage and documentation really does make it possible to identify Chateaubriand's holy places as a non-place, very similar to the ones outlined in pictures and slogans in our guidebooks and brochures."

The set-piece battlefields in *Medal of Honour* also have 'historical' landmarks (e.g. Omaha Beach) but as Michael Nitsche comments, the battles take place, as it were, like a theme park ride: "after Mike Powell has been shot by virtual snipers, killed by virtual machine guns, blown up by virtual mortars, and annihilated by virtual mines, I start to reflect upon the situation. The overall game might remain a kind of World War II theme park ride" (Nitsche 2008, 166). Again, the theme park space may aspire towards the creation of an identity but as Bolter and Grusin (1999, 177) state:

> Nonplaces, such as theme parks and malls, function as public places only during designated hours of operation [...] When the careful grids of railings and ropes that during the day serve to shepherd thousands of visitors to ticket counters or roller coasters stand completely empty, such spaces then seem drained of meaning.

From the above examples, it is evident that the wasteland scenario has underlying similarities with other types of space in RPG and FPS games. Think, for example, of the chillingly nondescript interior of Armacham Technology Corporation in *F.E.A.R.* (Monolith Productions 2005) where players find themselves devoid of links with the outside – almost a passer-by albeit in an eerily silent space punctuated with bursts of random activity. The randomness of events (especially in 'anomaly'-infested radioactive zones as in *S.T.A.L.K.E.R.*), multiplicity of meanings, the solitary contractuality with the game elements and the constant need to map and explore while traversing vast spaces seem to be common characteristics of most RPG and FPS games that have an even more heightened impact in the post-apocalyptic wasteland scenario; therefore, it is worth exploring the latter as a metaphor for videogame spaces.

Deeper into the Wasteland: Questioning the Non-Place Model

Just as the wasteland shows the above similarities with the non-place, it also highlights some key differences and actually serves to challenge previous positions based on the model. Extending the metaphor to more types of videogame spaces raises further questions. As Mortensen (2003) observes about MUDS and MMOs, it is difficult to call them non-places precisely because there is a sense of identity that runs deep in the guilds and communities in these virtual places:

> The players and the administrators weave the stories of their characters together, and the intruder, the stranger strolling by and deciding to linger finds that there is history to each and every one of the characters about him, history on several levels, just as it is to the people in a flesh-world geographical space. [...] while it's a long stretch to claim that a MUD is a physical place, to claim that it is a social place is easier. Not the least of signs to that is what I mentioned before, the territorial behaviour. There is also the social behaviour, the way the inhabitants tend to seek each other out in certain clusters, which are resistant to outside pressures or attempts to split them.

As far as the physicality of the 'placeness' is concerned, she cites de Certeau's conception of place as an instantaneous configuration of positions thus negating any objections to the fact that the space is not located on tangible ground. The MMO is not always as Mortensen describes; especially for a solitary newbie the vast spaces of Azeroth or Norrath might be daunting and wasteland-like. However, Mortensen's comment necessitates a rethinking of wasteland spaces as a metaphor for videogame spaces if it solely resembles the non-place described by Augé. This is not constrained to multiplayer spaces and to interaction with human players; single-player game environments may also provide some sense of identity and belonging.

On analysing further, significant differences emerge that make it necessary to analyse Augé's claims both in themselves and in terms of videogames. One of the different types of spatialities that Nitsche (2008, 16) outlines is called "fictional space [and it] lives in the imagination, in other words, [it is] the space 'imagined' by players from their comprehension of the available images." This corresponds to the construction of space from a narrative, as described by de Certeau. Only this narrative might be drawn from the player's non-game world or from an anthropological place outside the game. While Augé is right in differentiating the non-place from the anthropological place, at least as far as videogame spaces are concerned, it is important not to look at them as watertight and not to ignore the powerful impact of imagination in building a sense of identity in the game space – even more so in the wasteland scenario with its enlarged space of possibility.

There is another issue related to Augé's concept: not much is said about whether non-places can actually become anthropological places. One would like to think of the many so-called 'non-places' like the railway stations and transit points that later became huge cities; Kenya's capital city, Nairobi, which started as a small railway transit point and is now a major city is a case in point. Within the non-place, despite the solitary contractuality that Augé argues for, it is possible for deeper human bonds to develop. In the movie *The Terminal* (Spielberg 2005) an East European called Viktor Navorski is forced to live in New York City airport's international arrivals lounge until the US immigration agencies can resolve his situation. However, although living in Augé considers a typical non-place, Navorski builds many bonds and his life intertwines with those of many others. The Terminal becomes, for him, a 'place' as good as any other. As Ian Bogost (2006, 16) describes this:

> The recombinations of time horizons in the airport terminal allow Spielberg to paint the medium-term struggles of many characters, the long-term struggles of a few, and the short-term struggles of the airport itself. As different characters interact along one or more of these time horizons, the film's unit operations become apparent, and The Terminal reveals itself not as a film about a man struggling against governments for his identity, but as one about various modes of waiting.

Bogost sees the story as the glue for a configurative work about specific modes of uncorroborated waiting – for him, this begins to resemble a piece of software or videogame (ibid., 19). Such 'waiting' has in itself the potential of developing as yet unrealised possibilities into actions. It is more about the possible transition of non-places into places. In the wasteland scenarios in videogames, imagination can play a strong role in creating associations with the in-game characters, whether human (in multiplayer games) or NPCs, especially when the player joins an in-game faction such as the Brotherhood of Steel in *Fallout 3*, where it is possible to imagine some social ties with other characters in the group. In squad-based games like *Call of Duty 4* (Infinity Ward 2007), it is possible at times to relate to NPCs who are helping the player. Unlike the watertight conception of the non-place, the wasteland contains a key element that endears it as a spatial metaphor in videogames – it allows for many possibilities of change.

Another aspect in which Augé's conception of non-places struggles to describe the gamer's spatial experience is connected to the complex temporality of videogames. As noted earlier, Augé describes the temporality of the non-place as one where space seems to be trapped in time and where individual histories are, as it were, drawn from the inexhaustible stock of an unending history that is contained in the present moment. Curious as it may sound, in Augé's non-place, all history is subverted by an infinitely extended present. Seen in relation to videogames, there are both parallels and differences.

Paradoxically, temporality in videogames is a complex mesh of events that are different while remaining the same. It might even be tempting to see the entire videogame as an event stretched over a presentness – certainly all the actions in the game are being performed by the player in the immediate present although the storyline may have pasts and futures. The temporal structure of videogames is problematized with the saves, reloads and respawns of the player's persona. While it is true that the entire history of the game can experienced as parallel moments in the present, it does not necessarily have to be so.

With each repeated event in a reload, the same event is nevertheless experienced as a different and unique one. Games like *Prince of Persia: The Sands of Time* (Ubisoft 2003) and *Assassin's Creed* have storylines which consciously play with and subvert the linear experience of time. So instead of the homogenous presentness that Augé describes in his non-place, the videogame space is the locale for a temporal complexity where a repeated event is simultaneously the same and different and where time forms a mesh of presents, pasts and futures.

Elsewhere, I (Mukherjee 2008) have used Gilles Deleuze's framework from *Difference and Repetition*, to help understand this. What follows is a quick summary that relates the complex discussion of videogame temporality to the present context. To simplify Deleuze's (1994) concept, events exist within a virtual mesh of events where all events that consists of different iterations of the same events existing simultaneously as potential events. However, only some of these will be actualised (or in simple words, will happen for us) depending on the possibilities that are available at that point and on the conditions surrounding the event (which Deleuze calls 'singularities').

Unlike in real life, it is possible to reload event-sequences and in each instance of reloading, a saved game allows different possible events to be actualised from within the mesh of events. Deleuze's concept of difference and repetition is important in drawing a framework for the peculiar temporal structure of videogames. When a videogame instance is reloaded, even if the event actualised is similar to the one before it, there are still changes in the surrounding conditions (singularities) and all the different factors influencing the event make it different. The narrative and consequently the spatial experience are also different. The game space thus does not remain in a perpetual present; rather it turns into a multiplicity of spaces within multiple time-schemes.

Videogame Wastelands as 'Any-Space-Whatevers'

This is only one aspect in which Deleuzian thought necessitates a second look at the experience of videogame wastelands in terms of non-places. The above point, however, will help in developing a more complex understanding of videogame wastelands, building on and then challenging the already established framework of non-places. Deleuze and Guattari are key figures in any modern thinking on space and their classification of space into the constant combination of the uncontrolled 'smooth' space with the controllable and delimitable 'striated' space is popular even in videogame studies where major commentators such as Nitsche, Bogost and Mortensen have published on the subject.

This analysis, however, will look at a different aspect of Deleuzian conceptions of spatiality. The concept in question is taken from Deleuze's writing on *Cinema* and is called 'any-space-whatever' [*espace quelconque*]. There is some debate as to whether Deleuze developed this on Augé's concept of non-place because in his notes he credits a certain 'Pascal Augé.' Although critics are divided on this, some like Ronald Bogue and Réda Bensmaia have linked the concept to Marc Augé's non-place (Stivale 2006). Before commenting further on the link with Augé's non-place, however, it would be instructive to describe 'any-space-whatever.'

Deleuze analyses pre-World War 2 cinema in terms of what he calls the 'movement image' (he also has a subsequent category call the 'time image' which is less relevant to the present purposes). The movement image "is a form of spatialized cinema: time determined and measured by movement" (Totaro 1999). Deleuze's (1986, 1) understanding of movement is based on the Bergsonian idea that "movement occurs in the interval between the two [instants]" and therefore, we miss capturing the movement: in cinema, however, the in-between is perceivable as part of whole experience of movement. Between the perception of an object and the action that leads to a cinematic event, Deleuze posits an in-between state called the 'affection-image.' This is the state that is throbbing with multiple possibilities without having yet actualised any one of these.

The actualisation itself depends on a complex framework of restricting parameters that Deleuze calls singularities. These might be influenced by the game affordances, by remembered sequences of gameplay and by the player's experiential context at the time. One of the manifestations of the affection-image is that of the any-space-whatever. Ronald Bogue (2003, 80) describes this as a "virtual space, whose fragmented components might be assembled in multiple combinations, a space of yet-to-be actualised possibilities." Deleuze (1986, 101) himself elaborates on his concept in his description of the 'vast fragmented spaces' of Longchamp and Gare du Lyons in Robert Bresson's *Pickpocket*:

> Any-space-whatever is not an abstract universal, in all times, in all places. It is a perfectly singular space, which has merely lost its homogeneity, that is, the principle of its metric relations or the connection of its own parts, so that the linkages can be made in an infinite number of ways. It is a space of virtual conjunction, grasped as a pure locus of the possible.

From this it can be inferred that the any-space-whatever is not a formal model of spatiality and indeed like Augé's 'non-place', it is an experiential concept. Jeffrey Bell (1997) attempts to link this to Augé's non-place:

An 'any space whatsoever' [...] is an anonymous space people pass through [...] in such spaces -and this is what interested the anthropologist Augé – individuals become depersonalized [...] It is for this reason that Augé argued that the 'any space whatsoever' is a homogenous, de-singularizing space.

As mentioned earlier, whether Deleuze was influenced by Marc Augé's concept is still doubtful but Bell picks up Deleuze's reference to the fragmented spaces in the race course (Longchamps) and the railway station (Gare de Lyons) in comparison with Augé's non-places of transit. There is certainly a similarity in that both kinds of spaces are vast fragmented spaces and this is also true of the wasteland scenarios in videogames.

However, unlike Augé's 'homogenous, desingularising' space, the any-space-whatever has lost its homogeneity. It is loss of homogeneity that makes it rich with possibilities and Deleuze's 'pure locus of the possible' compares well with Katie Salen's and Eric Zimmerman's concept of the 'space of possibility' in game design.

In the affective zone of the any-space-whatever, the possibilities are actualised under the influence of the surrounding singularities, as described earlier. Like the non-place, the any-space-whatever is represented by fragmented zones that do not have any fixed meaning; they are usually liminal areas which are used for transit and where the traveller's relation with the space is that of solitary contractuality. The difference, however, lies in that the any-space-whatever supports difference and it need not constrain all history to an eternal present as Augé claims to be the case with the non-place. The any-space-whatever is not orientated in advance and it can create linkages in an infinitely multiple number of ways. Therefore, it does not preclude possibilities of Navorski making an anthropological place out of an airport lounge or of the videogame player converting the non-place of the game into a social place.

After the possibility within the any-space-whatever is actualised, it is possible to perceive identity in the spatial experience of the videogame. It is also possible to perceive a sense of history, contingent on the player's memory of the game events and the interaction with other players or non-player characters. In its experiential aspect, as opposed to its formal structural restrictions, the game space retains its ability to form 'linkages in an infinite number of ways' like the Deleuzian any-space-whatever. This considers the formal affordances of the game event, memory, the player's emotional and material environment among a host of other factors. Just as for Navorski the airport is not just a space where he acts out his daily routine but is simultaneously the locale for his experience, the videogame space is much more than a playing field. In fact, the very idea of a playing field, whether digital or otherwise, transcends the fixities of a rule-bound space and includes a host of experiences that form intrinsic parts of play.

As such, Augé's non-place or de Certeau's binaries of space and place both attempt to describe the fuller experience of space. Both conceptions, however, find it difficult to address the multiplicity that videogames involve without limiting the possibilities or creating mutually exclusive categories to explain them. The any-space-whatever with its characteristic loss of homogeneity addresses the fragmentedness of videogame space without taking away the potential of identity-formation and history. Further, it accounts for the multiple temporal iterations of the game space and at the same time, provides a model where the fragmented multiplicity and the emerging identity do not need to be separated.

At this point, it would be instructive to go back to the key question for this article: why are wasteland spaces such popular settings for videogames? The answer to this, it could be argued, lies in the way they function as any-space-whatevers. As dystopic wastelands, the spaces are barren and yet marked by a multiplicity of possibilities, mostly fraught with danger; the experience of moving through them leaves the player's nerves on edge, as it were. As in the airport terminal, there are various modes of waiting in the wasteland space and the space itself provides the locus where the player actualises the possibilities that create the game event at a specific moment.

The standard first-person shooters such as *Doom* are characterised by a fast-paced spatial progression where the speed often moves the focus away from the affective stage or the stage of 'becoming' in which the game actions are the result of the actualisation of possibilities rather than being essences. As such, this might lead to simplistic comparisons with the experience of a theme-park ride or a passing through other non-places such as an airport terminal. *Doom* gives us the impression of being a non-space, as Manovich suggests, precisely because although it is set in a post-apocalyptic space, the expansive wasteland-like feel is lacking. Slowing down the tempo, when the player has cleared an area and is moving ahead into another, the tension is palpable and the sense of the any-space-whatever pervades. The event that will be actualised is never a given.

Whether the player dies or carries on is determined by the singularities of the game's affordances and the player's experience; until the action is performed, the game space exists in an affective state or as an any-space-whatever. As opposed to *Doom*, the freeform wasteland space in *Fallout 3* or *S.T.A.L.K.E.R.*, therefore, slows down or crystallises the experience – it lets us perceive the affective stage. It is possibly to traverse vast desolate expanses where the apparent quietude is charged with the potential of action. You might be attacked by mutants or perish in a radioactive anomaly any moment.

As said before, even game settings that are ostensibly not wastelands use this 'stretching out', as it were, of time and space as in *F.E.A.R*, where in the corridors of Armachem Tech, the wasteland metaphor works aptly as a pure locus of the possible. The wasteland throbs with possibilities that are unlinked and unformed until the player and the surrounding environment intervene: it is an any-space-whatever. Such spaces make it clearer to perceive the workings of possibility and multiplicity in videogames. As any-space-whatever's, the videogame wastelands provide a locale for describing the workings of the complex experience of videogames that was hitherto not perceivable and hence was baffling on many accounts.

The Wasteland Metaphor as a Reassessment of Game-Space

Although the wasteland scenario has many similarities to the non-place described by Augé, the Deleuzian concept of the any-space-whatever helps by better defining it as a videogame metaphor. As the player enters the vast expanse of the wasteland, he or she is in a zone of possibility. The wastelands in *Fallout 3* or the *S.T.A.L.K.E.R.* games are zones invested with a multiplicity of meanings and randomness. At the same time, they are mostly bereft of any inherent identity or character – much like the transit points, theme parks and terminals that Augé describes. However, seen as an affective space or any-space-whatever, the wasteland is not devoid of potential to contain its own social places just as the airport lounge is converted into a home for the stranded protagonist of *The Terminal*.

Looking at the main quests of games like *Fallout 3* and *S.T.A.L.K.E.R.: Shadow of Chernobyl*, it is evident that the preferred aim of the game's plot is the restoration of fertility to the wasteland. The same goes for most wasteland narratives: Eliot's poem ends with a clamour for eternal peace or shantih. The preferred ending is, however, just one possible outcome among the many that the wasteland holds in its affective space. Seen is such terms, the similarities with videogame spaces are quite clear and the popularity of the wasteland setting in videogames is, therefore, hardly surprising. As such, when the experience of the Lone Wanderer in *Fallout 3* becomes representative of other experiences of ludic spaces, one can start thinking of the wasteland as a metaphor for videogame spaces and the way in which they are experienced.

References

2015, Inc. (2002): *Medal of Honour: Allied Assault*, PC: Electronic Arts.
2K Boston (2007): BioShock, Xbox 360: 2K Games.
Augé, Marc (1995): *Non-Places: Introduction to an Anthropology of Supermodernity*, London: Verso Books.
Bell, Jeffrey A. (1997): Thinking with Cinema: Deleuze and Film Theory, in: *Film-Philosophy* 1/1, www.film-philosophy.com/index.php/f-p/article/view/23/8.
Bethesda Game Studios (2008): *Fallout 3*, PC: Bethesda Softworks.

Bogost, Ian (2006): *Unit Operations*, Cambridge, MA/London: MIT Press.

Bogue, Ronald (2003): *Deleuze on Cinema*, New York, NY: Routledge.

Bolter, Jay D./Grusin, Richard (1999): *Remediation: Understanding New Media*, Cambridge, MA/London: MIT Press.

de Certeau, Michel (2002): *The Practice of Everyday Life*, Berkeley, CA: University of California Press [1980].

Deleuze, Gilles (1986): *Cinema 1: The Movement-Image*, London: Athlone [1983].

‒‒‒‒ (1994): *Difference and Repetition*, London: Athlone [1968].

‒‒‒‒/Guattari, Felix (1987): *A Thousand Plateaus: Capitalism and Schizophrenia*, Minneapolis, MN: University of Minnesota Press [1980].

Gearbox Software (2009): *Borderlands*, Xbox 360: 2K Games.

GSC Game World (2007): *S.T.A.L.K.E.R.: Shadow of Chernobyl*, PC: THQ.

Günzel, Stephan (2007): 'Eastern Europe, 2008': Maps and Geopolitics in Video Games, in: *Space Time Play: Computer Games, Architecture and Urbanism – The Next Level*, ed. by Friedrich von Borries, Steffen P. Walz and Matthias Böttger, Basel/Boston, MA/Berlin: Birkhäuser, 444-449.

Hillcoat, John (2009): *The Road*, Film: USA.

id Software (1993): *Doom*, PC: id Software.

Infinity Ward (2007): *Call of Duty 4: Modern Warfare*, PC: Activision.

Lammes, Sybille (2007): The Internet as Non-Place, www.mediaengager.com/spacesofnewmedia.pdf.

‒‒‒‒ (2008): Playing the World: Computer Games, Cartography and Spatial Stories, in: *Aether: The Journal of Media Geography* 3, 84-96.

Manovich, Lev (2001): *The Language of New Media*, Cambridge, MA/London: MIT Press.

Monolith Productions (2005): *F.E.A.R.: First Encounter Assault Recon*, PC: Sierra Entertainment.

Mortensen, Torill E. (2003): The Geography of a Non-Place, www.dichtung-digital.org/2003/issue/4/mortensen/index.htm.

Mukherjee, Souvik (2008): Ab(Sense) of An Ending: Telos and Time in Digital Game Narratives, *Writing Technologies* 2/1, www4.ntu.ac.uk/writing_technologies/back_issues/Vol.%202.1/Mukherjee/index.html.

Murray, Janet H. (1997): *Hamlet on the Holodeck: The Future of Narrative in Cyberspace*, New York, NY et al.: Free Press.

Nitsche, Michael (2008): *Video Game Spaces: Image, Play, and Structure in 3D Worlds*, Cambridge, MA/London: MIT Press.

Rockstar North (2004): *Grand Theft Auto: San Andreas*, PS2: Rockstar Games.

Salen, Katie/Zimmerman, Eric (2004): *Rules of Play: Game Design Fundamentals*, Cambridge, MA/London: MIT Press.

Stivale, Charles (2006): Duelling Augé's: Pascal and Marc (Addendum from Les Roberts), www.langlab.wayne.edu/CStivale/D-G/DuellingAugé.html

Spielberg, Stephen (2005): *The Terminal*, Film: USA.

Totaro, Donato (1999): Gilles Deleuze's Bergsonian Film Project, in: *Off Screen* 3/3, horschamp.qc.ca/9903/offscreen_essays/deleuze1.html.

Ubisoft (2003): *Prince of Persia: The Sands of Time*, GBA: Ubisoft.

Ubisoft Montreal (2007): *Assassin's Creed*, Xbox 360/PS3: Ubisoft.

———— (2008): *Far Cry 2*, PC: Ubisoft.

Valve Corporation (1998): *Half-Life*, PC: Sierra Entertainment.

The Game and 'The Stack'
The Infrastructural Pleasures of 'Pokémon Go'

Bjarke Liboriussen

In the summer of 2016, the phenomenal, global success of *Pokémon Go* (Niantic 2016) suddenly demonstrated just how effectively a game can recalibrate the way in which broad audiences engage with urban space. The game is played on mobile devices, primarily smartphones. The player's location is tracked by the device's GPS function and displayed as an avatar standing on a map. The map also reveals the location of nearby places of in-game interest, such as 'PokéStops' where resources can be harvested and Pokémon gyms where teams of players can play against each other. These places of in-game interest are typically laid on top of places of cultural, historical or social significance, for example, a supermarket, a library, a statue in a park, or a plaque marking where firefighters gave their lives to save others.

Virtual Pokémon creatures are spread out over the real world and when a Pokémon is nearby, the player can try to catch it by holding up their device and using its camera function. The screen displays the world as seen through the camera but overlaid with augmented reality (AR) graphics that includes a Pokémon to be caught. *Pokémon Go* has players physically moving about, with the health benefits physical activity entails, and in many instances walking into or paying attention to parts of their environments they had previously overlooked. More controversially, the game – currently played in a very early, perhaps somewhat premature version – has led players to enter private places without permission and to play in contexts (such as Holocaust memorials) or at times (such as press briefings) that many deem inappropriate.

In the following, I will use *Pokémon Go* as my core example as I connect Benjamin Bratton's recent Stack model of urban space with contemporary gaming (Bratton 2015). In an early, influential text, Espen Aarseth (2001, 169) proclaimed spatiality the core theme of computer games aesthetics: "Computer games [...] are allegories of space: they pretend to portray space in ever more realistic ways, but rely on their deviation from reality in order to make the illusion playable". But what kind of "realistic" space do computer games allegories? In Aarseth's two main examples, *Myst* (Cyan 1993) and *Myth* (Bungie Software 1997), the spatial realities allegorised by games include the landscapes, the contrast between nature and civilisation, and the contrast between indoor and outdoor. The approach usefully situates game spaces in a larger cultural history of space and place, a result pursued explicitly by Alison Gazzard (2013) in her monograph on mazes, where lines are drawn backwards in time from the digital mazes of today's computer games to mazes made of garden hedges and slabs of granite. Bratton's Stack model of urban space is a useful addition to game studies' analytical toolkit because it allows us to connect contemporary ludic spaces not only with spaces of the past but with contemporary urban spaces as well.

'The Stack'

In his book, Bratton captures the extraordinary changes that space itself has undergone in the twenty-first century, driven by the very digital technology of which computer games are part. Social media, GPS mapping, drones, tiny cameras and microphones, online shopping, mass surveillance, mass collection of data, *Google Earth*, visualisations of global data streams, and much more are changing the cognitive category 'space.' These phenomena are increasingly accessed through personal mobile devices, are increasingly interlinked (drones get camera eyes, Amazon employs drones, every instance of activity is logged and fed into data streams), and together they form what Bratton calls 'The Stack,' a megastructure comprised of six interconnected layers: Earth itself, with the very substantial energy and mineral resources needed for global computation, a cloud-layer where we find media empires such as Apple and Google, followed by the city-, address-, interface- and user-layers. I will use Bratton's Stack as the primary theoretical framework for a reading of *Pokémon Go*, and occasionally mention other kinds of games as well, but I will not exhaust the model's usefulness for interrogating the connections between gaming and urban space. I will use the six layers as a rough guide, starting with earth and moving my way upwards. Towards the conclusion, I will suggest that Bratton's technical account can be usefully complemented by attention to the pleasures available to those who insert themselves in dynamic structures, be they architectural or ludic.

Although Bratton points to many examples that are tentatively presented as evidence of how global computation congeals into 'The Stack,' he is not certain that the megastructure presently exists – or that it will ever exist. His six-tiered model is as much a description of something glimpsed at the horizon as it is as a design brief: as humanity only half consciously inserts itself (and planet earth) in 'The Stack,' Bratton calls for a more conscious approach, that is, for design to replace accident. Again, introducing Bratton's model by way of contrast to Aarseth's comments on computer games as allegories of space: Aarseth finds the expressive power of computer game spaces in the difference between real and illusion, Bratton's model is motivated by interest in the difference between present phenomena and a hypothesised future – and the possibility of shaping that future.

One of the most fundamental conceptual moves Bratton (2015, 65) performs, and one that immediately makes him interesting for game studies, is to prioritise the vertical, indeed, to aim for "a political geography for which the vertical is on equal footing with the horizontal and demanding its overdue tribute." Here, Bratton positions himself against, or at least in a complementary position to, social theory that has the network as its overall, guiding idea. This mode of thought has been on the rise since the 1990s and Manuel Castells (2010) remains a particularly clear and influential proponent of network theory. Using the most panoramic, historical canvas available, Castells suggests with broad strokes that the vertical hierarchy and the horizontal network have been competing as fundamental organising principles of social life since the dawn of life itself, each principle bringing unique strengths and weaknesses to society. As the two principles are mutually exclusive, is has never been possible to combine their strengths – until, that is, the advent of the Internet. In popular versions of network theory, flexible, flat, democratic, adaptable networks win out over inflexible and proto-totalitarian hierarchy, and the Internet has routinely been interpreted as a technology inherently on the side of networks. As the name 'stack' already implies, Bratton view networks not from a bird's eye perspective, giving an impression of two-dimensionality, but finds a slanted perspective. This allows Bratton to notice that global, networked computation is not so much dissolving borders, as the naivest network narrative would have it, but is multiplying and deepening them. A nation state does not, for example, only find the job of policing its border made more complex by 'The Stack,' the nation state also sees entire new layers into which it can project its sovereignty.

The slanted stack-perspective should be intriguing to a multidisciplinary field, game studies, that found a two-dimensional model at the centre of some of its foundational debates. That model is Johan Huizinga's (1998) 'magic circle,' which doubles as a model of how games are organised in space (arena, football field, playground etc.) and a model for their cultural and psychological functions in society (an activity divorced from work and other practical pursuits). Despite its usefulness in design teaching (Salen/Zimmerman 2004), the magic circle has often been found wanting as a model for contemporary, digital gaming with its often tight connections between play and everyday life. This has triggered critical reflection on how to improve the model, for example, by replacing smooth circles with puzzle pieces (Juul 2008) or by replacing it with Goffmanian frames (Glas et al. 2011). Thoroughly replacing the magic circle with 'The Stack' – replacing a two-dimensional model with a three-dimensional one – would produce a theoretical framework for a spatiality- and future-oriented version of Platform Studies (Montfort/Bogost 2009).

Bratton's work extends a tradition for critique of capitalism's structuring of space found at the crossroads of French philosophy and sociology. That micro-tradition took off in the 1960s and 1970s with Guy Debord and Henri Lefebvre, continue in the 1980s with Michel de Certeau and ends in the 1990s with Marc Augé's work on supermodernity. Apart from passing references to Debord and Lefebvre, Bratton (2015, 16) casually inserts himself in this tradition by placing his work at a point in time where "we are brought to a certain *end of nonplace*." Non-place is a concept suggested by Augé (1995) to describe a kind of emplaced placelessness characteristic of 'supermodernity.' In Augé's account, traditional (or 'anthropological') place used to be characterised by three kinds of ties: historical ties, social ties, and the ties that places have with other places. In contrast, non-places such as supermarkets and airports lounges are characterised by their lack of such ties. Upon entering a non-place, one is filled with a ('supermodern') sense of weight- and placelessness, notions that resonate closely with 'New Media' discourses emerging in the 1990s. Today, such notions have lost their explanatory power. It turned out, after all, that "even as strange geographies corrugate, fracture, and smear worldly scale and tempo, the ground isn't somehow evaporating into virtual information flux" (Bratton 2015, 16). In stack-terminology: every time a human or non-human *User* initiates a *session*, a *column* of activity shoots through the stack, down from the local to the global and back up again. These processes are not at all virtual but make serious demands on the resource of the earth and play an increasingly important role in the allocation of these resources – a point Bratton makes by including an earth-layer in his stack-model.

Layer 'Earth'

The stack's bottom layer is earth, where extensive coordination and extraction of energy and mineral resources take place. The stack's energy usage is growing very fast, is very extensive – measured in carbon consumption, the Internet in itself already costs us more than the global airline industry (ibid., 92) – and is very inefficient – in 2007, roughly one third of energy consumed in India was unaccounted for (ibid., 95). As the stack's energy consumption rises, energy flows are increasingly monitored and regulated by the stack in efforts to spend energy more efficiently. The total mapping of energy and resource flows, presented as digital visualisations, has cumulative, cognitive effects on human users: "the world itself is seen as *being* information" (ibid., 87). Many visualisations, for example, *Google Earth*, give a sense that a total overview of this world-information is possible (see also the *WebGL Globe*-project). Massively multiplayer online games (MMOs) such as *World of Warcraft* (Blizzard Entertainment 2004) can be added to the list of platforms that further a Stack sensibility towards the Earth. Such games allow players to travel vast online landscapes but a lot of playing time is typically spent harvesting herbs, mining minerals or killing animals and monsters. These resources appear regularly and according to fairly fixed patterns.

Being aware of the patterned nature of such flows of resources, for example, the places where iron ore appears, is very useful for the player. Instead of relying on basic awareness, it is, however, more efficient to keep track of where you have found iron ore in the past by using a bit of extra software added to the game, and it is much, much more efficient to have software upload this information to a central database where it is collated with information uploaded automatically from thousands of other players, and then have all the iron ore deposits presented on a map that forms part of the Graphical User Interface (GUI) of the game (on the stack's interface-layer). This service is a clear, if somewhat simplified expression of how the Earth layer connects with the rest of the stack. An even clearer example can be found in the fictitious massively multiplayer online role-playing game *T'Rain*, which is at the centre of Neal Stephenson's (2011) novel *Reamde*. Here real-world and game-world economics are designed to effortlessly connect, and the game world economics is based on a simulation of geology, making the *T'Rain* earth-layer information in a quite literal sense. The columns shooting up and down 'The Stack' of this fictional world might originate with actions of real-world users but echo in earth-layers that are hard to fix completely in either a *T'Rain* or real earth-layer; and that blurring of perception is precisely part of the cognitive effect of 'The Stack.'

Google Earth plays a major part in Bratton's study as the clearest example of a mapping exercise that creates a sense of total overview of planet earth. There are direct, biographical links between *Google Earth* and *Pokémon Go*. In 2004, Google acquired the company Keyhole and its core product, *EarthViewer 3D*, which was then relaunched as *Google Earth* in 2005. Keyhole had been founded in 2001 by John Hanke and others and Hanke would later become part of the team behind *Pokémon Go* (Bogle 2016). Use of *Google Earth* and *Pokémon Go* are characteristic of the kind of activities found in the stack's cloud-layer. When a user initiates a cloud session, the user's device becomes an access point to the cloud's vast resources of data and computation (relatively little goes on in your device itself). Setting up and maintaining such services is the job of vast corporations who do not so much generate as they collect and analyse information; as Bratton (2015, 125) puts it, for such corporations *"the index is the innovation."* Users are typically paying the cloud empires for their services not directly with cash but by contributing to the indexing of information: every time a Google Search result is acted on, the index grows a little bit more useful and a little bit more valuable. Similar mechanisms allow players of networked games to pay in cognitive labour rather than money.

Example: China

As more information is always better, all information must be best, feeding into the drive towards total overview that is part of 'The Stack's' ethos: Here things become contentious, as the imperial ambitions of cloud companies jar with the ambitions of more traditional empires. Bratton's core example is the relationship between Google and China. Google's corporate mission statement is "to organize the world's information and make it universally accessible and useful." Literal fulfilment of that mission requires access to all information in the world and its availability to every single person in the world, including China. At first, however, Google followed national requirements for offering search services in China: search companies must refuse to deliver results for Internet searches that contain certain words, for example, the names of individuals and organisations that the state sees as threats to social stability. Google then reversed its policy of compliance and eventually had to withdraw to Hong Kong where Google Hong Kong search is still available. Access to other Google services such as *Google Maps* and Gmail is occasionally possible in (parts of) China but not in any predictable and stable way. Although Bratton quotes one of the architects behind China's 'Great Firewall,' Fang Binxing as saying that "the Chinese Internet does not have the capability to disable a global Internet service whenever it wants to" (ibid., 113), the American cloud empires are not able to operate unhindered within Chinese territory either. What Bratton overlooks – being very focused on the fact that for the time being, every cloud empire with realistic ambitions of global dominance is a US-company – is the growth of Chinese cloud empires such as Baidu, Alibaba and Tencent, the so-called BAT. Bratton sees the Google-China conflict as one between

> two logics of territorial control. One of these sees the Internet as an extension of the body of the state [...] and another sees the Internet as a living, quasi-autonomous, if privately controlled and capitalized, transterritorial civil society that produces, defends, and demands rights on its [own] and which can even assume traditional functions of the state for itself (ibid., 112-13).

A critique of varying logics of territorial control is important but as the case of *Pokémon Go* shows, cloud conflicts can sometimes be understood in slightly more straightforward ways, as new means of enacting traditional national conflicts. *Pokémon Go* is unavailable in China, but Chinese players managed to play the game by tricking their GPS-enabled devices into functioning as if they were in Japan, then using a walking simulation to move about. Using these workarounds, one player came across the infamous Yasukuni Shrine where Japan honours those who have fallen for the country, including more than a thousand convicted war criminals; visits to the shrine by high-ranking Japanese officials, including prime ministers, frequently angers Japan's neighbours who were victims of Japanese war atrocities during the Second World War. This shrine happens to also hold the location of a Pokémon gym, one of the places over which teams of players fight for control. It was to the expressed delight of many Chinese social media users when a team of Chinese *Pokémon Go* players, using the illicit means just described, managed to take control of the Pokémon gym at the Yasukuni Shrine and post pictures of a Dragonite Pokémon named "Long Live China!!!!" at that location (Fu/Yamamitsu 2016).

Here an AR-game played on top of urban space already loaded with extraordinary amounts of cultural significance becomes a new tool for making a point in social media: not merely by writing a message on a social media platform but by writing a message onto reality itself (if we count AR as part of reality). That is fascinating in itself, and it might be a precursor of new, stranger online conflicts, but the underlying territorial logic is a very traditional one, with the nation state taking centre stage and public support for the nation informed by the history of past territorial violations. If anything, Chinese Pokémon occupation of the Yasukuni Shrine indirectly strengthens the power of the People's Republic of China government as it feeds into nationalist sentiments; "the Internet as an extension of the body of the state," as Bratton had it in the quote above. The traditional logic of state-driven territorial control hijacks transterritorial civil society for its own purposes. Something similar happened three days after the July 6th, 2016 launch of *Pokémon Go*, when the thinly veiled Chinese copy, *City Elves GO* (Tanyu.Mobi 2016) was launched. Although policies such as the 'Great Firewall' or the 2000-14 ban on foreign gaming consoles have political objectives, these objectives blend together with economic ones: shielding the domestic digital entertainment industry from foreign competition might allow the industry to develop domestic alternatives to US and Japanese entertainment services. A successful domestic digital entertainment industry might also help China project the soft power it attempts to accumulate with such urgency (Liborriussen et al. 2016). At least in the case of China, first evidence suggests that AR games such as *Pokémon Go* work towards extending the body of the state – a body with contemporarily soft and digital curves, that is – rather than towards establishing 'transterritorial civil society.'

Pokémon Go is played in the city-layer of the stack. Here Bratton (2015, 164) notes that "[t]he mobile device's interface [...] can index and express The Stack's organization of the city as the *City* layer with greater explicitness than any building-scale morphology." What Bratton has in mind when speaking of building-scale morphology, is the kind of buildings that adhere to principles of parametric architecture. Here architects find new news forms by shepherding digital simulations, resulting in design that makes and projects smart use of resources, for example, by repeating and varying particular elements in both efficient and visually pleasing ways. The result can be built space that feels like materialised digital flows rather than space whose design is merely supported by digital tools. Yet Bratton finds the role of mobile devices in directing the activities of urban populations even more emblematic of the 'The Stack's' impact on the experience of urban space. If there is a competition to most explicitly express a city-layer underpinned by earth and cloud and overlaid with address-, interface- and user-layers – and by extension to train the user to inhabit 'The Stack' – computer game spaces easily beat both parametric architecture and mobile device interfaces.

Users in 'The Stack'

MMOs' interfaces are frequently overlaid with dynamic information aimed at both spatial navigation and the efficient extraction of resources. Explorers of *Fallout 4*'s (Bethesda Softworks 2015) Boston or *Batman: Arkham Knight*'s (Rocksteady Studios 2015) Gotham navigate urban spaces with the aid of fictional aids – the nostalgic Pip-Boy for *Fallout*, hologram communication for *Batman* – that thematise both the character and its player as Users in 'The Stack.' It is only fitting that the fictional navigation device of the *Fallout* series, the Pip-Boy (Personal Information Processor-Boy), has become an icon of the series. The Pip-Boy is a rather bulky, wrist-worn device that collects and displays information such as maps (parts of the world you know) inventory (things in the world you have collected), and statistics (monsters killed, money earned, avatar attributes etc.). The Pip-Boy is emblematic of a stack-like attitude to the world-as-information. *Fallout 4* even comes in a deluxe *Pip-Boy Edition* that includes a Pip-Boy replica, essentially a plastic casing that holds the player's smartphone. When the player has downloaded the *Fallout* app, the smartphone can be worn as a Pip-Boy and support play by displaying maps, inventory and all the other information just listed. The player's smartphone, the core device for accessing the city-layer of the stack, has been transformed into the core device for accessing a game world. The smartphone's function is not changed by this, it is clarified: the smartphone as access point to the world-as-information, a world that can be measured, mapped and manipulated in its totality. The flip side is that the player-user becomes part of 'The Stack': as a contributing user to the evermore useful cloud indexes, as a collection of data, for example, biometrical data collected, displayed and shared by the smartphone and avatar attributes collected, displayed and shared by the smartphone/Pip-Boy.

To play a networked game, be it *Pokémon Go* or an MMO game, is to not only draw on the resources organised by 'The Stack' (resources ultimately, in a stack to come, corresponding to the entire world) but also to become a subject of the stack, to be addressable by 'The Stack'; we are now at Bratton's address-layer, above 'City' and below 'Interface.' To play the game, 'The Stack' must know your position. Ulf Wilhelmsson (2001) draws on Maurice Merleau-Ponty to articulate the idea that a player of a game inhabits 'point of being' rather than a 'point of view' (the term from film studies). The point of being is characterised by the capacity to act rather than the capacity to perceive. The significance of this distinction becomes clear when thinking about the difference between a game's three-dimensional space and its maps. Unlike the results of traditional cartography, in-game maps are not imperfect drawings of the world based on empirical observation but renderings of the world that carry just as much ontological weight as the game's three-dimensional space. Therefore, the player 'is' as much the avatar running through the streets of Gotham as the little dot moving on a corresponding, two-dimensional map. If, however, we think of being in terms of the capacity to act, there can be no doubt about where the player 'is': it must with the avatar, as this is where the player finds the highest potential to perform meaningful action in the world (Liboriussen 2014). With a networked game, however, the player's being in the game world rests on the cloud: if you do not appear to 'The Stack' you cannot exist in the world. Your position in the (game) world must be specified in the cloud, on some remote server, rather than in the memory of your own computer. It would seem that point of view does ultimately trump point of being, but it is 'The Stack's' point of view, not the player's.

The Interface-Layer

'The Stack' shares its point of view, its total overview, at the Interface layer: Here simplifications must necessarily be made to provide a useful image of the world. Such simplifications need to be scrutinised to ensure that we do not let the "persuasive graphic authority" of maps, as Cosgrove (2007, 104) puts it, blind us to the fact that even the *Google Maps* underpinning *Pokémon Go* are not pure, ideologically neutral representations of the world. It is tempting to think of maps as neutral representations, neat little mini-worlds seen directly from above, but we need to make sure we do not fall into this trap. This is hardly news. What is more novel about *Pokémon Go's* representation of space is the AR-layer. Bratton has already commented on the use of AR in *Ingress*, an earlier game developed by Niantic (2004), the company that also developed *Pokémon Go*. *Ingress* has a back-story summed up by Bratton (2015, 242) as "a science-fiction alien religious warfare story". That backstory fits perfectly with Bratton's basic concern regarding AR's future: that it is potentially the perfect tool for the communication of a fundamentalist worldview because it does not allow for any space between message and interpretation: "the metaphorical nuance of holy books is collapsed by the direct imprint of virtual words onto real things" (ibid., 242).

On this point, it is fascinating to read Bratton next to Huizinga: In his thesis, the contrast between sacred and profane allows for the emergence of civilisation. The magic circle plays an important role in maintaining that contrast. As civilisations mature, however, sacred and profane blur together, a process which is read as decline by Huizinga; commercialised Olympic Games become serious business, the noble arena of the stock exchange is reduced to a playground for rich kids. Bratton's concerns are related to Huizinga's, but Bratton is in a sense updating the sacred-profane problem by framing it with the stack. Where Huizinga is concerned about finding too many elements of one in the other, Bratton warns us against a technology that might not allow us to make any distinction between the two domains. With AR, we are not faced with a perverse mixing of the two but with the sterile literalness of fundamentalist worldviews against which no argument can be made because they do not need to rest on argument in the first place: the facts speak for themselves and the facts are directly accessible via 'The Stack,' as the word "enemy" AR-imprinted on another player of games or "unbeliever" AR-imprinted on all who do not follow the proper faith according to some database.

The Cloud and the Crowd

Pokémon Go is not narratively connected to fundamentalist warfare, but it does come with a geography that would have been impossible without 'The Stack.' When developing *Ingress*, Niantic needed a database of locations. They first turned to the cloud and collected "a data set of public artwork mined from geotagged photos on Google" (Bogle 2016). They then turned to their users for suggestions, received about 15 million and ultimately approved about five million. The most popular locations later became Pokémon gyms with the next most popular becoming Pokéstops. Critical questions could be asked about the selection of places: are churches more interesting (or less inappropriate, or more inappropriate) than mosques, is it more important to draw *Pokémon Go*-players to libraries than to shopping malls, is it more important to highlight a statue than a park? The answer to all such questions could be an oddly convincing exemption from individual, human responsibility: the cloud and the crowd – in short, 'The Stack', of which humanity as a whole is part – has created the geography of *Pokémon Go*.

After delivering his keynote at the International Symposium of Electronic Arts in Hong Kong in May 2016, Bratton was asked why he had titled his book *The Stack* and not *The Matrix*, and *Pokémon Go's* Stack-generated geography does have an oddly non-human, AI flavour to. As news stories about *Pokémon Go* players improperly trespassing on Holocaust memorials and dangerous building sites began to accumulate, journalists seldom tried to reach out to Niantic for comment from the game-designing individuals responsible for such actions. It was as if there was a collective intuition that no human individuals were responsible, that we had all done this by accidentally creating the stack.

What I sometimes find missing from Bratton's discussion of 'The Stack' is a sense of the pleasure that it can bring to find one's way through, or even succumb to, the flows of infrastructures. Inspired by the Virilio's work on acceleration and accidents, Bratton (2015, 233) mentions how the interfaces through which users access 'The Stack' cause stress, and that the very same interfaces "as a therapeutic response [...] are asked to soothe the stress [...] by presenting their remedy images of orderly resolution as data visualizations, as GUI, as mind maps, as tools and trackers." The idea that inserting oneself in the infrastructural flows of 'The Stack' merely soothes stress seems overly negative to me – and it is probably significant that I speak as someone who spends a lot of time researching games and their players. It is, however, not only in game studies can we find the idea that there are pleasures to be had in succumbing to structures. Although my examples of this will ultimately be drawn from games, it is useful to first take a look at how the notion of structure has developed in architectural discourse. Forty (2000, 276.) identifies three uses of the term "structure," the earliest being "any building in its entirety." Around the second half of the nineteenth century, an alternative meaning was added: "the system of support of a building" (ibid.). During the twentieth century, a third way of using "structure" was added and this is the meaning of the word relevant here, structure as "schema": "A schema through which a drawn project, building, group of buildings, or entire city or region become intelligible. The schema may be identified through any one of a variety of elements [...] none of [which] are themselves a 'structure,' only signs that give cause for the perception of 'structure'" (ibid.).

Architecture

Modernist architecture's grand old man, Le Corbusier, exemplifies the trend towards structure in Forty's third sense. When Le Corbusier (2008, 127) turns his attention from the singular dwelling and toward the urban, it is with a focus on and fascination with infrastructure, with "all the organs that up to now have been buried in the ground and inaccessible: water, gas electricity, telephone, pneumatic tubes, sewers, neighbourhood heating, etc." The quote is from the 1923 version of *Toward an Architecture*, in which Le Corbusier tentatively toys with the idea of making infrastructure visible and suggests that the time has come for grand new forms of urban plan. Later, in two books on the *Modulor*-proportional system (1948 and 1955), these ideas have come into full bloom. Describing his largest project, the city of Chandigarh, Le Corbusier (2000, 170) writes about "a cardiac system leading to the door of each of the habitation cells of a sector, but fitting in also with the constituent elements of the city – an urban entity." Just as water and electricity flow in the organs of the city, the movements of the inhabitants will flow according to machine-age plan. This kind of new, rational city plan will generate not only optimal flows of people, communication, power, etc., but also a kind of pleasurable or even spiritual connectivity in the lives of the inhabitants. Pleasures akin to that sense of connectivity are experienced by those who insert themselves in ludic flows of wandering AI monsters, regenerating resources, transportation opportunities, the regularities of player community activities – either in AR-based games or MMO games.

Pleasurable or not, giving oneself over to the dynamic structures underpinning a world has a totalitarian ring to it. In an illuminating accident, users signing up to *Pokémon Go* via their Google accounts originally granted Niantic full access to their Google Cloud-data, that is, users explicitly allowed the company to read all Gmail, access all Google Drive-documents, look at Google search history and *Google Maps'* navigation history, access private photos stored in Google Photos etc. (Reeve 2016). Although Niantic swiftly gave up the rights it had acquired seemingly unintentionally (Frank 2016), and although most users would probably not agree to paying for their cloud access with that amount of information, the accident can be used to think about how much we would be willing to make available to ensure stack-addressability (would it be alright to share *Google Maps* navigation history, perhaps photos shared in particular folders?) and if there is a point where it becomes suspect to avoid addressability ("nothing to hide, nothing to fear").

Surveillance

Bratton (2015, 192) does acknowledge that a "full-spectrum surveillance society, in which no biochemical misdeed goes unsearchable and unnoticed" is a possible outcome of the accidental design process leading towards 'The Stack.' This is an outcome Raph Koster (2016a) has regularly been warning against since he authored "Declaring the Rights of Players". Most recently, *Pokémon Go*, prompted Koster (2016) to quote the following from that older text:

> Someday there won't be any admins. Someday it's gonna be your bank records and your grocery shopping and your credit report. [...] Your avatar profile might be your credit record and your resume and your academic transcript, as well as your XP earned.

The entities that swallow all this information are the cloud empires, "Facebook, Google, and yes now Nintendo, The Pokémon Company, and Niantic [who] as they move into AR [become] basically like governments" (ibid.). They are like governments because they "have access to your private data [...] have controls on the economy, [...] can [unilaterally] affect real estate values, and [...] can set forth rules via commission or omission on how people interact" (ibid.).

Bratton (2015, 119) would agree with all that and even add other examples of the cloud taking over functions, such as cartography, that used to belong exclusively to states, but he would crucially add that the nature of states and governments, the nature of sovereignty itself, is under redefinition in the stack. Corporations taking on new roles previously held by states and states finding new ways to project their power are two outcomes of the same effect: 'The Stack' is becoming the source of sovereignty itself. Bratton's message is that dystopian outcomes is not a given but that 'The Stack,' although so far developed through a series of accidents, can be designed. If nothing else, the dystopian future is simply too easy to imagine, there must be other options, if we can imagine them. It bears repeating that game studies is well positioned to highlight the experiential dimension of that design, its pleasurable dimensions even. Koster (2016) remarks, again in connection with *Pokémon Go* as a precursor of what Bratton would call 'The Stack': "the best qualified people to design this brave new world are game designers, because the social network folks seem clueless about human behavior, the product people only want to sell to them, and the GIS people tend to forget they exist altogether."

Conclusion

Richard Bartle (2004), who famously co-designed the first MUD with Roy Trubshaw in 1978, tried to improve the possibilities of successful way-finding in the MUD by looking to the urban planner Kevin Lynch for advice. It is encouraging to know that such connections between game design and urban planning are made. Lynch talked of a person's sense of environmental image in a way that reminds of, yet is so far from, Bratton's (2015, 91) rather technically worded mention of "the diagrams and visualizations of the networked totality" found on the earth-layer. It is with a very different sense of human warmth Lynch (1960, 4) pronounces that: "A good environmental image gives its possessor an important sense of emotional security. He can establish a harmonious relationship between himself and the world" – How is that for a design brief?

By prioritising the vertical rather than the horizontal, Bratton's six-tiered Stack model of urban space offers game studies new conceptual resources for exploring the connections between contemporary gaming and everyday life. The model has been applied to computer games with special attention to the case of *Pokémon Go*. Computer games offer very clear examples of the mental attitudes associated with 'The Stack'; the sense of total overview and mastery of resources associated with the Earth and Interface layers came out in the use of software add-ons by MMO players. But games also offer clear expression of the ways in which Users become part of the stack on the address-layer, as they need to be addressable by 'The Stack' to play at all. Players physically inserting their *Fallout 4* smartphones into plastic parts of the game, after digitally preparing them with the *Fallout 4* app, were seen as an expression of users inserting themselves (including their data) in the stack. *Pokémon Go's* reception in China – workarounds used to occupy a highly symbolic shrine in japan, the launch of a Chinese copycat version, *City Elves GO* – has been used to show how 'The Stack' at times extends rather than threatens the logic of traditional state power. Finally, game studies is well situated to complement Bratton's account of 'The Stack' with attention to the experiential and pleasurable dimensions of inserting oneself in infrastructural flows.

References

Aarseth, Espen (2001): Allegories of Space: The Question of Spatiality in Computer Games, in: *Cybertext Yearbook 2000*, ed. by Markku Eskelinen and Raine Koskimaa, Jyväskylä: Research Centre for Contemporary Culture, 152-171.

Augé, Marc (1995): *Non-Places: Introduction to an Anthropology of Supermodernity*, London/New York, NY: Verso [1992].

Bartle, Richard A. (2004): *Designing Virtual Worlds*, Berkeley, CA: New Riders.

Bathesda Game Studios (2015): *Fallout 4*, PC: Bathesda Softworks.

Blizzard Entertainment (2004): *World of Warcraft*, PC: Vivendi.

Bogle, Ariel (2016): How the Gurus behind Google Earth Created 'Pokémon Go', in: *Mashable*, July 11th, mashable.com/2016/07/10/john-hanke-pokemon-go/#d MPq8UJAomq3.

Bratton, Benjamin H. (2015): *The Stack. On Software and Sovereignty*, Cambridge, MA/London: MIT Press.

Bungie Software (1997): *Myth*, PC: Bungie Software.

Castells, Manuel ([2]2010): *The Information Age: Economy, Society and Culture*, Vol. 1: *The Rise of the Network Society*, Chichester: Wiley-Blackwell [1996].

Cosgrove, Denis (2007): Mapping the World, in: *Maps: Finding Our Place in the World*, ed. by James R. Akerman and Rovert W. Karrow Jr., Chicago, IL: University of Chicago Press, 65-115.

Cyan (1993): *Myst*, PC: Brøderbund.

Forty, Adrian (2000): *Words and Buildings: A Vocabulary of Modern Architecture*, London: Thames & Hudson.

Frank, Allegra (2016): 'Pokémon Go' Raises Security Concerns among Google Users, in: *Polygon*, July, 11th, polygon.com/2016/7/11/12151442/pokemon-go-security-risk-data-information-ios-android.

Fu, Beimeng/Yamamitsu, Eimi (2016): Pokémon Go Is at the Center of an International Incident Because of Course It Is, in: *BuzzFeed*, July, 23rd, buzzfeed.com/beimengfu/pokemon-go-is-at-the-center-of-an-international-incident-bec?utm_term=.liZNnAMk8#.gdnwGn6da.

Gazzard, Alison (2013): *Mazes in Videogames: Meaning, Metaphor and Design*, Jefferson, NC: McFarland & Co.

Glas, René/Jørgensen, Kristine/Mortensen, Torill/Rossi, Luca (2011): Framing the Game: Four Game-Related Approaches to Goffman's Frames, in: *Online Gaming in Context. The Social and Cultural Significance of Online Games*, ed. by Garry Crawford, Victoria K. Gosling and Ben Light, London/New York, NY: Routledge, 141-158.

Huizinga, Johan (1998): *Homo Ludens: A Study of the Play-Element in Culture*, London: Routledge [1938].

Juul, Jesper (2008): The Magic Circle and the Puzzle Piece, in: *Conference Proceedings of The Philosophy of Computer Games*, ed. by Stephan Günzel, Michael Liebe and Dieter Mersch, Potsdam: Potsdam UP, 56-67.

Koster, Raph (2016): I Really Did Mean 'MMO', July, 14th, raphkoster.com/2016/07/14/i-really-did-mean-mmo.

–––– (2016a): Declaring the Rights of Players, August, 27th, raphkoster.com/games/essays/declaring-the-rights-of-players.

Le Corbusier (2000): *Modulor 2: Let the User Speak*, Basel/Berlin/Boston, MA: Birkhäuser [1955].

––––: (2008): *Toward an Architecture*, London: Frances Lincoln [1923].

Liboriussen, Bjarke (2014): Worlds and Maps, in: *The Johns Hopkins Guide to Digital Media*, ed. by Marie-Laure Ryan, Lori Emerson and Benjamin Robertson, Baltimore, MD: Johns Hopkins UP, 530-533.

––––/Andrew White/Dan Wang (2016): The Ban on Gaming Consoles in China: Protecting National Cultural Security and Industrial Policy Within an International Regulatory Framework, in: *Video Game Policy: Production, Distribution, and Consumption*, ed. by Steven Conway and Jennifer deWinter, New York, NY/London: Routledge and Taylor & Francis, 230-243.

Lynch, Kevin (1960): *The Image of the City*, Cambridge, MA: MIT Press.

Montfort, Nick/Bogost, Ian (2009): *Racing the Beam: The Atari Video Computer System*, Cambridge, MA: MIT Press.

Niantic (2004): *Ingress*, Andriod/iOS: Google.

–––– (2016): *Pokémon Go*, Android/iOS: Nintendo.

Reeve, Adam (2016): Pokemon Go is a Huge Security Risk, July, 8th, adamreeve.tumblr.com/post/147120922009/pokemon-go-is-a-huge-security-risk.

Rocksteady Studios (2015): *Batman: Arkham Knight*, PC: Warner Bros. Interactive.

Salen, Katie/Zimmerman, Eric (2004): *Rules of Play: Game Design Fundamentals*, Cambridge, MA: MIT Press.

Stephenson, Neal (2011): *Reamde*, New York, NY: Morrow.

Tanyu Mobi (2016): *City Elves GO*, Andriod/iOS: Tanyu Mobi.

Wilhelmsson, Ulf (2001): *Enacting the Point of Being: Computer Games, Interaction and Film Theory*, PhD-Thesis, University of Copenhagen.

No End of Worlds

Michael Nitsche

This paper argues for a flip side of the relationship between physical play space and digital game space. In play, we engage with specific game worlds and their functionalities. We embrace our new role in their settings and 'transform' ourselves. Many – including myself (Nitsche 2009) – have explored this effect. This paper argues that the transformation is a two-way street. It is not unidirectional into the gaming system where the player takes on a virtual role. Most of all, it is not limited to the player and their identity. Instead, fictional videogames spaces can transform 'outwards' and redefine our living rooms and ultimately our understanding of physical space as such. The main goal of this essay is to outline two different approaches of this outwards directed transformation, exemplify their differences in related game designs, before it will close with the new questions that these spaces pose.

Against Turkle's (1996) visionary statement that 'Real Life' can be 'just one more window' I argue that we are in the process of losing the comfort of the window 'frame.' Instead, Real Life and its spaces are imbued with digital media and neither of these two can be seen as separate. This should not be misinterpreted as a continuation of an existent tradition of mediated space. When Tolstoy takes us on a stroll of the battlefields at Waterloo in the end of *War and Peace*, his prose may affect the way we understand the very same space today but the book as medium does not significantly affect this space. In contrast, videogames' materiality continues to expand into the physical realm. Whether it is through the Kinect cameras, the Guitar Hero controller, or through the eye of an Augmented Reality application – digital media spaces expand in manifold ways into the physical, re-shaping, re-using them. In the form of location aware cell phones, this conquest of the physical is becoming mainstream on levels even beyond video gaming. The paper will break down the influence into two seemingly distant positions: that of the arbitrary space allocation and of specific spatial adjustments.

Anywhere Space

The project *Next Generation Play* (NGP), conducted by the Digital World & Image Group at Georgia Tech, was one example for a near ubiquitous computing inter-action design. The project allowed players to collect media elements from a range of sources, including an interactive TV-application, a barcode scanner, and from web sites. Media include images, texts, sounds, or videos. Once collected, these media can be arranged into playlists in a collaborative way using Android cell phones. Players create own playlists and program their media experience collabo-ratively anytime as long as internet connectivity is provided.

Older paradigms typically saw media production, programming, and distri-bution centralized. NGP was a design- and implementation-exercise in a spread-ing of media experiences in an uncontrolled and decentralized way. While the consumption might have been shared, the selection of what media to experience was traditionally not shared. Hence the fight for the remote control in TV, which is being replaced by individual multi-screen media consumption. Especially in the TV-production and consumption processes were spatially separated and confined: the studio vs the living room.

NGP dissolves many of these traditions. Instead of a single regulated source of media, the surrounding world is seen as a constant source of media elements. Beyond the experience of advertisement panels, large displays, programmed soundscapes, and countless signs and icons that litter urban architecture and that try to deliver a message of some kind, NGP proposes that these manifestations can be used as physical links into an underlying media landscape. Online the image of the poster for a new blockbuster movie is often a button – a 'transcoded' entity (Manovich 2001) – that links to a trailer for that product. NGP builds on that con-cept or transcoding, adding interactive TV- and web-features, and not only con-siders a media element a possible link to another underlying media experience, but also allows players to collect these media connections, share them, and assem-ble them later into new forms (fig. 1a-b). In this system, one can collect a trailer from a poster in the subway station, a book from an educational TV-program, a music piece from a book, and a song text from the band's official web site. Once collected, the player is free to arrange the items in any way they want, sharing them with others, and play them back whenever and wherever desired.

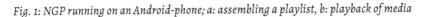

Fig. 1: NGP running on an Android-phone; a: assembling a playlist, b: playback of media

We termed the interaction with media artefacts a 'media play space' and this play space stretches across different locations and boundaries. Following a philosophy close to the idea of an Internet of Things, it treats physical forms like signifiers for associated data that can be transcoded to feed a media application.

This architecture makes spatial conditions almost arbitrary. Media as play objects can be embedded almost anywhere, available anytime, and be shared, arranged, and activated wherever and whenever needed. Locations are infused with media but the way this infusion happens is through a form of arbitrary parallel world. The same principle is at work at many Augmented Reality systems – such as *Pokémon Go* (Niantic 2016) or *Wikitude* (Wikitude 2008) – that add media to certain locations and objects, but remain unaltered by the original space. AR systems do not necessarily demand an alteration to the spaces they augment, but they provide a parallel additional layer to it.

A special challenge to this spatial arbitrariness is the design of Alternate Reality Games (ARG). Part of their concept is Elan Lee's tongue-in-cheek mantra "This is not a game." It implies that the spatial restrictions to a given spatial frame are gone through an extensive game fiction that often spreads across all kinds of media and design:

> My definition is very loose. An alternate reality game is anything that takes your life and converts it into an entertainment space. If you look at a typical video games, it's really about turning you into a hero; a super hero, a secret agent. It's your ability to step outside your life and be someone else. An ARG takes those same sensibilities and applies them to your actual life (Ruberg 2006).

In ARG, the space and the media can be tightly interwoven. Players have to be in certain locations at certain times to receive specific phone calls, for example. At the same time, ARG live through the creation of a wide player base that operates as a team using all elements of web communication. They mix highly specific events with 'available for all'-media design.

NGP does not aim to convert the player permanently but instead to make a parallel media play space available at all times. It does not demand players to "step outside your life and be someone else" and does not ask them to play a role. Instead it allows a collaboration on an artificially created media play space. In contrast, in Lee's vision of an ARG the stage expands outwards, becomes continuous in the 'Real Life.' One continues to play a role in a fictional setting. But in both cases the physical world is re-shaped even when the servers are down and the game has ended.

Changing Space

ARGs offer already a glimpse into how games can infuse the 'real' world. At this end of the spectrum, we look at how games affect the organization and spatial understanding of our homes, workplaces, cities, and other structures. To illustrate the point, I will concentrate first on the living room. Whether it is the space we need to play our Kinect, or a multi-player split screen set up on other consoles – games demand spatial re-structuring of our living rooms.

One example for this development inside our homes is the change of furniture. New media posed new challenges to interior designers that have evolved into everyday arrangements from the bookshelf to the media console, including the development of the chair in relation to media:

> With the advent of television many homes are presented with the problem of seating a number of people in a limited area. My chair is particularly well suited for handling such occasions in that the chair takes up a minimum amount of room and can simply be placed on the floor, the chair being foldable for storage purposes (Meyer 1957).

Fig. 2: Meyer's original television chair design, 1957

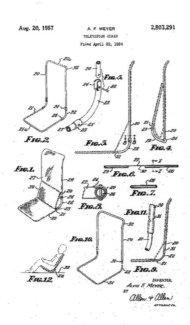

In the case of the 1958 TV-chair (Fig. 2), the particular media usage – having friends over for a TV-viewing – is still seen as a temporary event and the furniture is provided as a fill in to support it. TV had not conquered the living room and viewing functionality was deemed necessary only temporarily – much like the mechanically folding cinema seats provide today. Likewise, many more recent game-chairs use a 'rocker' design that often allows owners to fold and store the chair easily. It might appear that digital games are still seen as temporary inhabitants of our living rooms, but we can see a development into a permanent transformation, too.

The more dominant the media form, the more persistent the specialized furniture and interior design. In the case of the TV-chair, this has led to more dominant recliner seats and home-theatre set-ups. While early television audiences were not even sure where to put the new TV-set (Barfield 2008), many of today's architectural features for home interiors optimize TV-viewing in specific domestic areas (Spigel 1992). It is not particularly difficult to see how this will demand a comparable adjustment to the living room. In the case of game chairs, for example, there are changes in function and design noticeable.

Fig. 3: Ultimate Game Chair V3, 2008

The *Ultimate Game Chair V3* (fig. 3) offers reclining options and twelve integrated motors to provide a kind of large-scale force feedback. Other chairs feature integrated speakers or wireless connectivity. But no matter where the game media infusion of the home will lead us, it illustrates the extension of game space into physical worlds. As the sales sheet for the *Ultimate Game Chair V3* claims, the product attempts both: it "blends into any living space" while it also allows you to "get in the game and feel the action." Through these kinds of physical transformations our living rooms (and the more specialized 'game room' spaces) are adjusted to the needs of specific game world extensions.

While the first movement outlined above was one toward arbitrariness in the mapping of the physical and the virtual, this movement is one of physical transformation supporting the game world. Here the specific space changes to adjust to the given media and their content.

Not unlike the architecture of theme parks that is optimized to a certain pre-structured experience design, these game worlds that "become flesh" are all encompassing multi-sensual modifications toward a specific game experience. As they evolve, this concept of gradually materializing game worlds reframes our existing physical surroundings. Adidas sport shoes carry AR-worlds; Webkinz plush toys become 'alive' online; game-chairs have become fused hybrids of game interface and sitting utility. The game world is integral part of my non-digital everyday world as we stumble over USB-cables and *Skylanders* (Toys for Bob 2011) figurines in our children's room and make decisions about our coffee tables with the functionality of the Kinect in mind.

Making Sense

In opposition to the traditional vision of Virtual Reality as a replacement world in which we log in and tune out, a *Matrix*-ghost world, I have suggested two different perspectives regarding games' spatiality in relation to the physical world: one is a seemingly boundless cross-media view (exemplified in handheld games and especially cell phone applications); the other is the growth of a hybrid space in our homes (exemplified in game chairs and furniture). One sees an expansion of the game space into arbitrary physical territories, the other sees the invasion of detailed elements into our domestic space. How, then, can we include these kinds of developments in a spatial game design?

An often chosen point of connection is the player's body as the interconnecting hinge around which the game's spatial design has to evolve. It has been identified as a central design criterion for digital media (Dourish 2001) and has long become a central point in interaction design, spawning whole academic departments. Instead of questioning this approach, we shall take it as a given and ask how a player-centred design for game spaces might look when considering the here suggested two spatial approaches.

In Game Studies, Juul (2009) provides a brief pointer to space-driven mimetic interfaces that support game spaces' invasion in the living room. I do not necessarily see the need for more mimetic game control but instead for consistent mapping of these controls. Players do not need to control virtual avatars the same way they would control their physical body. However, the way in which they control the avatar has to provide a meaningful cognitive connection. The result of that connection is one of *diegesis*, not *mimesis* (knowing that a pure format of either is impossible). Some example cases should help to illustrate this. To highlight the differences both examples will be taken from mobile phone games.

Real: Another Edition (Tecmo 2004) extends the ghost hunting of the underlying *Fatal Frame* (Tecmo 2001) game franchise into a location-based cell phone game (fig. 4a-d). The game can provide hints to players where to search for virtual ghosts. Players then set out to hunt those ghost manifestations, which are overlaid in a hybrid reality way over the imagery available in their physical surrounding.

Fig. 4: Real's game play; a: fighting a ghost with the cell phone camera, b-d:
overlay of the ghost world over the visible physical surroundings

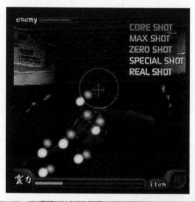

Players have to find the locations of new ghosts, discover the individual ghost as it appears on the phone's screen, and 'shoot' it with the camera. Mirroring the very same design principle behind the purely digital game franchise *Fatal Frame*, where the player uses a magical camera to defeat ghosts as they appear in the 3D-polygon world, *Real* takes the interaction principle one step further as it now locates the ghosts in the physical surroundings of the player. It clearly cites traditions of spirit photography but literally projects these spirits into any physical surrounding, thereby changing the nature of this surrounding (it is depicted as haunted) without relying on a specific adjustment of the location as such (any spot could be haunted).

Kitsune (Roberts 2010) is an example for a location-based game that overlays whole territories on each other. To play *Kitsune* players have to navigate physical space in order to engage with the virtual world (fig. 5a-c). The overall concept of the two overlapping worlds was informed by the idea of a border zone (fig. 6), much like the Japanese *satoyama*.

Fig. 5a: screen shot of the game running on the Android-phone, b: Kitsune *at work in Piedmont Park, c: playing* Kitsune

Fig. 6a: aerial view of Piedmont Park, b: Kitsune's *fictional virtual map*

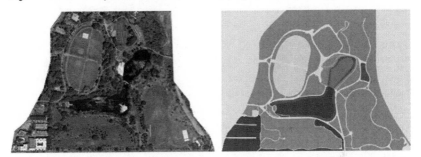

Accordingly, the game cites Japanese folklore in its virtual world as it stages players as multiple hunters and one player can become the hunted fox spirit, *Kitsune*. Where *Kitsune* differs from other part- or full-location-based cell phone systems – such as *Parallel Kingdom* (PerBlue 2008), *Can You See Me Now?* (Mixed Reality Lab 2003) or *Ingress* (Niantic 2004) – is that it puts emphasis on the physical behaviour of the players on location and reflects it in the virtual game world. For example, the virtual avatars become transparent and invisible whenever their players stand still in the physical world for a certain time (and the accelerometer does not sense movement). Likewise, catching the fox depends on the casting of a virtual net between the hunters, using the cell phones, their direction, and their accelerometer. Thus, not only is location used as a physical player interface, but so are gestures and full-body movement.

Both games are typical examples for ubiquitous computing and the games that evolved from these new technologies. At the same time, they illustrate two very different spatial concepts outlined in the first half of the essay. *Real* is based on arbitrary spaces. Its very core design – just as the one at work in the *Fatal Frame* series at large – is the challenge that any ghost might appear at anytime, anywhere. *Kitsune* uses the landscape architecture of the existent Piedmont Park in Atlanta, but transforms it into a specific hybrid space. While *Kitsune* is not an example for a domestic space transformation, it nevertheless shows all the same signs for specific space referencing. It can only be played in Piedmont Park.

Ending in Questions

The spaces outlined here depend on play. They are diegetic, fictional worlds that are remarkable in their almost adverse spatial concepts, but depend on comparable game functionality when it comes to the question how they are played and how they come into being.

Both depend heavily on sensing technology to allow the digital system to make better sense of the surroundings. While cell phones lack numerous features that are standard in game consoles, they are superior in two ways: one is constant connectivity, the other is a range of sensors from microphones, to cameras, accelerometers, compass, or multi-touch. Overall, game consoles are playing catch up with these features. Newer generations, such as the Nintendo Switch, focus on new implementations of already existing functionalities, such as mobility and basic movement detection. These advances will continue but to realize the above noted spatial grounding of future games in our living rooms or in 'anywhere' scenarios, we would need spatial sensing in future console games. For example, cameras will not only detect players and their movements but also elements of furniture and interior design; cameras and other sensors will not only detect body weight, posture, speed of movement but also room temperature, light levels, acoustic conditions to adjust play conditions to them. Whether the spatial design follow the arbitrary spaces philosophy or the specific domestic space invasion: the system needs methods to engage with the surroundings in order to re-interpret them.

I am asking to consider game worlds as co-inhabitants of our living spaces and for technology to realize this in more detail. This is not a technological quantum leap but already very feasible as indicated in the projects and games discussed above. For example, cell phones already offer a range of the called for sensors – and more. It is more a question of realizing the potential how to enable games to become valid extensions of our spatial spheres.

References

Barfield, Ray E. (2008): *A Word from our Viewers: Reflections from Early Television Audiences*, Wesport, CT: Praeger.

Dourish, Paul (2001): *Where the Action Is: The Foundations of Embodied Interaction*, Cambridge, MA/London: MIT Press.

Juul, Jesper (2009): *A Casual Revolution: Reinventing Video Games and their Players*, Cambridge, MA: MIT Press.

Manovich, Lev (2001): *The Language of New Media*, Cambridge, MA/London: MIT Press.

Meyer, Alvin F. (1957): *Television Chair*, patents.google.com/patent/US2803291.

Mixed Reality Lab (2003): *Can You See Me Now?*, Android/iOS: Blast Theory.

Niantic (2004): *Ingress*, Android/iOS: Google.

–––– (2016): *Pokémon Go*, Android/iOS: Nintendo.

Nitsche, Michael (2009): *Video Game Spaces: Image, Play, and Structure in 3D Worlds*, Cambridge, MA: MIT Press.

PerBlue (2008): *Parallel Kingdom: Age of Thrones*, Android/iOS: PerBlue.

Roberts, Andrews (2010): *Kitsune*, Android: Georgia Institute of Technology.

Ruberg, Bonnie (2006): *Elan Lee's Alternate Reality*, gamasutra.com/view/feature/130182/elan_lees_alternate_reality.php.

Spigel, Lynn (1992): *Make Room for TV: Television and the Family Ideal in Postwar America*, Chicago, IL: University of Chicago.

Tecmo (2001): *Fatal Frame (Project Zero)*, PS2: Tecmo.

–––– (2004): *Real: Another Edition*, Android/iOS: Tecmo.

Toys for Bob (2011): *Skylanders: Spyro's Action*, Wii et al.: Activision.

Turkle, Sherry (1996): *Life on the Screen: Identity in the Age of the Internet*, London: Weidenfeld & Nicolson.

Wikitude (2008): *Wikitude*, Android/iOS: Wikitude.

III. Territories

Itineraria Picta
Itineraria Scripta

Mathias Fuchs

In his text on orientation from 1786 Immanuel Kant (1963, 8) reflects about how we orient ourselves when reasoning, and starts to build up his argument from observations about geographical orientation:

> In the proper meaning of the word, to *orient* oneself means to use a given direction (when we divide the horizon into four of them) in order to find the others – literally, to find the *sunrise*. Now if I see the sun in the sky and know it is now midday, then I know how to find south, west, north, and east. For this, however, I also need the feeling of a difference in my own subject, namely, the difference between my right and left hands.

Way-Finding

The Kantian text reads as if the philosopher would have shared a cartographic convention from the 14th century that used to display the Saviour's left and right hand to connect to the hands of the map-reader. Maps like the *Ebstorf Worldmap*, which originates around 1300 (probably produced in the homonymous Benedictine monastery in Lunenburg Heath), render double meaning to the hands, feet and the head of the person embracing the globe (fig. 1): Firstly, the human members refer to the bodily incarnation of a divine being. Secondly, they serve as virtual pointing devices for the reader who is equipped with human hands and feet. The gestural answer to the question of where this or that is, is pointing at it with the hand.

Fig. 1: Ebstorf Worldmap

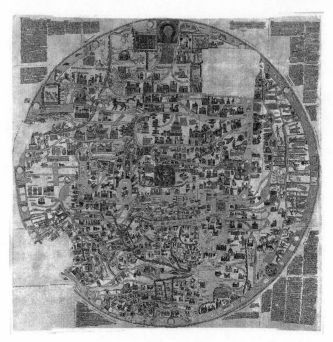

Kant observes that the difference in directions is not reflected in differently looking signs (as the printed words 'left' and 'right' would) but that a subjective understanding of direction is the basis for an understanding of the difference between
left and right. Kant continues:

> I call this a feeling because these two sides outwardly display no designatable dif-
> ference in intuition. If I did not have this faculty of distinguishing, without the need
> of any difference in the objects, between moving from left to right and right to left
> and moving in the opposite direction and thereby determining a priori a difference
> in the position of the objects, then in describing a circle I would not know whether
> west was right or left of the southernmost point of the horizon, or whether I should
> complete the circle by moving north and east and thus back to south (ibid., 8-9).

Kant is obviously not interested in providing a toolset for lost hikers, but he is
interested in the role of subjectivity for the process of reasoning. This is of relevance for the ideas on mapping and cartography that this essay wants to develop.
Historic maps and navigation techniques in computer and videogames are to a
substantial degree influenced by a priori concepts of space. Cartography and
computer game design are attempts of coming to terms with our position in space

and the possibility of navigating within space. Irrespective of the aesthetic and educational qualities of maps and games, we want to describe them in rather dry terms as 'tools for orientation in unknown territory.' The territory, that they might help us find a way in, can be real (as with geographical maps) or symbolic (as with maps in computer games). Susan Sontag (1980, 112) reminds us that not everybody will use maps as orientation tools and refers to Walter Benjamin for whom maps would be a tool for getting lost. However, for most travellers, explorers or computer game players, maps are instrumental in finding a way. They are *itineraria* – as the Romans called them – 'way-finders' and 'route-planners'. We rely on the information maps contain to find places we are looking for and use them to navigate towards these places.

Maps exist in a multitude of forms and can be built upon or include different perspective, topography and environment. They can be linear, two-dimensional, three-dimensional in a perspective mode, three-dimensional and isometric, or of a mixed mode in between the above. For those familiar with the typology of space as proposed by Aarseth, Smedstad, and Sunnanå (2003), the criteria of perspective, topography and environment will sound familiar. These criteria are supposed to be of key relevance in regard to distinguishing between different types of computer games. A glance at historic maps will disclose the very same triplet of criteria to be of crucial importance for a qualitative analysis of *mappae mundi*, 'maps of the world.' A small number of historic maps that exemplify aspects of perspective, topography and environment are examined below.

World-Finding

The T-O maps is a type of maps used since the sixth century – prominently by Isidor of Sevilla (fig. 2) – and still into the 13th century, displayed what was then considered to be *omnis orbis terrarum*: the world. The perspective was one of omnipresence. A circular line orbited what was in the world: Asia, Europe and Africa. The shape of the continents does not refer to real geography and outlines the T-O shape, which could be read as 'Terrarum Orbis.' Topological information outweighs geographical information. In these early examples of maps, no non-navigable environment is present.

Fig. 2: T-O Map from Isidor's Etymologiae, print by
Günther Zainer, 1472

The world map from Albi (fig. 3), originating in the 8th century, is slightly more detailed than the T-O-maps. It contains little geometrical information, and provides almost no analogue information regarding distance, scale and direction. The topological space is discrete, as if countries are states in a binary system one can inhabit by being inside or outside only. Lybia, Carthago and Numibia are equally sized blocks of land without any differentiation in regard to the shape of the countries. Geometrical features like rivers and mountains are neglected. Even though this representation of the world is of pictorial nature with only a few words filled in, little information can be retrieved from the lines and shapes of the drawing.

Fig. 3: World map from Albi, 8th A.D.

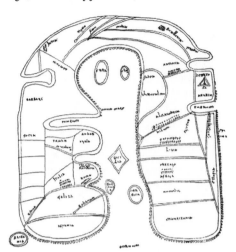

Fig. 4: 13th A.D.-reproduction of Tabula Peutingeriana's segment IV, including the city of Rome on the right-hand side of the middle ground strip

Even though maps like the topographically transformed *Tabula Peutingeriana* (fig. 4) or the world map from Albi did not grant completeness of a world perspective with contemporary eyes, they allowed for omnipresence inside the cartographic system. This need not necessarily be so. There are, and have been, maps which favoured a vagrant view as opposed to an omnipresent view. The successful *Falk Plan* (fig. 5) can be taken as an example of this.

Fig. 5: Falk Plan of Berlin in the hands of the author

The earliest forms of antique itineraria did not contain pictorial information to guide the travellers, but textual information only. Itineraria scripta were descriptions of travel routes in written format. The texts were copied and sold to travellers on their voyages. There were central information points in the city of Rome set up as official points of reference. Even in the late Middle Ages itineraria scripta were popular amongst pilgrims. A document written by an anonymous pilgrim from Bordeaux in the late 13th century and published in printed form in 1589 gives us an impression of how these early maps operated: "Itinerarivm a Bvrdigala Hiervsalem vsqve, et ab Heraclea per Aulonam, et per vrbem Romam" describes the way from Bordeaux to Jerusalem via Heracleum and Rome:

> mutatio ad sextum leugae vi / mutatio hungunuerro leugae vii / mutatio bucconis leugae vii / ciuitas tholosa leugae vii / mutatio ad nonum milia viiii / mutatio ad vicesimum milia xi / mutatio cedros milia vi / castellum carcassone milia viii / mutatio tricensimum milia viii / mutatio hosuerbas milia xv / ciuitas narbone milia xv [*Change direction after the sixth leuga of the road (i.e. after 9000 double steps or 18000 steps) /change after nine thousand steps / you reach the castle of Carcassone / you reach the city of Narbonne.*]

This is how this itinerarium tells us where to go to. It is obvious that such a description was not reliable at all, and phrases like "dextra est arbor palmae [*to the left is a palm tree*]" in the 595th line of the itinerarium makes you wonder how you would ever arrive in Jerusalem with the help of such a navigational device? Giving directions via text might create problems, but they have a high level of persuasiveness due to the fact that words make us feel being addressed by a person. This might be the reason for textual directives to remain powerful tools in times when visual information seems to be the ideal solution for navigation and wayfinding. The *itin-*

eraria scripta of the computer game ZORK (Infocom 1980) share a lingual ductus with the "Itinerarivm a Bvrdigala Hiervsalem vsqve" when they state: "From the Torch room, go South, / then East and get the coffin. / Return West, / then continue South to the Altar."

Text adventures like ZORK link the computer mediated experience with the tradition of mysteries and storytellers. Itineraria picta, graphical representations of routes increasingly replaced the older itineraria scripta and took over as the main device for spatial orientation. It seems however that the description of a 'tour' has never completely been replaced by description as a 'map.' Even in *Google Maps* the textual directions coexist with geographically realistic forms of representation.

Touring

Michel de Certeau (1988, 119) reports that an investigation by philosopher Charlotte Linde and linguist William Labov into how New Yorkers describe their apartments, found out that 97% of the descriptions are of the type of a *tour*: "You turn right and come into the living room." According to his source only three percent are of the 'map' type: "The girl's room is next to the kitchen." (ibid.). De Certeau interprets this observation as a piece of evidence for the predominance of acting versus seeing. The tour would reflect an action – and the map a view of the world.

A map about the surroundings of Norwich's Great Hospital, built in 1290, shows how geographical information was depicted in the 17th century (fig. 6). The topographic information given renders a fair impression of distances, location and orientation. The map shows places as a continuum of buildings, meadows, fields and roads. Even though there is no central perspective rendering the 3D-illustration, a sense of realism has been accomplished.

Fig. 6: St. Giles Hospital Norwich in a map from 1630

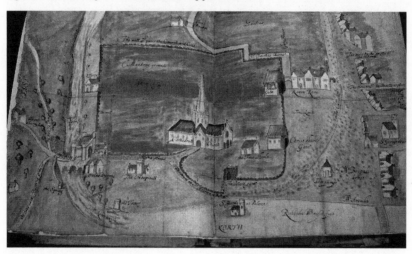

It is however noteworthy, that the map is not a radical *itinerarium pictum*, but a mix of text and image. Street names and names of buildings are placed at the appropriate locations on the map. It also seems that the map loses pictorial representation towards the borders of the depicted area and becomes textual the farther we move away from the centre (fig. 7).

Fig. 7: Norwich and the "waie to the Castle"

The mixed form of pictorial and textual information seems to be of high practical value if we compare it to forms of pure text (e.g. "Itinerarivm a Bvrdigala Hiervsa-lem") or to exclusively pictorial mapping attempts. An abstract non-realistic map with no words on it is useful only to the cartographer himself. It has little value for anyone except for the initiated.

Secret maps, cryptic descriptions of routes and the private notes of game geeks fall into the category of maps with a low level of general transparency. It is, however, another communality of maps and games that signs need not necessarily be readable by anybody, and that hints, ambiguity and delusion are part of the game (fig. 8).

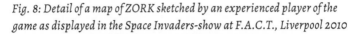

Fig. 8: Detail of a map of ZORK sketched by an experienced player of the game as displayed in the Space Invaders-show at F.A.C.T., Liverpool 2010

Space-Walks

The celestial map *Planisphaerium Coeleste* by Frederik de Wit (fig. 9) was targeted at a specialist audience. The map has a perspective of omnipresence, is precise in regard to astronomical distances and shapes of objects depicted and is rich in environment. The clouds surrounding the hemispheres are of a non-navigable character, they provide background atmosphere and aesthetic added value to the map. The same could be said for the elaborate artwork on the astronomical constellations. The etching of the Bear, Scorpio or Lion does not contribute to the cartographic information, it adds however to the look and feel of the map. A nice detail of the map is the methodological discourse displayed as a set of small spherical elements labelled 'Hypothesis Copernicana,' 'Hypothesis Ptolemaica' and so on, a brave statement in the 17th century that accounts for the mapmaker's political position.

Fig. 9: Celestial map by Frederik de Wit, c. 1680

A comparison of contemporary computer games maps with historic maps shall demonstrate that perspective, topography and environment play a crucial role in each of these fields of spatial representation and space-related ideational construction. The map distributed as a survey for the *Grand Theft Auto: Liberty City Stories* (Rockstar Leeds 2005) computer games is loaded with environment, i.e. non-navigational information about Liberty City (fig. 10).

Fig. 10: GTA-orientation map for Liberty City

The map contains hints about celebrities, gangster bosses and power structures (fig. 11), and resembles baroque European maps displaying portraits of the countries' kings and clerical leaders. The map's background is another source for environmental information that is not related to the pseudo-geographical form of representation adopted here.

Fig. 11: Detail of map for Liberty City

The perspective of the Liberty City map is persuasive of an omnipresent approach, whereas the game itself is obviously an example for vagrant navigation in a fully immersive 3D-environment. Quite different regarding the perspective of the game is *Civilization IV* (Firaxis Games 2005), where the player finds himself vagrant and looking down upon a 3D-space, displaying spatial information suggestive of a quasi-central perspective with stereotypical drop-shadows. Environmental, numeric and text information are displayed at the same time.

Fig. 12: Detail from Civilization IV

The spatial concept is interesting as it reminds us of *itineraria picta* and *itineraria scripta* in different sections of the screen. Landmark buildings, mountains and rivers clearly belong to the pictorial realm whereas a line like '57 turns left' (fig. 12) could well be taken from the *Itinerarivm a Bvrdigala Hiervsalem*.

The map that guides the players in *Civilization* could be taken as a fine example for a discursive system, where Derrida would be expected to detect play. There is obviously gaming in *Civilization IV*. There are also players, when the computer game is played. In terms of Derridean philosophy there is however another type of play taking place (and time) on a semiotic and cartographic level. Anette Baldauf (1997, 141) refers to Derrida's writing, when she employs him as an advocate against 'clean cartography;' since according to Derrida, there is difference, an active movement involving spacing and temporalizing. The presence of one element cannot compensate for the absence of the other. A gap or interval remains that escapes complete identity: "Constituting itself, dynamically dividing itself, this interval is what could be called *spacing*; time's becoming-spatial or spaces's becoming temporal (*temporalizing*)" (Derrida 1973, 143).

In addition to pictorial and written text information being contained within the maps, it became apparent with recent technologies that wayfinding subjects are embodied actors – moreso than with previous technologies. Gestural interfaces, touch screens and ludic interfaces reinstall bodily input into systems of navigation that seem to have become completely disembodied. Mobile- and smart-phones with touch-screens, NAVSAT-technology, geotracking, and the user sensitive interfaces of Kinect-machines and Wii-remotes cling on the users' bodies and reintroduce the Kantian 'left and right hand' where there was the left half of the brain left only.

Fig. 13: Hands-on navigation in Mirror's Edge

The reason why videogames in first person perspective, like *Mirror's Edge* (DICE 2008), display the player's hands (fig. 13) can hardly be found in an increase in playability. Professional players report that the 'weapon hands' should better be switched off as they only distract from hitting precisely. There is however a psychological effect of increased immersiveness with the hands of the player being visible in the scene. There is probably also a benefit for orientation and for a subjectivisation of orientation, when left and right hand of the player subject can be mapped to the territory, as in *BioShock Infinite* (Irrational Games 2013). This is what Kant refers to in the statement quoted in the beginning of this article as 'feeling of a difference' (fig. 14).

Fig. 14: Neo-Kantian orientation in BioShock Infinite

Conclusion

We observe a rediscovery of the player subjects' hands in videogames, mobile apps and locative media apparatuses. This has crucial effects on the range of perspectives that technical und ludic systems can offer. Locative Games can per definition not provide an omnipresent perspective as they are built upon the subject and the thrills of disorientation as much as on the challenge for orientation. In the pieces Blast Theory set up, the modes of verbal versus visual geographic representation do not simply coexist in one cartographic artefact, but they are different systems of map-making to be selected by the players. The player subject is drawn into the navigational apparatus. Systems of spatial representation turn into tools to compete with each other. Games like *Uncle Roy All Around You* (Blast Theory 2003) assign the modes of spatial representation to player groups and turn the system of orientation into a constituting factor of agonistic gameplay (fig. 15a-b).

Fig. 15a-b: Locative media, gestural interaction and human actors on the move in URAY

The interface for accessing the realm of different perspectives and experiences is however not a digital interface like the ASCII keyboard or the screen. It is a manual interface in the narrow sense of the word *manus*, which creates a link in between the embodied orientation of the user and the disembodied directiveness of the system.

References

Aarseth, Espen/Smedstad, Solveig Marie/Sunnanå, Lise (2003): A Multidimensional Typology of Games, in: *Level Up: Digital Game Research Conference*, ed. by Marinka Copier and Joost Raessens, Utrecht: Universiteit Utrecht, 48-53.

Baldauf, Anette (1997): Identität verräumlichen und Raum identifizieren: Mit Derrida gegen die Illusion einer 'sauberen Kartierung', in: *Atlas Mapping*, ed. by Paolo Bianchi and Sabine Folie, Vienna: Turia + Kant, 141-149.

Blast Theory (2003): *URAY: Uncle Roy All Around You*, Android: Equator IRC.

de Certeau, Michel (1988): The Practice of Everyday Life, Berkeley, CA/Los Angeles, CA/London: University of California Press [1980].

Derrida, Jacques (1973): Différance, in: id.: *Speech and Phenomena: and Other Essays on Husserl's Theory of Signs*, Evanston: Northwestern UP, 129-160 [1968].

DICE (2008): *Mirror's Edge*, Xbox 360: Electronic Arts.

Firaxis Games (2005): *Civilization IV*, PC: 2k Games.

Infocom (1980): *ZORK*, PC: Infocom.

Irrational Games (2013): *BioShock Infinite*, PC: 2K Games.

Kant, Immanuel (1963): What Does It Mean to Orient Oneself in Thinking?, in: id.: *Religion and Rational Theology*, Cambridge et al.: Cambridge UP, 7-18 [1786].

Rockstar Leeds (2005): *Grand Theft Auto: Liberty City Stories*, PSP: Rockstar Games.

Sontag, Susan (1980): Under the Sign of Saturn, in: id.: *Under the Sign of Saturn*, New York, NY: Ferrar, Strauss & Giroux, 119-134 [1978].

Distance and Fear
Defining the Play Space

Sebastian Möring

This paper proposes to take the play space into consideration when analysing computer games. While analysing computer games using *Being and Time* by Martin Heidegger one realizes that his notion of fear describes a situation that seems to be essential for many action games. Fear as an objective structure can be stated if something harmful is in a definite range with something else that can be injured or killed by it. Fear exists as long as the harmful entity is at a critical distance and as long as the fearsome (e.g. 'killing') is possible, but does not happen. Between the threatening entity and the threatened entity emerges a certain space which I regard as the 'play space.' The play space as opposed to the often architecturally described 'game space' can firstly be regarded as the vital space in a game and secondly as a distance that must be ensured for the game to be continued.

The play space emerges in the game space between a player-controlled entity and the game limits as well as within the game space between a player-controlled entity and harmful objects. It is within this space that actions take place and options re-main available. While the game is being played the dimensions of the play space dynamically change due to changes in gaming situations. Heidegger divides this space into a near and a far space and thus allows the distinction of a space of necessity in very close distance and a space of possibility within a greater distance. Additionally, I propose further distinctions regarding the properties of 'play space' with the help of proxemics.

Game Space and Play Space

In *Rules of Play* Salen and Zimmerman's (2004, 478-481) demonstrate that the term 'play space' defines a space which includes play actions and excludes real-life actions with real-life consequences at the same time: Such a space can be a children's room, or a playground in the park. Its primary characteristic is that it is a safe space in which actions have no real-life consequences and can therefore also contain elements which are a cultural taboo. The main purpose of this play space is play. This play space is not necessarily structured to play a particular game, but rather to provide a space where numerous games can emerge out of play or can be played in it due to its specific properties. On an urban football cage, for instance, one could also play basketball or hopscotch and so on.

In his work *Casual Revolution* Jesper Juul (2010, 16-18) mentions the player space which is situated in front of the gaming console. Michael Nitsche (2008, 16) suggests five conceptual planes for the analysis of game spaces: a) 'rule-based', b) 'mediated', c) 'fictional', d) 'play' and e) 'social'; with using the term 'play space' (d) to address the "space of the play, which includes the player and the video game hardware". As opposed to Juul the play space for Nitsche serves as the space of communication between the player on the one side of the screen and the game on the other side, in order to "connect the material world and the fictional one" (ibid., 13). Like Salen and Zimmerman, Nitsche refers to the difference of the material or real world and the fictional world of the game. However, Nitsche's theory is confined to videogames while Salen and Zimmerman refer to non-videogames.

In videogames the term 'game space' mostly describes their architectural structure. It is furthermore "defined by the mathematical rules that set, for example, physics, sounds, AI, and game-level architecture" (Nitsche 2008, 16). Nitsche calls this the rule-based plane of the game space (a). Unicursal labyrinths which provide the fundamental spatial structure for many first-person-shooters are an example for such spaces.

However, I neither want to talk about the space in front of the videogame console and television nor explicitly about the rule-based game space. This paper focuses on the play space that emerges in agonistic games like many action and real-time strategy games. The perpetuator of this space is the fear-structure that emerges from the gameplay of these games, within the limits of the game space as well as in between the player-controlled objects and threatening entities.

Competition and Fear

Referring to Martin Heidegger's *Being and Time* (2008) one can apply the existential structure of the 'being-in-the-world' [*Dasein*] to computer games and assume that a game exists as long as it is played. It occurred to me that Heidegger's notion of fear describes a phenomenon commonly observed in action games (or other agonistic games like real-time strategy games). Fear is a mode of the 'disposedness' [*Befindlichkeit*] of a Dasein (derived from its fundamental existential situation in the light of inevitable death, which Heidegger calls 'Angst' as the 'basic disposedness' [*Grundbefindlichkeit*]). This concept is best described as a mood in which a Dasein is always already in the world. Thus, Dasein experiences its world and itself always in a mood. I propose that the mood of fear is a fundamental structure in agonistic computer games like action and real time strategy games.

Fear is not understood as an often psychologically explained emotion for example induced by some kind of horror, which applies at the shell or the representational layer of computer games (Aarseth 1997, 40; Mäyrä 2008, 17-21). Even if both, the mechanical layer (core) and the representational layer (shell) of the game, are sometimes hard to keep apart I am looking at fear at the level of the game mechanics/structure (Aarseth 2011, 59), or the "core, or game as gameplay" (Mäyrä 2008, 17). With Ernest Adams (2010, 19) gameplay can roughly be understood as consisting of a) the challenges which a game provides as well as b) actions to overcome these challenges although not all actions are "tied to specific challenges". With the help of Caillois' difference *ludus* and *paidia* it is possible to derive a notion of gameplay which is based on implications of these terms (Caillois 2001). The play element is derived from the notion of *paidia*, which is considered as "unstructured and lacking in rules" (Slethaug 1993, 65). The game element is derived from the notion of *ludus*, which "has certain moves, rules and goals" (ibid. 1993, 65).

As opposed to Caillois (2001, 53), who considers *ludus* and *paidia* two different kinds of play, gameplay is here understood as consisting of a) the game, which itself consists of the game rules as well as the ruled game space, the challenges and possible game actions and b) the play, which can be considered as the actualization of a possible action from the space of possibility that is enabled by the game at a certain moment of the game at play. In line with the distinction of games as objects and games as processes (Aarseth 2001; 2011) the game part of gameplay signifies the game as an object (the potential game) and the play part of gameplay signifies the game as a process (an actual game at play).

Following Huizinga (1998, 31-35 and 46-75), *agon* or contest "bears all the formal characteristics of play" and therefore accounts for the play element in all kinds of cultural institutions featuring agonistic figurations such as war, the stock market, poetry etc. For Caillois (2001, 14–17) *agon* is characteristic specifically for games of 'competition' featuring an agonistic structure as opposed to games of 'chance' (*alea*), games of 'simulation' (*mimicry*) and games of 'vertigo' (*ilinx*). As such one can say the gameplay of games of *agon* is characterized by elements of competition.

Furthermore, Huizinga (1998, 51) emphasizes the close relationship between contest and fear when he observes that the Greek terms *agon* and *agonia* share an "intimate connection," in that the "latter word originally meant simply 'contest', but later 'death-struggle' and 'fear'". Studying the concept of dramatic suspense in the Scholia of the *Iliad* German philologist Andreas Fuchs (2007, 29) offers a similar insight. The terms 'fear' or 'anxiety' and 'competition' have the same etymological root: which is the Greek term *agōn*. As there is an etymological relationship between competition and fear, one can assume that fear is a fundamental structure in the gameplay of games of competition like in action games or turn-based and real-time strategy games. However, Heidegger's notion of fear is based on Aristotle, who in his *Rhetoric* (book 2, chpt. 5) defines it as follows:

> Let fear be defined as a painful or troubled feeling caused by the impression of an imminent evil that causes destruction or pain; for men do not fear all evils, for instance, becoming unjust or slow-witted, but only such as involve great pain or destruction, and only if they appear to be not far off but near at hand and threatening, for men do not fear things that are very remote; all know that they have to die, but as death is not near at hand, they are indifferent. If then this is fear, all things must be fearful that appear to have great power of destroying or inflicting injuries that tend to produce great pain. That is why even the signs of such misfortunes are fearful, for the fearful thing itself appears to be near at hand, and danger is the approach of anything fearful.

Aristotle's definition of fear as a 'painful or troubled feeling' is caused by something dangerous or 'fearful' which is 'imminent,' i.e. something that is possible to happen but has not happened, yet. The imminence thereby is seen as temporally imminent as well as spatially imminent. His definition clearly states that fear requires the fearful thing or event to be near rather than far. Additionally, Aristotle's examples show that particularly agonistic relationships are predestined for fear, like this is the case in relations between rivals, enemies, or between stronger and weaker, as well as relations of inequity, vengeance or dependency.

To explain fear in Heidegger's *Being and Time* in the shortest possible manner I shall quote Hubert Dreyfus' (1991, 176) commentary on Heidegger's work, who explains the three-fold structure of fear as follows:

> *The fearing as such* [...] is the mood that lets something matter to us as fearsome. [...] *That which is feared* [is] [s]omething specific coming at us, in some specific way, from some specific sector of the environment. [...] *That which is feared for* [is] Dasein itself as threatened in some specific respect. This need not be some part of the body. Fear can threaten Dasein's self-interpretation by threatening its projects.

I am mainly interested in that *which is feared* and that *which is feared for*. The latter can be regarded as a) the player who fears for his being in the game; or b) the playing of the game, that is the game at play, which is constantly threatened in its very existence and therefore is the 'subject' of fear.

The objects of fear or that *which is feared* are harmful objects in the game space threatening an object in the game that is not to be hit, injured or killed. These objects often point at the direction of the objects that should not be hit. Heidegger calls them 'detrimental' [*abträglich*] in relation to the object that is not to be hit (these objects are usually represented as characters, avatars or geometric objects).

Fear is at play if the harmful object is at an approachable distance from where it can be harmful or not. Heidegger calls this a 'threat'. The emerging uncertainty – whether the approaching harmful object(s) will finally be harmful or not – is fundamental of fear. Temporally seen, the fearsome is always in the future. As soon as it happens it does not exist anymore. Seen from the spatial point of view the fearsome is always within a certain distance from where it can harm or not. For Aristotle as well as Heidegger the fearful/harmful is near (no matter if temporally near or spatially near) which makes it an essentially spatial constellation which often occurs in situations of competition and consequently in respective games.

To demonstrate this on computer games I will look at the popular game classic called *Tetris* (Pajitnov 1984). The top limit of the game space can be regarded as that *which is feared*. It is not to be touched by the bricks the player has to fit into each other in order to complete the lines leading to their deletion and therefore opening of more space. In between both entities the upper limit of the game space and the highest brick is a space that has not much been defined, yet. However, this space seems to have an important function since the game's instruction could simply be: "Maintain the play space!" This is the most important space of the game at play and its maintenance is necessary for the game's existence. In *Tetris* at play, the player is not interested in the bottom lines within the game space, since she must manage the expansion and contraction of the space between the upper limit and the highest brick. She is interested in the play space, which she has to ensure and where the game play actions take place.

The Play Space: The Space between

According to Sybille Krämer (2005, 12), a German philosopher, we refer to "the Fluxus of a swinging, often returning to itself and repeating motion" when we talk about play. In her opinion the dynamics of play require a to-and-fro motion – and to explain her reasoning she refers to Helmuth Plessner's saying of "keeping oneself in-between [*ein Sich-Halten im Zwischen*]" (ibid.). This 'in-between' which I regard as the play space is maintained thanks to the fear structure derived from Heidegger. This point of view is strengthened by Hans-Georg Gadamer (2004, 107), a student of Heidegger, who applies a notion similar to the play space as proposed in this paper, which is translated as 'playing field':

> Games differ from one another in their spirit. The reason for this is that the to-and-fro movement that constitutes the game is patterned in various ways. The particular nature of a game lies in the rules and regulations that prescribe the way the field of the game is filled. This is true universally, whenever there is a game. It is true, for example, of the play of fountains and of playing animals. The playing field

on which the game is played is, as it were, set by the nature of the game itself and is defined far more by the structure that determines the movement of the game from within than by what it comes up against – i.e., the boundaries of the open space – limiting movement from without.

Two aspects of this quotation are important for my argument. Firstly, Gadamer says that the nature or the character of the game is primarily defined by the "the structure that determines the movement of the game from within" (ibid.). This can be read as a statement for the shift of attention from the game space to the play space. Secondly, the to-and-fro movement which especially characterizes the "playful character of the contest" (ibid., 105) is the result of "rules and regulations that prescribe the way the field of the game is filled" (ibid., 107). Consequently, fear has to be seen as the rule that provokes the characteristic to-and-for motion of the play space in games of competitions.

In *Tetris* at play are the compulsory actions enacted to guarantee a minimal distance between the highest blocks and the upper detrimental game space limit. It should be noted that in *Tetris* the bricks can be considered as threatening the upper limit, which is also the threatened object. However, if we regard the whole game at play as a Heideggerian Dasein – whose basic purpose is to be 'there' [*da*] or to be at play (i.e. game as a process) – it does not matter which of the entities is the feared or the fearsome since it is the possible dangerous physical contact of the two that could in the worst case end the game's existence or the game session. Therefore, the contact of the two is actually fearsome.

Regardless of whether one *plays* the game or one plays *with* the game, one always has to consider the fundamental condition of possibility of maintaining the play space as a basis for all other play activities. Consequently, this mainte-nance of the play space can be seen as an essential part of what Olli Leino (2010, 134) terms the *gameplay condition* based on Sartre's (2003) *Being and Nothingness*. Thus, I propose a shift of attention from the game space to the play space. Nev-ertheless, the game space provides the play space with general limits. Hence, the characteristics of the game space within which play takes place have to be taken into consideration, too. The top limit of *Tetris*' game space is a good example for this. On the other hand, during the game the play space emerges primarily between an entity that is threatened by the possible contact with a harmful entity as well as the limits of the game space.

Further Examples

This play space also exists in first-person-shooter games such as *Battlefield: Bad Company 2* (DICE 2010) or platform games like *Super Mario Bros.* (Nintendo 1985). In these games, the play space is maintained either by eliminating or by evading opponents. In a first-person-shooter game based on a unicursal labyrinth the diameter of the play space contracts when facing an opponent who herself or whose projectiles come closer. After eliminating the opponent, the play space expands until another opponent appears. Thus, the characteristic movement of the play space is an oscillation of contraction and expansion.

The essence of the given agonistic games is to negotiate the play space. In order to guarantee the continuation of a game at play (its existence) the play space should not collapse. Depending on the lifes a game at play has left a collapse of the play space can in the worst-case lead to a game over. However already a play over (e.g. losing one life but still having at least one life left which is much more common in contemporary single-player action games) results in an interruption of the game which equals a game over if the game is not continued.

In the Snowblind-level of *Battlefield: Bad Company 2* the player and an object in the game space requires protection from the opponents: The mission of the group of soldiers the player-controlled entity belongs to is to save a crashed satellite from being destroyed by the opponents. In this case, the play space emerges between the opponents, the player character, and the satellite. In Heidegger's (2008, 181) terms this is a case of 'fearing-for'. So we have a player-controlled-object and a game-space-object that are not to be eliminated by the opponents. If either the player character or the satellite is destroyed the level cannot be completed. I have shown how the play space is understood in this paper. To define the play space further I propose two concepts by Heidegger and proxemics.

Striking Distance:
Heidegger's 'Nearness', the Far and the Near Play Space

Heidegger's idea of nearness does not necessarily signify an object that is located at the smallest distance from our body, but rather an object or entity which we have to cope with every day in the process of living our lives. Thus, nearness has different characteristics, which are actually not meant to be distances in a Cartesian space. By using a telephone to call somebody, the telephone is physically near. Heidegger would say it is ontically near. However, ontologically nearer to us is actually the person we are talking to via the telephone. In fact, we first realize the telephone's existence when its service is disrupted while trying to make a call. It changes from readiness-to-hand into presence-at-hand and comes into the nearness of the Dasein's attention. Hubert Dreyfus (2007) identifies at least four modes of nearness in *Being and Time*: 'accessibility nearness', 'mattering nearness', 'attention nearness', and 'availability nearness'.

When applying this nearness to the play space in computer games, I find that the most harmful entities are the ones nearest to the player character or another threatened object. Mostly, they go along with those at the shortest distance from the entity that must not be hit. However, this must not necessarily be the case. For example, in *Battlefield: Bad Company 2* those opponents, pointing bazooka at the player avatar are the nearest, and because of their high destructiveness they are the most dangerous threat. However, there are other opponents who are closer to the player-character but who are less dangerous. This is an example for the difference of attention and mattering nearness as opposed to a small distance in a Cartesian sense.

As I have shown when discussing fear, only those entities that are in an effective distance from the threatened entity are considered to be near and can therefore be fearsome. Thus, the play space can be differentiated into the near and the far. Far means that a harmful entity is not at an approachable distance and near describes the opposite. The near is thus a *striking distance*.

Proxemics

With the help of proxemics the play space can be further defined: Edward T. Hall the founder of intercultural communication as an academic discipline developed a system, which allows the description of distance behaviour of different cultures in different contexts. Inspired by the Swiss zoologist Heini Hediger, Hall (1990, 8) distinguishes four distances: intimate distance, personal distance, social distance and public distance. In the following, I will compare these distances to game situations starting with the farthest distance. Although these are distances derived from Cartesian space, they coincide with different degrees of a mattering nearness as outlined by Heidegger.

Public Distance: Public distance starts from twelve feet away from a person's skin and is unlimited in its expansion. According to Hall "public distance [...] is well outside the circle of involvement" (ibid., 123). For sports like football, this would be beyond the limits of the playing field, which literally is the place for the spectators in a football stadium. Public distance is far away from the place of action. Considering football, it literally does not even belong to the game space since it actually describes the distance of the audience, the public. Thus, it could be considered the outside or the excluding boarder either of the game space or the play space as the space of game play action.

Using football as an example the goalkeeper of the attacking team is situated in the public space, as long as he is not attacking. In this moment he does not take part in the current play situation, he becomes a spectator. For videogames this counts for all entities that do not affect the game play at all and those that are not involved in a particular game play situation. In *Tetris* this is true of the lowest bricks that can neither be deleted, nor can they receive another brick or will be able to do so in the next moves. In *Super Mario Bros.* this can apply to opponents that are outside the visible screen but will be coming in soon.

Social Distance: Social distance is in the range of four to twelve feet and is normally used in situations of business communication (ibid., 121). I consider this the including border of the play space. To give another example from my apparent favourite game football, the following situation can be considered to be at a social distance. A defender from the opposing team starts an attacking scene in his own half. From the moment where the player with the ball reaches a distance – maybe around the centre circle – from where he could possibly shoot, he is in the social zone. Therefore, the ball-guiding player in relation to the opposing goal defines the social zone. In *Super Mario Bros.*, this would be the opponent who has just arrived on screen while the game world is moving. However, if this opponent arrives on screen, there can be other opponents who are already within personal distance. The player can already act in relation to it.

Personal Distance: Personal distance is stretched between 18 inches and approximately four feet (ibid., 119). It is applied when couples from western cultures stand in public. If somebody else gets this close to our partner, either we know him and his intentions or we would like to get to know him because we may have been suspicious of his intentions. During personal conversation, we keep this distance, which is about an arm's length. The metaphor of arm's length distance applies well to boxing where the aim is to keep the opponent at such a distance.

The personal zone in *Tetris* comes into play if there is still enough distance at the top that one can try to play a certain tactic, for example only deleting four lines at once with the so called 'I-brick' which looks similar to the capital letter 'I.' This means waiting for it to come and meanwhile risking touching the upper limit of the game space.

Intimate Distance: In everyday life, intimate distance emerges between our skin surface and around 18 inches from one's body (ibid., 116). We only allow people, with whom we are intimate with, to get this close to us. Otherwise, we feel highly threatened and may try to expand the distance. Transferred to a videogame, this would be the zone where a threatening object hits or is close to hitting the threatened object. There is nearly no possibility to escape, to shoot it or jump on it. In the example of *Tetris* this would be the distance of about one empty line of blocks to the upper limit. In *Super Mario Bros.*, it is comparable to the shortest possible distance between an opponent or a projectile and the threatened object before touching each other. In this case, immediate action is needed to avoid losing a life or ending a game. In most cases, it is already too late.

Hall also calls the intimate zone "the distance of love-making and wrestling, comforting and protecting" (ibid., 117). The wrestling example reminds me of 'beat'em up' games like the *Tekken* series (Namco 1994) or *Street Fighter 2* (Capcom 1991). Here the game would not take place or at least not allow a decision to be made if the harmful and threatened entities did not get in touch with each other in the intimate zone.

By adopting the concept of proxemics, the play space is distinguishable into different zones of threat. Hall's premise is that all cultures do have a certain distance behaviour, which is to some degree "rooted in biology and physiology" (Hall 1990, 3). Consequently, distance behaviour can be considered an anthropological constant. However, the distances are experienced differently in different cultures. Hall (ibid., 116) empirically observed these distances originally among "non-contact, middle-class, healthy adults, mainly natives of the north-eastern seaboard of the United States." Therefore, absolute distances expressed in feet and inches are only valid for this specific culture.

Considering games as specific cultures, one can thus also assume that the absolute distances vary among different games whereas the experienced distances stay similar. If one compares boxing and football it obvious that the striking distance in both games varies in absolute measures. Whereas in boxing I always have to be less than an arm length away from the opponent in order to be in striking distance the absolute striking distance in the association football simulation *FIFA 13* (EA Canada 2012) can already start outside of the penalty area whose border is simulated 18 yards away from the goal. However, in the example of real association football, for instance, the absolute striking distance can itself vary in different cultures. Culture can here already mean that different teams in the same league follow a different philosophy or culture of playing football.

Imagine there is a team that more often than other teams shoots from outside of the penalty area whereas another team usually tries to score a goal from within the six yards box in the penalty area. The absolute striking distance of the former team is thus farther away from the goal line than the one of the latter team. Given these teams belong to Hall's sample from the USA, the striking distance of the former team matches the public distance of the culture the team is a part of and the latter team's striking distance matches the social distance of the cultural average. Nevertheless, within the game one can say that the intimate, the personal, the social, as well as the public distance are being recoded according to the norms of the game and the specific play philosophy or culture.

Play Space as Space of Necessity

Comparing the distances described by Hall and the striking distance derived from Heidegger, harmful objects seem to arrive more and more at a mattering nearness the more they move from social distance to intimate distance. – Compared to the play space the concept of the space of possibility seems to be very similar. I will now discuss the concepts of the space of possibility by Salen and Zimmerman as well as Nitsche and relate them to my notion of play space.

According to Salen and Zimmerman (2004, 67) "[c]reating a game means designing a structure that will play out in complex and unpredictable ways, a space of possible action that players explore as they take part in [a] game". The space of possibility emerges from the designed game structure and contains all possible actions of a game even if they were not intended. Discussing the space of possibility Salen and Zimmerman think of the game as a whole and not of the game at play in a particular situation. Thus, they regard the entire game space as a space of possibility where particular intended or unintended game actions are possible. Of course, possible actions depend on the respective context. Not all game actions are possible at each place in the game space.

Describing the spatial patterns rails/tracks, labyrinths/mazes, and arenas Nitsche (2008, 188) concentrates primarily on the architectural game space as a "structural force of interactive events" and its capacity "to channel interaction." He discusses the example of a bridge which is an architectural structure influencing a games possibility space with respect to the particular abilities of the player-character. Nevertheless, it remains a space of possibility in which the player can choose what actions to commit when and where next.

However, due to their perspectives Nitsche as well as Salen and Zimmerman (2004, 67) do not take into account that the play space, emerging between threatening objects and threatened objects, in many action videogames is transformed from "a space of possible action" into a *space of necessary action*, the latest at intimate distance if the player intends to play on. If a threatening object is incoming the player will have less choices to make since the priority is to guarantee the continuity of the game: Firstly, the fearsome situation is drawing the attention of the game onto the relation of an incoming threatening object and the threatened object. Thus, the *space of necessity* coincides with the mattering nearness of the play space. The player has to make an adequate choice to avoid the fearsome to happen. In the worst case, it could disrupt or end the game. Choosing to collect coins as a kind of displacement activity from animal behaviour would definitely not be adequate. Secondly, the player does not have the possibility to do nothing given that she wants to play on. Therefore, the player's possibilities are limited by the situation of an incoming threat. This situation of fear and threat requires the choice to defend herself by fighting or avoiding the threatening object. Thus, the space of possibility has turned into a space of necessity.

Defining the Play Space

As I have shown the play space as proposed in this paper is a space, which describes the striking distance between a threatening object and a threatened object and therefore coincides with the Heideggerian structure of fear. This space has to be ensured as a necessity in order to play a game. The play space as a distance can be limited by spatial constraints of the game space, the abilities of action of the player-controlled objects as well as the player's own mastery of the controls or the game. It is furthermore a space that is directed towards the most threatening object in a certain situation of the game at play. The play space can be distinguished into four distances that differentiate game play situations according to their character of nearness and threat. It is therefore to be considered as a dynamic space, which constantly changes its dimension as it expands and contracts. A threatening object at intimate distance from a threatened object turns the space of possibility into a space of necessity.

Furthermore, the play space can be thought of in terms of a cognitive space as the distance between the current state of the game and a possibly harmful event or game state. As such also games of a purely cognitive nature as well as games in which the harmful is rather metaphorically close than literally would be included in this model. For instance, in *SimCity* (Maxis 1989) the wellbeing of the game depends on keeping an eye on the budget and avoiding running out of cash. Consequently, there can be situations in which the possibility to run out of cash is much more likely to happen and therefore closer than in others. For instance, a sudden catastrophe like the zombie invasion can decimate the city's population significantly. If this city is already run on a tight budget the sudden lack of taxpayers lets the possibility of insolvency appear much closer (Leino 2010, 127).

Finally, with Gadamer one can see the fear structured play space from the perspective of the game and as such as its method to keep itself in play. As is known Gadamer (2004, 106) advocated for a primacy of the game over the player in that the game plays the player and not the other way around: "The attraction of a game, the fascination it exerts, consists precisely in the fact that the game masters the player. [...] The real subject of the game (this is shown in precisely those experiences where there is only a single player) is not the player but instead the game itself."

Especially agonistic single player games such as *Battlefield: Bad Company 2* and *Tetris* can be considered as pieces of software, which constantly threaten to stop running as soon as they have been started, in that they constantly contract the play space that the player through her actions tries to expand again. With Gadamer (2004, 107) one can consider this a sneaky strategy of the game with the purpose to keep being played since "the purpose of the game is not really solving the task, but ordering and shaping the movement of the game."

References

Aarseth, Espen J. (1997): *Cybertext: Perspectives on Ergodic Literature*, Baltimore, MD: Johns Hopkins UP.

–––– (2001): Computer Game Studies, Year One, in: *Game Studies. The International Journal of Computer Game Research* 1/1, gamestudies.org/0101/editorial.html.

–––– (2011): Define Real, Moron! Some Remarks on Game Ontologies, in: *DIG-AREC Keynote-Lectures 2009/10*, ed. by Stephan Günzel, Michael Liebe and Dieter Mersch, Potsdam: Potsdam UP, 50-69.

Adams, Ernest (²2010): *Fundamentals of Game Design*, Berkeley, CA: New Riders [2006].

Caillois, Roger (2001): *Man, Play, and Games*, Urbana, IL: University of Illinois Press [1958].

Capcom (1991): *Street Fighter II: The World Warrior*, Arcade: Capcom.

DICE (2010): *Battlefield: Bad Company 2*, PC: Electronic Arts.

Dreyfus, Hubert (1991): *Being-in-the-World: A Commentary on Heidegger's Being and Time, Division I*, Cambridge, MA: MIT Press.

–––– (2007). Lecture 9: Spatiality I (Lecture from the course *Philosophy 185 Heidegger*), archive.org/details/Philosophy_185_Fall_2007_UC_Berkeley.

EA Canada (2012): *FIFA 13*. PC: Electronic Arts.

Fuchs, Andreas (2007): Zur Missachteten poetologischen Qualität antiker Kommentare: Das Verständnis der Dramatischen Spannung in den Ilias-Scholien, in: *Gespannte Erwartungen: Beiträge Zur Geschichte Der Literarischen Spannung*, ed. by Kathrin Ackermann and Judith Moser-Kroiss, Vienna: Lit, 15-35.

Gadamer, Hans-Georg (²2004): *Truth and Method*, London/New York, NY: Continuum [1960].

Hall, Edward T. (1990): *The Hidden Dimension*, New York, NY: Anchor Books [1966].

Heidegger, Martin (2008): *Being and Time*, New York, NY: Harper Perennial [1927].

Huizinga, Johan (1998): *Homo Ludens: A Study of the Play-Element in Culture*, London: Routledge [1938].

Juul, Jesper (2010): *A Casual Revolution*, Cambridge, MA: MIT Press.

Krämer, Sybille (2005): Die Welt, ein Spiel? Über die Spielbewegung als Unumkehrbarkeit, in: *Spielen: Zwischen Rausch und Regel*, ed. by Deutsches Hygiene Museum Dresden, Ostfildern-Ruit: Hatje Cantz, 11-17.

Leino, Olli (2010): *Emotions in Play: On the Constitution of Emotion in Solitary Computer Game Play*, PhD Diss., IT University of Copenhagen.

Mäyrä, Frans (2008): *An Introduction to Game Studies: Games in Culture*, Los Angeles et al.: SAGE.

Maxis (1989): *SimCity*, PC: Maxis.

Namco (1994): *Tekken*, Arcade: Namco.

Nitsche, Michael (2008): *Video Game Spaces: Image, lay, and Structure in 3D Game Worlds*, Cambridge, MA/London: MIT Press.

Nintendo (1985): *Super Mario Bros.*, NES: Nintendo.

Pajitnov, Alexey (1984): *Tetris*, Electronica 60: Pajitnov.

Salen, Katie/Zimmerman, Eric (2004): *Rules of Play: Game Design Fundamentals*, Cambridge, MA/London: MIT Press.

Sartre, Jean-Paul (2003): *Being and Nothingness: An Essay on Phenomenological Ontology*, New York, NY/London: Routledge [1943].

Slethaug, Gordon E. (1993): Game Theory, in: *Encyclopedia of Contemporary Literary Theory*, ed. by Irene Rima Makaryk, Toronto/Buffalo/London: University of Toronto Press, 64-69.

The Rhetoric of Game Space
Lotman's Spatial Semantics as a Method for Analysing Videogames

Niklas Schrape

The spatiality of videogames came prominently into focus in the last years (Günzel 2008a, 2008b and 2012; Wiemer 2008; Ljungström 2005 and 2008; Nitsche 2008; Gazzard 2013), while at the same time their potential for political expression was examined (Bogost 2007 and 2008; Klevjer 2002; Frasca 2001; Flanagan 2009; Schrape 2012). Up until now, however, rhetorical analysis centred mostly on visual interfaces and systemic behaviours. But space is a unique property of games and new media (Manovich 2001) that can't be put in one or the other category. Instead, it is both: a mimetic presentation, which guides the player's understanding and a systemic structure that constrains and channels play. As it is crucial for the experience of many games, it can be assumed that space can be an integral part of a game's rhetoric. But how can game space work as a rhetorical device? This article investigates the question theoretically and through an exemplary analysis of a game that clearly makes use of the rhetorical power of game space and does so in a very transparent way: Serious Games Interactive' *Global Conflicts: Palestine* (Serious Games Interactive 2007). As method for rhetorical analysis, the Spatial Semantics by Estonian semiotician Yuri M. Lotman are explored. First, however, it will be argued, what a spatial approach to the rhetoric of videogames is.

The Overlook of Game Space in Procedural Rhetorics

Rhetorical analysis of videogames was introduced by Gonzalo Frasca (2001) and expanded on by Ian Bogost: His book *Persuasive Games* from 2007 as well as his article on *The Rhetoric of Video Games* from 2008 are considered to be landmarks within Game Studies. Therefore, even if there now exist further examinations of the topic (Flanagan 2009), Bogost's approach will be the central point of reference in this article. First, however, in order to recognise what is unique about the rhetoric of videogames, it is necessary to remind oneself about the meaning of 'rhetoric.'

If we talk about the rhetoric of movies, pictures, games or even fashion, we often mean inscribed ideological positions. In this case 'rhetoric' denotes content, not form. The actual system of rhetoric, however, is a 2500-year old heuristic to organise speech and text, regardless of its content. Aristotle (1991) described it as technique of strategic communication with the intent to persuade through reason, emotion and the image of the speaker. He defined it as the counterpart to dialectics, as a method not to attain knowledge, but to create plausibility. In contrast to logical reasoning, its premises are therefore not analytic truths, but accepted believes. The rhetorical reasoning, the enthymeme, is not deductive by nature, but reductive: It makes the unknown understandable by leading it back to the familiar (Kopperschmidt 2005, 31f.). Originally it was restrained to speech, but since Augustine of Hippo it became transformed to a general text theory. In modernity, it degenerated to mere stylistics, before it vanished in the face of positivism (Barthes 1994). In the last century, however, it was rediscovered by theorists like Chaim Perelman (1990; Perelman/Olbrechts-Tyteca 1991) and Stephen Toulmin (2007) and became applied not only to verbal text, but also to pictures (Barthes 1978), design objects (Buchanan 1985) and film (Joost 2008; Kaemmerling 1971; Kanzog 2001).

In its broadest sense, rhetoric can be described as a *textual strategy* – in the sense of Umberto Eco – to guide the recipient's understanding in an intended way. But this implies that the object of rhetorical analysis would have to be considered as some kind of text. This, of cause, leads back to the age-old question of Game Studies: Are videogames texts? And if they were not, wouldn't it be a colonial act to apply rhetorical analysis (Eskelinen 2001)? There exist a lot of definitions of videogames: as space images (Günzel 2008a and 2012), formal systems (Juul 2005a; Crawford 1984), cyberdramas (Murray 1997) or cybertexts (Aarseth 1997; Kücklich 2006). The very existence of so many definitions highlights two things: "videogames are a mess" (Bogost 2009) – and *every definition is bound to a contingent theoretical perspective*. They all can be understood as epistemological analogies in order to grasp a new subject (Poser 2006). They lead back the unknown (videogames) to the familiar (text, space, pictures). In this vein, it shall not be said that videogames are rhetorical texts, but just that they can be analysed as such.

Here, rhetoric is conceptualised as a general text theory bound to the perspective of persuasion through argumentation. As every textual strategy is reliant on an intended effect and there can't be a formal analysis without at least an implicit (and subjective) understanding of the meaning of a given text, rhetoric depends on hermeneutics in the broadest sense (Eco 1979). In order to analyse the rhetorical form, we have to understand the content first. This highlights a fundamental paradox: The hermeneutic circle presupposes the existence of a fixed material text (Dilthey 2003). But this is exactly what is not given in ergodic artworks like videogames (Aarseth 1997; 1999). If the visual surface of the videogame is always changing in response to the player's actions and is therefore not fit to be the prime reference point of a rhetorical analysis – where else could persuasion be at home in games?

This question worked as entry point for a new concept of rhetoric, developed by Frasca and Bogost: Frasca (2001) defined games as *simulations* and declared them to be a whole new mode of representation – not through signs, but through rules. In *Unit Operations*, Bogost (2006, 98) clarifies this notion of simulation as "a representation of a source system via a less complex system that informs the user's understanding of the source system in a subjective way." With this invocation of subjectivity, he reclaimed the necessary ideological inscriptions in simulations as objects for rhetorical analysis. For Bogost and Frasca, simulations in general and videogames in particular perform a procedural rhetoric, not based on words but rules and processes. Taking up the notion by Salen and Zimmerman (2004), Bogost assumes a "possibility space of play" including "all of the gestures made possible by a set of rules" (Bogost 2008, 120). The structure of this possibility space can be understood as model that the player explores through his or her actions in play:

> Video games are models of real and imagined systems. [...] [W]hen we play, we explore the possibility space of a set of rules – we learn to understand and evaluate a game's meaning. Video games make arguments about how social or cultural systems work in the world – or how they could work, or don't work. [...] [W]hen we play video games, we can interpret these arguments and consider their place in our lives (ibid., 136).

At the heart of the procedural rhetoric lies the *procedural enthymeme* – an adaption of the rhetorical reasoning or syllogism to videogames: "the player *literary* fills in the missing portion of the syllogism by interacting with the application, but that action is constrained by the rules" (Bogost 2007, 34). The game proposes a starting position and a goal and the player has to try out how to reach the goal, but every solution he or she finds is already part of the game's possibility space.

The concept of the procedural enthymeme is extremely helpful for analysis, but it has a flaw: Bogost (2007, 18) defines an enthymeme as deductive reasoning with omitted proposition. In the sentence "We cannot trust this man, as he is a politician", the major premise would be omitted (ibid.). It's a compressed reasoning, actually consisting of three steps: (1) "Politicians are not trustworthy", (2) "This man is a politician", (3) "Therefore, we cannot trust this man" (ibid.). Bogost equates the starting position in a game, the player's struggle to beat it and the goal with the major and minor premise and the conclusion of a syllogism (the result is a concept that resembles the so-called practical syllogism, discussed in Aristotle's *Nikomachean Ethics* [Poser 2006, 53]).

However, his understanding of an enthymeme differs from the one Aristotle had. The original enthymeme simply describes a kind of reasoning that is based on probable and familiar premises, not analytic truths – in contrast to logic and dialectic (Ueding/Steinbrink 1994, 226). According to Roland Barthes (1994), the elliptic enthymeme, which Bogost refers to, developed much later in antiquity. At this point in time, rhetoric was already highly formalised as part of the educational system – and it is exactly this formalisation that makes the procedural enthymeme possible in the first place. As it is formally defined, it could be identified in nearly every game, regardless of its content. Doesn't even *Tetris* (Pajitnov 1984) contain a procedural enthymeme, persuading the player to staple blocks in a way defined by rules? As valuable as it is, it therefore doesn't answer the question, why the player should understand any procedural representation as referring to something real and making a plausible claim about it. The emphasis in the Aristotelian enthymeme, on the other hand, is not on how to trick the listener via an omitted premise, but on how to make an argument seem probable and plausible – and this is a task that can't be formalised as easily.

Therefore, while the procedural approach is generally convincing, a too strong focus on the systemic nature of games might result in the danger of overlooking other aspects, which are just as crucial. Very obviously, the level of visual representation is the one that motivates the player to draw references from in-game experiences to concepts of reality. As rules are formal, and often hidden from the player, they can't motivate a reference by themselves. The visualisation in the graphical interface, however, can perform this task: the game has to show what it is about. However, this is not such a trivial task, as it may seem. A closer look at one of the games, Bogost uses as examples, highlights a complex strategy of visualisation that motivates a very specific understanding by the player: *McDonald's Video Game* (Molleindustria 2006) asks the player through the structure of its rules to realise the fast-food industry as inherently destructive – it effectively performs a procedural enthymeme. What makes the game such a great satire, however, are not only its rules, but also its cartoonish visualisations that make the game appear cute, harmless and – in regard to the actions represented – extremely cynical. In other words: The game shows its irony through the very way it represents itself. The notion of 'irony' is fitting, as – according to Culler (2000, 73f.) – it is characterised by an obvious contradiction between two parts. Here, the cute visualisations stand in glaring contrast to the tasks the player has to perform and the goals he or she has to reach. Furthermore, the *McDonald's Video Game* contains quite a lot of textual background information and even a "Why this game?" section, where the documentary *Super Size Me* (Spurlock 2004) and books like Naomie Klein's *No Logo* (2002) are suggested for reading. These references can be understood as grounds or evidences that back up the game's implicit argumentation (Kopperschmidt 2005; Toulmin 2007). The game strives for plausibility. This observation highlights an important feature of any argumentation that is not prominently reflected in Bogost's writing: An argumentation consists not only of a claim, but at least of another proposition that backs it up. It is a chain of propositions, supporting each other in the attempt to create validity. Bogost clearly demonstrates how a game can make a claim through the structure of its possibility space. But this perspective has to be supplemented by a careful consideration of the way the graphical interface motivates real-world-references and modes of understanding (irony) and by an analysis of the whole argumentation of a game understood as chain of propositions (Schrape 2012).

Most important, however, is another blind in procedural rhetorics: the overlook of the game space as a rhetorical function. As simulations, games contain models. A quick glance on architecture shows that a model can be spatial – not only in the metaphorical sense of the possibility space, but as actual space of movement. Following Bogost and Frasca, such spatial models necessarily have to be subjective and ideological. But how can a spatial model be analysed from a rhetorical perspective?

Compared to other forms of texts, spatiality is quite a unique property of videogames – and a baffling feature. This becomes evident in the fact that Juul (2005a, 188-189) describes it as an exceptional and special case within his theory of videogames: "*Space* is a special issue between rules and fiction. [...] [L]evel design, space, and the shape of game objects refer simultaneously to rules and fiction. This is a case in which rules and fiction *do* overlap." For this very reason, game space is of extreme importance for any rhetorical analysis. Following Bogost and Juul, it could be assumed that within game space, procedural, visual and textual rhetoric merge into one.

Further, from a methodological point of view, game space seems to be a perfect object for analysis, as its basic structure quite often is fixed: the player can move through it, but not change fundamentally. This offers great opportunities for analysis as it qualifies the game space for the application of the hermeneutic circle; it can be repeatedly observed and analysed – but how?

Lotman's Spatial Semantics as Method to Analyse Game Space

One promising framework for the analysis of spatial rhetoric in videogames are the Spatial Semantics by Yuri M. Lotman. Surprisingly, the Estonian semiotician has not come up as a reference point in Game Studies yet. Lotman developed a unique take on narratology and rhetoric – one that doesn't solely focus on sequences in time as organising principle of narrative, but also on structures in space. As many games are fundamentally spatial, this recommends Lotman as starting point for their rhetorical investigation.

Yuri M. Lotman founded the so-called Tartu-Moscow Semiotics School, gathering renowned theoreticians of his time and developing collectively a theoretical framework for the semiotics of culture. Relatively independent from French and American semiotics, this school melted sign theory with cybernetics, information theory and formalism (Eimermacher 1986). The two works, which are most relevant in the context of spatial rhetoric, are *Universe of Mind*, where Lotman developed a semiotic theory of culture, and *The Structure of the Artistic Text*, where he explained his spatial take on literary analysis.

For Game Studies, Lotman is not only of interest because he developed a spatial narratology, but also because of his theory of play. Similar to Gadamer (1989), he developed his concept of art out of a discussion of play. According to Lotman (1977, 61) in play as well as in art, two modes of behaviour are at work: a practical and a fictional. Artists, readers and spectators would perform a similar "synthesis of practical and conventional" (ibid. 65) – fictional – behaviour. They all would know that games and artworks are not real, but nevertheless treat them as such to a certain degree. Play, on the other hand, would be characterised by the attributes of fictionality, safety, controllability, the existence of mental models, the possibility to try out (to simulate) and its tendency to conditionate. A comparison with concepts of 'play' by Caillois (2001) and Huizinga (1955) cannot be done in this article, but the parallels are obvious.

Of greatest interest is Lotmans emphasis on models: For him, an artwork would not simply depict or describe an aspect of reality, but model it. He understood modelling as a process of translation, where something is reformulated according to an artwork's or an artform's inherent (semiotic) rules – its specific system of denotates (Lotman 1977, 46). For him, the singular artwork is a model, built within conventions of art form, style and genre – the model building system. The *primary model building system* of our culture would be common language; every art form would be *a secondary model building system*, based on already coded material. Lotmans considerations apply perfectly to games, if they are understood as simulations. Their models are built out of algorithmic as well as semiotic rules, depending on technical restrictions and the conventions of game and interface design – the secondary model building system of the videogames. Moreover, what a game models is already pre-coded, already understood as something and conceptualised within language. From this perspective it therefore proves to be imprecise to say that a simulation is "a representation of a source system via a less complex system" – it more correctly should be described as a secondary computational model (run through time), built within given technical conditions and conventions, which represents pre-existing, culturally coded models of some entity. The important point here is not Lotman's conviction that verbal language should be the primary model building system, but that any representation must be a secondary model, derived from an already existing mental model that is depending on culture. To put it another way: Models (and simulations) do not simply represent reality, but models of this very reality that never can be grasped in objective totality – models model models.

Considering that play is Lotman's starting point in developing a theory of narrativity and culture, it isn't surprising that it fits well to the analysis of games. Not only in his take on narratology, but also in his cultural theory where Lotman focuses on spatiality. Essential for his thinking is the notion of boundaries, which would shape cultures and worldviews: Lotman (1990, 123) envisioned any culture to be imbedded in a uniquely structured semiotic universe, consisting of various languages (or codes) interacting and relating to each other – the *semiosphere*. The semiosphere of any culture would have a boundary, which would mark a distinction to another culture, but would also be a place for translation between them. In itself the semiosphere would be divided by countless sub-boundaries, marking differing sub-cultures within. These boundaries would always be moving and could take on various forms, but their basic function would stay persistent and be universal:

> Every culture begins by dividing the world into 'its own' internal space and 'their' external space. How this binary division is interpreted depends on the typology of the culture. But the actual division is one of the human cultural universals. The boundary may separate the living from the dead, settled people from nomadic ones, the town from the plains; it may be a state frontier, or a social, national, confessional, or any other kind of frontier (Lotman 1990, 131).

Obviously, Lotmans notion of boundaries is not limited to geographical space. But if inscribed into real space, they would foreground the ideological, religious or cosmological structure of a culture's semiosphere:

> When a semiosphere involves real territorial features [...], the boundary is spatial in the literal sense. The isomorphism between different kinds of human settlement [...] and ideas about the structure of the cosmos has often been remarked on. Hence the appeal of the centre for the most important cultic and administrative buildings. Less valued social groups are settled on the periphery. Those who are below any social value are settled on the frontier of the outskirts [...], by the city gate, in the suburbs. [...] However, some elements are always set outside. If the inner world reproduces the cosmos, then what is on the other side represents chaos, the anti-world, unstructured chthonic space, inhabited by monsters, infernal powers or people associated with them (ibid., 140).

What is striking about Lotmans descriptions of boundaries is that immediately pictures of the fictional worlds of videogames come to mind, especially role-playing-games with complex settings like *Dragon Age: Origins* (BioWare 2009) or *World of Warcraft* (Blizzard Entertainment 2004). These worlds are full of boundaries in the aforementioned sense: Boundaries between safe cities and the dangerous wilderness, between the overworld and the dungeon, between the territory of the Alliance and the Horde etc. Ljungström (2005) accomplished a detailed analysis of the spatial structures in *World of Warcraft*. In recourse to the seminal architectural work *A Pattern Language* by Christopher Alexander (1977), he described, among other things, how the fictional world of Azeroth is divided into opposing fields and how the major cities Orgrimmar and Ironforge are structured into several zones with clear identity, separated from each other by boundaries with just a few entry points. But boundaries can also exist in time, according to Lotman (1990, 140): "'Normal' space has not only geographical but also temporal boundaries. Nocturnal time lies beyond the boundary". A game like *Minecraft* (Mojang 2009) is evidently structured around the fundamental boundary between day- and night-time.

Not only whole semiospheres, but also fictional universes that model them can be described as compositions of boundaries. For Lotman, the relations between these boundaries form the potential for *events* – which, in their specific sequence, build the *sujet* or plot of a narrative. An event, on the other hand, would be constituted by the crossing of a boundary within the fictional universe (Lotman 1977, 233). Typically, such a fictional universe would be divided into opposing *semantic fields*. An example: the semantic fields of a basic vampire story are the world of the living and the world of the dead. The crossing of the boundary between these fields constitutes an event. Interestingly, this crossing can be performed in two directions within the same fictional universe: the living can venture into the world of the dead and the dead into the world of the living. As it becomes obvious, the spatial relations within the very same semantic fields hold the potential for different series of events – which in turn combine to diverse sujets.

According to Lotman, two types of characters can be distinguished in narratives: (1) mobile ones, who can move through the fictional universe and across its boundaries and (2) immobile ones, who he describes as "functions of that space" (Lotman 1990, 157). The hero of a story, of cause, is always a mobile character:

> A hero [...] can act that is, can cross the boundaries of prohibition in a way that others cannot. Like Orpheus or Soslan from the epic of the Narts, he can cross the boundary separating the living from the dead, or like the Benandanti he can wage nocturnal war with witches, or like one berserk he can fling himself into battle, defying all rules. [...] He may be a noble robber or a picaro, a sorcerer, spy, detective, terrorist or superman – the point is that he is able to do what others cannot, namely to cross the structural boundaries of cultural space. Each such infringement is a deed, and the chain of deeds forms what we call plot (ibid., 151).

This description is not only perfectly fitting for most narratives, but also for many videogames. Here, the player takes on the role of the hero, the mobile character, while the non-player-characters (NPCs) are immobile in most cases. If a NPC stands in front of a shop, just waiting for the player to come along and to trigger a dialogue, if a wolf is striving back and forth in the forest, following a prescribed movement-pattern, until the player reaches a defined attack-range, then such NPCs can be considered as functions of the game space in quite literal sense.

In games, to cross a boundary can mean to enter a dungeon or a city, to travel from one map to the next – or even to steal a car in front of the police (triggering a specific element of gameplay, namely a car chase). Boundaries come along with obstacles, which can't be overcome by anyone except the hero (the wolf has to be killed, the door to be lock-picked, the dragon to be defeated). This concept reminds of Aarseths (1997, 90ff. and 1999) master tropes of the cybertext: the *aporia* and the *epiphany*, the hopelessness in face of an obstacle, and the revelation through its overcoming.

What Lotmans spatial approach to narratives allows, is to separate the fictional world of a story from its actual plot – and to analyse its spatial structure as a generator for a variety of different plots. This spatial view on narratives fits far better to games, then a temporal one: Juul's (2005b) objections against the latter one do simply not relate to Lotman. He probably would assert that videogames often contain highly structured fictional universes and put the player in the position of a mobile character (the hero), but that it is the player him- or herself, who performs the deeds and triggers events while crossing the boundaries, constituting a new and different plot in every playthrough. How well this approach fits becomes evident, when Lotman (1977, 241) even considers the possible failing of the hero, in his words: "drops out of the game.'

Nevertheless, it is important to consider the specifics of videogames' fictional universes: even in their simplest form, they tend to possess boundaries – but often in a different way then in other media. In *Space Invaders* (Taito 1978), for example, the whole dynamic is driven by the player's struggle to keep the hostile alien forces from crossing a boundary – namely the bottom line of the screen. According to Lotman, its transgression would mark the only real event in play, signalled by the game-over screen. In many such early arcade games, the hero is a hopeless defender – and the narrative therefore cannot move forward, but is trapped within a potentially infinite delay of its own end. In other games, the structures of levels, sublevels and areas can be conceived as semantic fields, separated through boundaries associated with obstacles, which the player tries to overcome. In *Super Mario Bros.* (Nintendo 1985), 32 levels, grouped in eight supra-levels (worlds) with four sub-levels (stages) each, structure the fictional universe of the Mushroom Kingdom. Every level can be understood as arrangement of obstacles, which the player has to overcome in order to cross the boundary to the next one. Two observations become obvious: First that the fictional world of *Super Mario Bros.* is actually highly repetitive – it isn't structured in just two distinct semantic fields (as in the Dracula example), but every field is divided into various sub-fields that mostly differ in details and degrees. These sub-fields with their own boundaries and obstacles protract the transgression of the fundamental boundary – in this case: the entry into Bowsers Castle in the last stage of the final world. The spatial structure of the Mushroom Kingdoom is not built for the performance of a dynamic and dramatic narrative, but for the very delay of it. The same is true for *Castlevania* (Konami 1986), demonstrating that the fictional worlds of vampire stories too bend to the *secondary model building system* of the videogame. It nevertheless is important to point out that even in these early games, the dichotomy between semantic fields persists, even if it is discretised in a number of gradual varying sub-fields in order to prolong play. This leads to the second observation: Play doesn't happen in the moment of transgression of the boundary, but before – and potentially indefinitely so.

Even if there are important differences in the way videogames and traditional narratives are spatially structured, Lotman's spatial semantics can be a valuable method of analysis. Martinez and Scheffel (1999, 140f) summarised and operationalised Lotman's approach. They distinguish three dimensions of semantic fields: (1) the topology, (2) the semantics and (3) the topography. The topological level encompasses fundamental spatial relations ('up' vs. 'down'). The semantical level covers evaluations and connotations ('good' vs. 'evil'). The topographical level contains explicit denotations ('heaven' vs. 'hell'). In a semantic field, all three dimensions converge into one – but they can be separated for analytic purposes, in order to highlight the ideological structure of some fictional universe. A glance at espionage thrillers of the cold war era hints, how topological structures ('West' vs. 'East'), evaluative semantics ('Good' vs. 'Evil' – or vice versa) and topographical denotations (USA vs. USSR) can contain ideologies. In the analysis of game spaces, however, it is not so easy to distinguish all three levels, as the ones of topography and semantics tend to merge together in just one visual, whose evaluating and denoting dimensions often can't be completely separated.

In the following, Lotman's spatial semantics will be put to use in the exemplary analysis of just one game in order to highlight its analytic potentials: *Global Conflicts: Palestine* (Serious Games Interactive 2007). The game is a perfect example and proving ground for the method, as it possesses a quite simple and very clearly structured game space and refers to a real geopolitical region. The general applicability of the method will be discussed afterwards in the conclusion.

Exemplary Analysis: 'Global Conflicts: Palestine'

Serious Games Interactive's *Global Conflicts: Palestine* is a game with clear pedagogical intend (one of the game's developers, Simon Egenfeldt-Nielsen [2007], is a leading researcher regarding the educational and pedagogical potential of computer games [Egenfeldt-Nielsen et al. 2008]) The developers openly state their intentions in the manual: to give the player insight in the complexity of the Israeli-Palestinian conflict, tell the stories of its participants and most importantly not to take sides. In short: The game's intention is to abolish the prejudices of the player.

He or she takes on the role of a journalist, investigating the conflict. The game is structured in six episodes, dealing with topics like the clash between Jewish settlers and Palestinians in rural areas, the influence of checkpoints and security measures on the daily life of residents, the motivation of suicide bombers etc. Each episode consists of two phases of play (fig. 1). In the first phase, after selecting a newspaper to write for, the task is to interview characters, strategically select dialogue options and choose quotes. In the second phase, articles must be built out of these quotes. Strategic reasoning is necessary, as the player's articles reflect political opinions and influence two scores: an Israeli and a Palestinian one. These scores have impact on the behaviour of characters, therefore taking sides changes what happens next. What follows is a non-playable phase in which the article gets evaluated, before an eyewitness report is quoted that relates to the episode's topic. The main part of the game, however, is the first phase, which can be differentiated in two modes. In the first one, the player has to move the avatar through the game space to meet up interviewees. In the second mode, choices have to be made in dialogue menus, presented in cinematic style.

Fig. 1: The structure of an episode

Playable Phase	Phase I: Research	1. Mode: Navigation	• Decision about newspaper • Navigation through game space • Dialogue, gathering quotes
		2. Mode: Dialogue	• Side quests
	Phase II: Writing		• Strategic selection of quotes
Non-Playable Phase	Evaluation		• Feedback about success and consequences
	Eyewitness report		• Thematically relating to the episode

Many critical decisions take place in the second game mode, which, together with the non-playable phase, will be neglected in this article. Instead, it will focus on the importance of space in the first mode.

In *Global Conflicts: Palestine*, the game space contributes to a fictional universe that can be analysed with Lotman's spatial semantics. The significance of this approach is immediately evident if one takes a look at the game's map (fig. 2). It allows the player to orient him- or herself by a secondary view from the bird's eye perspective (Günzel 2008b). Like in many strategy and role-playing games, in this view, the game space is abstracted to an information field, empty, deterritorialised and reduced to its formal function (Wiemer 2008). It's the perfect starting point for the examination of fundamental topological structures.

Fig. 2: The map

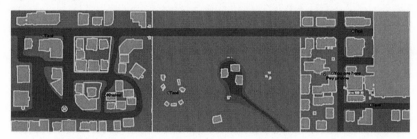

The game space is separated in three fields: two opposing ones and an interspace. By cartographic conventions, the left and the right ones can be recognised as cities, linked by a street. The middle field can be split up further, as there are two gatherings of buildings on the left and in the middle. The isolated buildings at the bottom and the right shall be ignored to simplify matters. Obviously, the game space is structured by a left vs. right opposition, which is mirrored in the middle-field. The condensed topology and the maze-like patterns in the cities are thereby typical for game spaces. The topological structure of the game space can be visualised as thus (fig. 3):

Fig. 3: Topological structure of the game space

	(Channel)		
Field A	*junction*	*junction*	Field B
	Field C	Field D	

The *primary* view of the game space is its three-dimensional presentation – it is the place, where the actual movement takes place (Günzel 2008b). Through this view, the game's topography can be examined. The city in field A reveals itself to be dominated by concrete buildings, speckled by small shops with sings in Arabic and cheap looking display windows (fig. 4a). There are dozens of waste containers (fig. 4b), some market stands and a few basic playgrounds. Many pedestrians look stereotypical Arab: women wear headscarfs, men white robes. Ambulances bear the sign of the Red Crescent, the Arabic pendant to the Red Cross. All these elements are more than simple detonates, as they also evoke connotations of poverty connected to Arabs.

Fig. 4a-b: Topographical details in field A

Dozens of graffiti charge the topography with political references. One picture, for example, shows a child, being under fire by guns (fig. 5). The ambiguity of the picture is reduced by an *anchorage* through strongly encoded signs (Barthes 1978): the Palestinian flag, carried by the child, and the Star of David, painted on the guns. As a visual metonymy, the graffiti indirectly denotes Palestinians and the Israeli army, while connoting helplessness and aggression. As a whole it evokes an antithesis between the ethnic groups.

Fig. 5: A graffiti on the wall

The majority of the graffiti, however, consist of writing, some in Arabic, but most in Latin scripture. They refer to the Israeli-Palestinian conflict and inscribe the Palestinian's rage within the topography. The antithesis *us vs. them* reoccurs in variations. The relationship between the own group and the other is summed up in the phrase: "Israeli killing us?!!?" The Israelis are presented as aggressors and killers, capable even to child murder ("Where is our children"), while the Palestinians are associated with positive attributes, like the will to freedom ("give me liberty [...]"), willingness to make sacrifices ("or give me death"), conviction and resistance. Regarding their rhetorical function, the graffiti disambiguate the meaning of field A, which now can be identified as a Palestinian city or town. As details, they also evoke an *effect of reality* (Barthes 1989). Most importantly, however, they model the Palestinian perspective on the conflict.

Field B stands in total opposition to field A. It is also a city, but the buildings are ancient and ornated. There are no garbage containers, but clean playgrounds and shops with well-tended showcases (fig. 6a). Lots of trees line the streets, a huge market place dominates the city scape. Magnificent buildings stand on proper squares and at some of the corners soldiers are watching out. In the middle, a huge church can be found (see fig. 6b) and at the right brim a gigantic wall, in front of which men in Jewish orthodox dress are praying. Many of the pedestrians wear the kippah. There are no graffiti in this field.

Fig. 6a-b: Details in field B

The details in the topography of both fields motivate a specific understanding: as Palestinian town and as Jerusalem. The game thereby alludes to visual stereotypes to guide the player's understanding. (In the sense of Putnam [1975] stereotypes do not necessarily imply prejudices. As mental concepts with reduced complexity, they enable understanding in the first place.) Field B is disambiguated by famous historical sights, like the Western Wall or the Church of the Holy Sepulchre. Most players will understand it to be Jerusalem. This is remarkable, as its structure does not resemble the real one in any way. While Jerusalem is a big city, field B only consists of 22 buildings – thus equating it in size with the Palestinian town. It is a model, built within the convention of a highly condensed game space. The model works like a synecdoche, as it evokes the idea of a whole (Jerusalem) by the showing of familiar parts (the Western Wall). It's the fundamental rhetorical pattern: control of understanding by recourse to the familiar.

The details also motivate evaluations: The trash, the sparse display windows and the simple concrete buildings connote poverty, while the lush display windows, the ornamental buildings, the trees and the huge market connote wealth. Further, the graffiti connote anger and despair, while the soldiers and military vehicles trigger associations of power.

Verbal texts during the game affirm that field B is Jerusalem while field A is named Abu Diz – actually a small town within the Palestinian territory, which boarders Jerusalem. Moreover, field C is discovered to be a Palestinian village and field D to be an Israeli settlement. Both are mirroring detailings of A and B: While the village is presented as poor with simple buildings and lots of trash containers (fig. 7a), field D reveals to be a clean and tidy settlement behind barbed wire (fig. 7b).

Fig. 7a-b: Details in field C and field D

The semantic fields, therefore, are structured as a doubled opposition between Israelis and Palestinians. The antithesis A-B is repeated in C-D. This pattern can be described as spatial parallelism. As a whole, the game space constitutes a model of the conflict's region, in which Israelis and Palestinians are strictly opposed (fig. 8).

Fig. 8: The spatial parallelism

	(Channel)		
Field A			Field B
	Field C	Field D	
Poverty	Poverty	Wealth	Wealth
Anger	Anger	Power	Power
Palestinian	Palestinian	Israeli	Israeli

A single street, however, links field A and B, leading to checkpoints. Here, the movement of the player is channelled through junctions. With Ljungström (2005) and in recourse to Alexander (1977, 549 and 277) these junctions can be understood as gateways, enforcing an 'entrance transition' and thus enabling the player to recognize that he or she moves to a different area. The checkpoints have to be passed several times during play. This enforced repetition can be described as *spatial amplification*, as it accentuates the checkpoints relevance. Topographically, soldiers and watchtowers characterise the junctions, denoting the military while connoting power. Before the checkpoint of Jerusalem, there is a long queue of Arabs. This implies, that Palestinians want or need to get into Jerusalem and cannot pass freely (fig. 9a-b).

Fig. 9a-b: The checkpoints

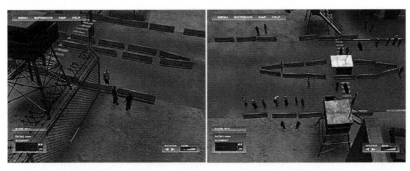

The checkpoints mark an obstacle, whose overcoming should constitute an event. It's impossible for the waiting Palestinians to cross the boundary, so their impermeability is hinted. Strangely though, the boundary is no real obstacle for the player. When arriving, sometimes a dialogue situation is triggered: A soldier asks for the player's papers, whereupon he or she can comply or ask for the reason. In the latter case, the soldier gives an explanation, but in the end the player has no alternative as to hand over the press card – whereupon he or she is allowed to pass.

What is the function of this reoccurring intermezzo? Why should an obstacle be established only to be solved automatically? Why an aporia is hinted, but abolished so quickly that an epiphany can't arise? Whatever the deficit in game design might be, the rhetorical function is evident: The short scene works as an *example*, the inductive counterpart to the enthymeme (Bogost 2007, 18). It illustrates the situation of the people in this region. It refers to a general template, but actualises it in an atypical way. To be able to cross the boundary as journalist is marked as exception. Therefore, the repeated scene motivates a reasoning: "If I can pass the checkpoint because I' m a journalist, people who aren't can't." The impermeability of the boundary paradoxically gains evidence because it doesn't count for the player. While the player's journalist can move between the semantic fields, the other characters are bound to just one. This fact is the motivation for many quests during the game.

What is the rhetorical function of the game space? First, it's a potential for events, to be actualised during play. Second it constitutes a model of a real geopolitical situation and therefore motivates the player to relate his or her experiences to reality. It is, however, a highly selective condensation of geopolitics from a very specific perspective. In a way it 'describes' the geopolitics to create the basis for further argumentation. Every argumentation presupposes such a description of its topic and, as any description is bound to a contingent perspective, this already implies presuppositions (Kopperschmidt 2005, 66). Knape (2000, 121) calls this a thematic instruction and describes it as fundamental part of any rhetorical text. In classical theory it equals the *narratio*, the telling of the cause, as foundation for the *argumentatio*, the strategic persuasion. The spatial model fulfils this very function, as it 'describes' the Israeli-Palestinian conflict as antithesis between homogeneous groups.

Moreover, this dichotomy is mirrored in the scores that are presented on the screen and in front of the game space – they belong to what Galloway (2012, 39ff.) calls the *intraface*, an interface within the interface. An Israeli and a Palestinian score measure the relationship of the player to these groups. If he or she helps them through various tasks or if he or she writes benevolent articles, the scores raise – influencing the reactions of the dialogue-partners during the rest of the game. If, for example, the player attains a high Israeli-score, characters, who are affiliated with Israel will react friendlier, opening up more dialogue options and vice versa. The scores model the conflict as antithetical opposition between two homogenous groups – and the player has to orient his or her actions towards this score in order to play successfully. The game thereby constructs a dilemma: there seems to be no other choice than to choose allegiance. Both, the model of the conflict in the game space and in the scores are antithetical – this mirrored and doubled structure can be described as a *transdiegetic parallelism* (Schrape 2012, 205 and 331).

Up until now, the representation of the Israeli-Palestinian conflict in *Global Conflicts: Palestine* seems to be simplified in an extreme way. With Lotman, one could say that the modelling of the geopolitics and cultural conflicts happened in accordance with the conventions and necessities of the secondary model building system of the videogame: The opposition of just two factions forces the player to make hard decisions, while the coupling of the factions to clearly defined places in game space allows for effective orientation. If the game would try to model the real complexity of the conflict, with dozens if not hundreds of factions and sub-factions, and a realistic geopolitical model, in which the Palestinian areas are so much intersected with Israeli settlements that they resemble a Swiss cheese, the player could be confused. Nevertheless, up to this point, the troubling fact remains that despite the good intentions of the designers, the modelling of the conflict in game space and game mechanics results in a distorted representation, reduced to a binary opposition between two homogenous groups.

The story, however, doesn't end here. The binary opposition is just the basis for further argumentation. During the game, the player gets to know a diverse set of figures: a young Israeli soldier who wants to be an artist, a veteran who longs for peace, his wife who is a human rights activist, an ambitious soldier who justifies all means for security, a hateful Palestinian who despises the Israelis, a grumpy old Arab who disapproves of violence, a young Arab boy who loses himself in fantasies about martyrdom, etc. The ensemble of characters covers the whole spectrum of political positions. The player has to discover that there are fanatics on both sides. He or she will learn about the demoralising effect of constant threat on Israeli families, but also about the frustration, poverty and misery of the Palestinians in the occupied territories. Hamas activists will explain their motives to him or her as well as the Jewish settlers. Most importantly, he or she will learn about the longing for peace on both sides. In the end, the player won't be able to stop a Palestinian boy from throwing away his life and thereby experience the destructive power of fanaticism first hand. The simple antithesis between Israelis and Palestinians does not hold water throughout the game, as the player is cued to deconstruct it. The rhetorical strategy of *Global Conflicts: Palestine* therefore encompasses two steps: First, the game affirms the player's likely prejudices and reduces the complexity of its topic to a simple antithesis. Then, it guides the player to question this very antithesis. The spatial rhetoric of the game therefore builds the necessary foundation for its more differentiated narrative rhetoric. In the terms of Chaim Perelman (1990, 127ff.) the latter one performs an *argument of dissociation*, the splitting of concepts, believed to be self-evident.

Finally, the game concludes its argumentation through back-ups of its authenticity: After every episode, a thematically related eyewitness-report scrolls through the screen. The fourth episode, for example, is concerned with the motivations of the Palestinian suicide bombers. At one point, the player meets a boy who religiously justifies the acts. After finishing the episode, the player is confronted with an eyewitness-report making exactly the same claims – even up to the very phrasing. The authenticity of this report, again, is backed up by a reference (which can be looked up in the web). *Global Conflicts: Palestine* presents itself as well-researched, realistic and authentic. It thereby asks the players to relate their in-game experiences to their understanding of reality – and thus aims to motivate a transfer between the world of the game and the world outside of it.

Conclusion

Global Conflicts: Palestine is not the singular example for a rhetorical function of game space. Many games with elaborated game-worlds come to mind. One good example would be *Dragon Age: Origins*, which, with the mythical country of Ferelden, presents a highly structured fictional universe, where it is the main task of the player to cross boundaries between different semantic fields. On a fundamental level, the universe is divided between an upper part, populated by humans, elves and others, and an underworld, where demons live (the darkspawn), while the caves of the dwarves function as a kind of interface between those fields. The plot-development is driven by the transgression of the boundary by the demons, which invade the upper world. The task of the player is, of cause, to stop the demons. In order to do so, he or she also has to venture into the underworld, thus transgressing the boundary in opposite direction. On a macro-level, the movement between those fields drives the plot of *Dragon Age: Origins*. What makes the game interesting however, are the various sub-fields within the world. Ferelden is full of boundaries, the player has to cross – and many mark highly political oppositions. The realm of the dwarves (the city of Orzammar), for example, is divided into an upper and a lower part (dust town). In the first one, live the respected members of society, in the last one the castles. Below dust town are the 'deep roads' – abandoned, dangerous tunnels and caverns, where the demons live. The player, of cause, has the ability to transgress the boundaries – if he or she is able to overcome the various obstacles (an attack by rouges, when first entering dust town). To cross those boundaries does not only move the plot forward, but is also understood by various NPCs as a political act (no respected dwarf enters dust town).

Another example would be the city of Denerim, in which the opposition between Israeli and Palestinian territories, described above, is nearly mirrored. Here, however, it is one between Humans and Elves. The latter ones live in a ghetto within the city as marginalised group, while the rest belongs to humans. Like the game space in *Global Conflicts: Palestine*, Denerim is structured by an antithetical topology, merged with a highly evaluative topographical representation, in which the poor, helpless and disadvantaged are contrasted with the rich and powerful. A detailed analysis of *Dragon Age's* spatial rhetoric can't be accomplished in this article, but it surely would unravel a complex fictional universe, structured by oppositions between countless sub-factions, resulting in a complex arrangement of boundaries and therefore a great potential for events and plot-development.

But spatial semantics can also be put to use in games, which at first glance do not have a complex game-world to explore. Gonzalo Frasca's famous satirical experiment *September 12th* (Newsgaming 2003) is a good example. Here, the player can shoot missiles from a god's eye perspective at terrorists in an Afghan city (see fig. 10). The obstacle being that it's nearly impossible not to hit civilians by accident, which causes witnesses to transform into terrorists. In his discussion of the game Bogost (2007, 86f.) points out that it conveys a simple but powerful message by its rule-structure: the war on terror is the cause of terror – and the player learns this the hard way through a rhetoric of failure.

Spatial semantics, however, allows for further analysis: In *September 12th*, the movement of all characters are regulated by a grid-like spatial structure, which ensures their evenly allocation. This is of the utmost importance for the game's rhetoric, as agglomerations of civilians or terrorists could enable the player to hit just one of the groups. The player's actions, on the other hand, are not affected by this horizontal topology, as missiles can be shot on any location. Therefore, there also exists a vertical topology, separating two semantic fields: the invisible player's field of omnipotence and the visible characters' field of regulated movement. The launch of a missile can be understood as a crossing of the boundary between those fields and therefore as an event. A missile's hit causes a building to crumble, but only on a topographical level, as the ruin still channels the characters' move-ments – the game space's topology stays fixed.

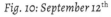

Fig. 10: September 12th

The topographical presentation contributes to the game's rhetoric, as it motivates references to reality. Like in *Global Conflicts: Palestine*, visual stereotypes enable the understanding of the semantic field as Afghan city: women wear blue bur-qas, terrorists white headscarfs, while simple rectangular buildings, palm trees, market-stands and a sandy colour scheme evoke familiar images of Afghanistan. As the characters within the city can only react to the player's actions by dying or turning into terrorists (that are no threat to the player), this semantic field is connoted with passiveness and weakness. The invisible player's field, on the other hand, is associated with power. Its nature remains strangely unclear, as the only signs motivating any reference are the militaristic cross-hairs on the screen. The game's title, however, suggests that it represents the West or the US military in reaction to 9/11.

All in all, the game space constitutes an antithetical model of the geopolitics of the so-called war against terror, in which Afghans are mere objects to play with for a nearly omnipotent West. In this reading, *September 12th* is not only a critique of the assumptions behind the war on terror, but also a model of power relations that actually reaffirms Western feelings of supremacy. During play, this impression is challenged to some degree, as military force turns out to be contra-productive – but the asymmetry of the model is untouched by this experience.

As it becomes clear, the use of space is just one part of a game's rhetoric – alas a crucial one. This is not surprising, as games are complex hybrids between dif-ferent medial forms and their rhetoric therefore grounds on all of them at the same time. The rhetoric of game space shouldn't be analysed independently from the rules, the narrative, the visualisations or non-interactive elements (like cutscenes). There is no necessary contradiction between a procedural, a narratological, a spatial or a visual take on a game's rhetoric. All these perspectives have to be considered, as they are relating to different aspects of the videogames. In their multifaceted wholeness, videogames prove to be wonderfully rich objects of analysis and rhetorical potential.

References

Aarseth, Espen J. (1997): *Cybertext: Perspectives on Ergodic Literature*, Baltimore, MD: Johns Hopkins UP.

—— (1999): Aporia and Epiphany in *Doom* and *The Speaking Clock*: The Temporality of Ergodic Art, in: *Cyberspace Textuality. Computer Technology and Literary Theory*, ed. by Marie-Laure Ryan, Bloomington, ID: Indiana UP, 31-41.

Alexander, Christopher (1977): *A Pattern Language: Towns, Buildings, Construction*, New York, NY: Oxford UP.

Aristotle (1991): *The Art of Rhetoric*, London/New York, NY: Penguin Books.

—— (2004): *Nikomachean Ethics*, London/New York, NY: Penguin Books.

Barthes, Roland (1978): Rhetoric of the Image, in: id.: *Image Music Text*, New York, NY: Hill&Wang, 32-51 [1964].

—— (1989): The Reality Effect, in: id.: *The Rustle of Language*, Berkley, CA: University of California Press, 141-148 [1968].

—— (1994): The Old Rhetoric. An aide-mémoire, in: id.: *The Semiotic Challenge*, Berkley, CA: University of California Press, 11-94 [1970].

BioWare (2009) *Dragon Age: Origins*, PC: Electronic Arts.

Blizzard Entertainment (2004): *World of Warcraft*, PC: Vivendi.

Bogost, Ian (2006): *Unit Operations*, Cambridge, MA/London: MIT Press.

—— (2007): *Persuasive Games: The Expressive Power of Videogames*, Cambridge, MA/London: MIT Press.

—— (2008): The Rhetoric of Video Games, in: *The Ecology of Games: Connecting Youth, Games, and Learning*, ed. by Katie Salen, Cambridge, MA: MIT Press, 117-140.

—— (2009): Videogames Are a Mess: Keynote presented at Digital Games Research Association Conference at Uxbridge, UK, September 1, 2009, bogost.com/writing/videogames_are_a_mess.shtml.

Buchanan, Richard (1985): Declaration by Design. Rhetoric, Argument, and Demonstration in Design Practice, in: *Design Issues* 2/1, 4-22.

Caillois, Roger (2001): *Man, Play, and Games*, Urbana, IL: University of Illinois Press [1961].

Crawford, Chris (1984): *The Art of Computer Game Design: Reflections of a Master Game Designer*, Berkeley, CA: Osborne/McGraw-Hill.

Culler, Jonathan (2000): *Literary Theory: A very short Introduction*, New York, NY: Oxford UP.

Dilthey, Wilhelm (2003): The Development of Hermeneutics, in: *Philosophies of Social Science: The Classic and Contemporary Readings*, ed. by Gerard Delanty and Piet Strydom, Maidenhead/Philadelphia, PA: Open University, 99-101 [1900].

Eco, Umberto (1979): ,Lector in fabula:' Pragmatic Strategy in a Metanarrative Text, in: id.: *The Role of the Reader: Explorations in the Semiotics of Texts*, Bloomington, IN: Indiana UP, 200-260 [1979].

Egenfeldt-Nielsen, Simon (2007): *Educational Potential of Computer Games*, London: Continuum.

Egenfeldt-Nielsen, Simon/Jonas Heide Smith/Susana Pajares Tosca (2008): *Understanding Video Games: The Essential Introduction*, New York, NY: Routledge.

Eimermacher, Karl (1986) [Ed.]: *Semiotica Sovietica 1. Sowjetische Arbeiten der Moskauer und Tartuer Schule zu sekundären modellbildenden Zeichensystemen (1962-1973)*, Aachen: Rader Verlag.

Eskelinen, Markku (2001): The Gaming Situation, in: *Game Studies* 1/1, gamestudies.org/0101/eskelinen.

Flanagan, Mary (2009): *Critical Play: Radical Game Design*, Cambridge, MA/London: MIT Press.

Frasca, Gonzalo (2001): *Video Games of the Oppressed: Videogames as a Means for Critical Thinking and Debate*, Master-Thesis, Georgia Institute of Technology, School of Literature, Communication and Culture, ludology.org/articles/thesis/FrascaThesisVideogames.pdf.

Gadamer, Hans-Georg (²1989): *Truth and Method*, New York, NY: Continuum [1960].

Galloway, Alexander R. (2012): *The Interface Effect*, Cambridge, MA: Polity Press.

Gazzard, Alison (2013): *Mazes in Videogames. Meaning, Metaphor and Design*, Jefferson, NC: McFarland & Co.

Günzel, Stephan (2008a): The Space-Image. Interactivity and Spatiality of Computer Games, in: *Conference Proceedings of the Philosophy of Computer Games 2008*, ed. by id., Michael Liebe and Dieter Mersch, Potsdam: Potsdam UP, 170-188.

–––– (2008b): Raum, Karte und Weg im Computerspiel, in: *Game over! Perspektiven des Computerspiels*, ed. by. Jan Distelmeyer, Christine Hanke and Dieter Mersch, Bielefeld: transcript, 113-132.

–––– (2012): *Egoshooter: Das Raumbild des Computerspiels*, Frankfurt a.M./New York, NY: Campus.

Huizinga, Johan (1955): *Homo Ludens: A Study of the Play-Element in Culture*, Boston, MA: Beacon Press [1939].

Joost, Gesche (2008): *Bild-Sprache: Die audio-visuelle Rhetorik des Films*, Bielefeld: transcript.

Juul, Jesper (2005a): *Half-Real: Video Games between Real Rules and Fictional Worlds*, Cambridge, MA/London: MIT Press.

———— (2005b): Games Telling Stories, in: *Handbook of Computer Game Studies*, ed. by Joost Raessens and Jeffrey H. Goldstein, Cambridge, MA/London: MIT Press, 219-226.

Kaemmerling, Ekkat (1971): Rhetorik als Montage, in: *Semiotik des Films: Mit Analysen kommerzieller Pornos und revolutionärer Agitationsfilme*, ed. by Friedrich Knilli, München: Hanser, 94-109.

Kanzog, Klaus (2001): *Grundkurs Filmrhetorik*, München: Schaudig & Ledig.

Klein, Naomie (2002): *No Logo: Taking Aim at the Brand Bullies*, New York, NY: Picardor.

Klevjer, Rune (2002): In Defense of Cutscenes, in: *Proceedings of Computer Games and Digital Cultures Conference 2001*, ed. by Frans Mäyrä, Tampere: Tampere UP, 191-202.

Knape, Joachim (2000): *Was ist Rhetorik?* Stuttgart: Reclam.

Konami (1986): *Castlevania*, NES: Konami.

Kopperschmidt, Josef (²2005): *Argumentationstheorie zur Einführung*, Hamburg: Junius.

Kücklich, Julian (2006): Literary Theory and Digital Games, in: *Understanding Digital Games*, ed. by Jason Rutter and Jo Bryce, London/Thousand Oaks, CA/New Delhi: Sage, 95-111.

Ljungström, Matthias (2005): The Use of Architectural Patterns in MMORPGs, Paper Presented at the *Aesthetics of Play*-Conference in Bergen, Norway, 14th-15th October, aestheticsofplay.org/ljunstrom.php.

———— (2008): Remarks on Digital Play Spaces, in: *Conference Proceedings of the Philosophy of Computer Games 2008*, ed. by id., Michael Liebe and Dieter Mersch, Potsdam: Potsdam UP, 190-209.

Lotman, Yuri M. (1977): *The Structure of the Artistic Text*, Ann Arbor, MI: University of Michigan [1972].

———— (1990): *Universe of Mind: A Semiotic Theory of Culture*, Bloomington, IN: Indiana UP.

Manovich, Lev (2001): *The Language of New Media*, Cambridge, MA/London: MIT Press.

Martinez, Matias/Scheffel, Michael (⁶1999): *Einführung in die Erzähltheorie*, München: Beck.

Murray, Janet H. (1997): *Hamlet on the Holodeck: The Future of Narrative in Cyberspace*, New York, NY et al.: Free Press.

Mojang (2009): *Minecraft*, PC: Mojang.

Molleindustria (2006): *McDonald's Video Game*, Browser: Molleindustria.

Newsgaming (2003): *September 12th: A Toy World*, Browser: Newsgaming.

Nintendo (1985): *Super Mario Bros.*, NES: Nintendo.

Nitsche, Michael (2008): *Video Game Spaces: Image, Play, and Structure in 3D Worlds*, Cambridge, MA/London: MIT Press.

Pajitnov, Alexey (1984): *Tetris*, Electronica 60: Pajitnov.

Perelman, Chaim (1990): *The Realm of Rhetoric*, Chicago, IL: University of Notre Dame Press [1977].

————/Olbrechts-Tyteca, Lucie (1991): *The New Rhetoric: A Treatise on Argumentation*, Chicago, IL: University of Notre Dame Press [1958].

Poser, Hans (2006): *Wissenschaftstheorie: Eine philosophische Einführung*, Stuttgart: Reclam [2001].

Putnam, Hilary (1975): The Meaning of 'Meaning, in id.: *Minnesota Studies in the Philosophy of Science, Language, Mind and Knowledge*, Vol. 7, Minneapolis, MN: The University of Minnesota Press, 113-193.

Salen, Katie/Zimmerman, Eric (2004): *Rules of Play: Game Design Fundamentals*, Cambridge, MA: MIT Press.

Schrape, Niklas (2012): *Die Rhetorik von Computerspielen: Wie politische Spiele überzeugen*, Frankfurt a.M./New York: Campus.

Serious Games Interactive (2007): *Global Conflicts: Palestine*, PC: Serious Games Interactive.

Spurlock, Morgan (2004): *Super Size Me*, Film: USA.

Taito (1978): *Space Invaders*, Arcade: Midway.

Toulmin, Stephen E. (2007): *The Uses of Argument*, Cambridge, MA: Cambridge UP [1958].

Ueding, Gert/Steinbrink, Bernd (³1994): *Grundriß der Rhetorik: Geschichte, Technik, Methode*, Stuttgart/Weimar: Metzler.

Wiemer, Serjoscha (2008): Strategie in Echtzeit: Ergodik zwischen Kriegsspiel und Wirtschaftssimulation, in: *Strategie Spielen: Medialität, Geschichte und Politik des Strategiespiels*, ed. by Rolf F. Nohr and id.: Berlin: Lit, 213-248.

Morphology and Meaning in 'Castle Wolfenstein 3D'

Paul Martin

This chapter takes as a starting point the images of episode six level three of *Wolfenstein 3D* (id Software 1992) pictured in fig. 1 and asks "what does the morphology of this level mean?" Potential answers may be found by approaching the images from two different perspectives. The first is as a cartographic image. The second is as a traversable space (fig. 2). To understand the level as a cartographic image this chapter will begin by approaching the picture on the left as a hidden feature or 'Easter egg' and discuss the process by which this Easter egg becomes visible and the way in which this process helps to structure different players' relationships to the game and to the designers. To understand the level as traversable space, space syntax, a method put forward by Hillier and Hanson (1984) for spatial analysis of buildings and urban formations, is employed to describe the relationship between morphology and the experience of moving through the level.

Fig. 1: Episode 6, level 3 of Wolfenstein 3D *as seen through MapEdid*

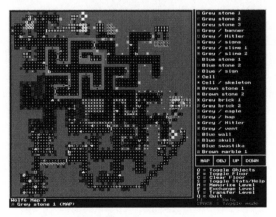

Fig. 2: Wolfenstein 3D *'on the ground'*

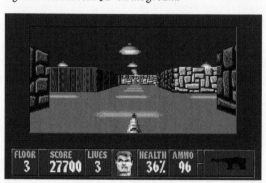

The Cartographic Image and Cultural Space

Videogames frequently contain hidden features and content, known as Easter eggs. These hidden features do not advance the gameplay or confer extra powers on the player-character. Rather, it is the fact of their secrecy, and the sense of discovery and achievement they give rise to, that is the source of their pleasure. Easter eggs can be accessed in one of two ways. The first is through extensive play. Here, the Easter egg is a reward for skills and knowledge that is accessible from within the game. The most famous example of this type of Easter egg is the secret room in *Adventure* that featured a message from the game's author: "created by Warren Robinett" (Robinett 2003, vii). This room was difficult to access because it required the player to pick up a hidden pixel-sized dot from one room and carry it to a different one in order to open a secret door. The second type of Easter egg requires specific knowledge or technology that is not available from within the game. In *Streets of Rage 3* (Sega 1994), for example, several of the bosses are playable on inputting certain button combinations shortly before dying. In the Japanese version of the game, *Bare Knuckle 3*, one of these playable bosses is the gay stereotype Ash, but he is removed (both as a playable and non-playable character) from the western versions of the game. However, he can be unlocked as a playable character on the western versions using a cheat cartridge such as the Game Genie. In the first case the bosses are unlocked through knowledge gained from outside the game, for example in game magazines; in the second case Ash is unlocked through technology from outside the game; that is the Game Genie. Most Easter eggs are some combination between knowledge and skills gained within the game and knowledge gained outside the game. For example, to fight Reptile in *Mortal Kombat* (Midway Games 1992) the player must win in the Pit stage when the moon is partially occluded without losing any energy and without blocking an attack. In this case, even knowing how to access the Easter egg from an outside source does not guarantee the player will be able to access it without a great deal of skill in the game. Also, the same Easter egg may be accessed by some players without recourse to outside resources – through perseverance, skill or blind luck – and by others through knowledge gleaned from walkthroughs, game magazines and conversations with other players.

Easter eggs often take advantage of the spatial nature of games, with secret rooms being a popular feature. However, level 6-3 in *Wolfenstein 3D* is a different kind of spatial Easter egg to Robinett's secret room. Here, it is not the rooms that are hidden, but rather the form of the overall space. Or rather the level exists in two different registers – the traversable space and the cartographic image – the first unhidden and the second hidden. Once discovered, both are simultaneously available but not simultaneously accessible. That is, when I am traversing the first level may be aware of its cartographic appearance, but the full resonances of this image do not come home to me. Similarly, when looking at the image on the left of fig. 1 I can imagine what it would be like to traverse, but this is a theoretical rather than practical or phenomenological knowledge of the level as traversable. It is tempting to think of this doubleness as a spatial pun, though the flickering between alternate meanings that is delightful in the pun is not present in this 'double space' since to move from one register to the other is a more laborious task.

Empirically speaking it may be the case that many players come to 6-3 firstly through the cartographic image. However, for most players it is firstly – and perhaps exclusively – encountered as traversable. In any case it is certainly intended to be primarily a traversable space, with the cartographic image a discoverable Easter egg. Even if a player discovers the cartographic image before traversing the game space, it would still be recognised as belonging to the secret, less accessible register. How, then, is this Easter egg accessed? There are four possibilities. First: some players may be able to piece together in their head the overall map-image while traversing the level. Second: players may draw a map as they traverse the level. Third: players and non-players may access the game's code through the creation or use of 'map editor' software designed to view the levels as maps rather than as environments seen 'on the ground.' Fourth: players and non-players may see representations made with pen and paper or map editor software and distributed in magazines or over the Internet. The first two of these possibilities are examples of the first kind of Easter egg, which is discovered through the player's efforts within the game. The third mode of access – through map-editor software – and the fourth – through published images – are examples of the second kind of Easter egg, which is discovered through knowledge and technology from outside of the game.

I am not arguing that the cartographic image in 6-3 is in itself particularly sophisticated. Easter eggs always have some content associated with them – a cool animation, an interesting image, unlocked characters – but the value of an

Easter egg is not necessarily connected to its actual content. Often what is more important is the amount and kind of effort required to access it. *Grand Theft Auto III* (Rockstar North 2001) plays with this fact, making some of its most inaccessible Easter eggs wilfully anticlimactic. Jumping through one fake wall in Vice City leads to a room containing a chocolate egg. Ascending to the top of the Gant Bridge in San Andreas reveals a sign saying, "There are no Easter eggs up here. Go away."

Certainly, the swastikas in 6-3 may be controversial in its use of this sensitive image in an insensitive way, and this may be linked into a reading of *Wolfenstein 3D* as ushering in a particular phase in videogame history where the moral responsibility of the game industry became an important talking point. *Wolfenstein 3D* was released in the same year as *Mortal Kombat*. The U.S. congressional-hearings on the marketing of games to minors would take place in the following year and the ESRB rating system would be launched the year after that. While *Wolfenstein 3D* was not mentioned in the hearings, the 'bad-boy' attitude of its designers is certainly a part of the way in which a new angle on videogames as a harmful form of entertainment emerged in the early '90s (Kushner 2004).

However, the content of this Easter egg is perhaps of less importance than the way in which it categorised its fans. Easter eggs are always about elitism and they always differentiate fans according to some criteria. Depending on the type of Easter egg, these criteria are a mixture of skill, time spent with the game, community membership, cultural knowledge and technological or technical ability. The cartographic image of 6-3 may have been discovered by players around the world in any of the ways listed previously, but it garnered widespread attention through the hacking community who soon after the launch of the game began to release software to edit levels. The most popular and long-lived of these was MapEdit, initially developed by Bill Kirby (Kirby 1992).

In this context, the swastika Easter egg seems to be a nod to the initiated who can access the image through use of this type of software. John Carmack and John Romero, the main founders of id Software, both had an affinity with the hacker community, and, while the enthusiasm with which this community modified *Wolfenstein* may have been unexpected, it was nonetheless welcomed (Kushner 2004). Secrets for those who could access images of the level from above may not have been intended to create a hacker community around the game – they may simply be an in-joke for the developers – but they certainly helped to establish two tiers amongst *Wolfenstein*-fans – those who knew the code and those who didn't. There have always been people interested in modifying games, but *Wolfenstein 3D* seemed to specifically go about rewarding people who engaged with the game on this other level. For example, id Software did not bring legal claims against people who distributed *Wolfenstein 3D* mods online, despite advice to the contrary (Kushner 2004). The accessibility of the swastika image to those who knew the code was just one way of establishing hackers as a special kind of gamer.

However, *Wolfenstein 3D* also contains an example of this benign relationship between hacker and developer breaking down. Perhaps the most famous of *Wolfenstein 3D*'s mazes comes in episode two, level eight, which contains over 150 secret rooms (see fig. 3). This maze contains a boss, an extra life and, in a room that is particularly difficult of access, a message instructing the player to call Apogee, the publishers of the game, and say a code word. According to Joe Siegler, an employee at Apogee, this was originally intended as a competition, but the idea was abandoned almost immediately because software like MapEdit meant the otherwise near-impossible to reach secret room became relatively accessible, resulting in hundreds of calls before Apogee had even decided on a prize (Stoddard 2005). The level works in a contrary way to 6-3: Here the map image reveals a second meaning to the level for those players who have the wherewithal to access the cartographic image. This creates a sense of collusion between the designers and a certain 'class' of gamer. But here, the image as revealed by the hacker undermines the designers' intention. This intention is to reward not the players who, through hacker-developed tools, step outside the game and look 'down into it' but the players who spend hours running around the maze looking for secrets from within the 'legitimate' game space. In 6-3 the hackers and the designers are on the same side, but in 2-8 they stand in opposition.

Fig. 3: Level 2-8; with this map it is relatively easy to traverse an otherwise impenetrable maze

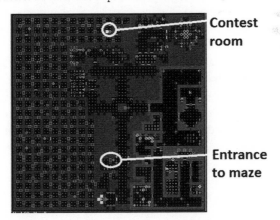

Contest room

Entrance to maze

While *Wolfenstein 3D* established a categorical difference between how different people engaged with the game this was by no means set in stone, and the secrets gleaned by those in the know were quickly shared with the community at large, as the 'call Apogee' episode demonstrated. This process only became more streamlined with the development and spread of the World Wide Web. The hit that *Wolfenstein 3D* made with hackers also directly led to the inclusion in subsequent id games of a more hacker friendly architecture (Kücklich 2005). Games in the *Doom* (id Software 1993) and *Quake* (id Software 1996) franchises were specifically made to be moddable, even to people without a great deal of programming ability. Over the course of the 1990s looking 'down into' the game became as legitimate and almost as accessible an activity as playing the game.

6-3 as Traversable Space: Isovist Analyses

The cartographic register of 6-3, then, points to a particular moment in the history of modding, in which the hacker was both recognised as a special kind of gamer and the fruits of hacking began to be widely distributed throughout the gaming community. But the cartographic image has more immediate formal effects on the game that have nothing to do with controversial Nazi imagery, Easter eggs, or the history of modding. These effects are to do with how a configuration of seven swastikas structures a player's experience of the level visually and kinaes-thetically. But how do we get at the range of experiences that the morphology of a particular game space makes available to the player? One way is to create various models of the level as a spatial system. These models help to calculate measures that describe the player's relationship to the environment and how this changes as the player moves about the level. In this way morphology, which is characteristically spatial, is connected to performance, which is characteristically temporal.

The first model attempts to describe how the visual information provided to the player changes. This represents the level as a set of isovists, or view sheds. By looking at the area of these view sheds we get an idea of the amount of visual information the player has over the course of the level. This is based on isovist analysis as put forward by Benedikt (1979) and developed elsewhere (Batty 2000).

Fig. 4a-b shows a simple corridor system as described through isovists analysis. The isovists in the first image show the area that can be seen from two points. The second image breaks the system into a set of points and represents the area of the isovist from each point in the system. Warmer colours represent larger isovists.

Fig. 4a-b: Isovists in a simple corridor system

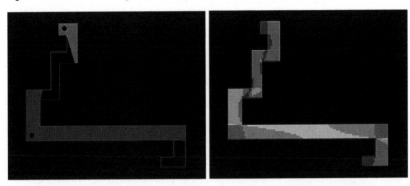

In terms of amount of visual information available to the player, the swastikas in 6-3 set up a steady pulse over the course of the level. As the player moves from the end to the crook of the arm, from the crook to the middle of the arm, from the middle to the crossroads, and then back toward the next end, the visual field continually expands, contracts, and expands again. If we take the most efficient route from the entrance to the exit of this level as indicative, the player's visual field expands and contracts in this way several times. Firstly, the player passes through the swastikas marked A, B and D, then enters the very different visual environment of the lower corridor. Here, the visual information is never as plentiful as it is in the main 'swastika area,' but is instead fairly uniform across three corridors connecting two small rooms. The player must reach the end of this sequence, collect a silver key, and then return to the main area. Here, there is the same expansion-contraction of the visual field as before, though this time the sequence is punctuated by the wide corridor marked X between D and E. At the end of F, the player either exits or collects a second key and returns, this time passing through five swastikas in the same expansion-contraction sequence, to the secret exit near the start (see fig. 5).

Fig. 5: *Expansion and contraction of visual fields as player traverse level three (white lines show the most efficient route)*

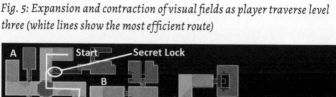
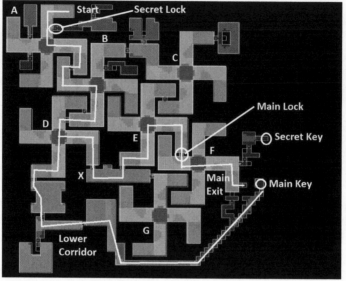

This is an unusual level in *Wolfenstein 3D* not only because of how the level looks 'from above,' as a picture, but also because of how the symmetry of that morphology sets up a repetitive rhythm in terms of the amount of visual information the player has. This in itself can be disorientating, since radically varying amounts of visual information in different areas of the level would act as a landmark that aids navigation. The repetitiveness of the expansion-contraction pulse does not provide this variation and so cannot be relied upon as a means of orientation. Of course, there are other aspects of the environment – such as different colours and textures of walls, different enemy spawn points and patrols, and different statues, pictures, furniture and pickups – that do provide variation across the level and so run counter to this repetitive rhythm.

If we look at the nine other levels in the episode, there is not nearly so regular a pulse in terms of isovist area. In the other levels asymmetry in morphology gives rise to an unpredictability that is central to the game's aesthetic.

We find the 'expansion-contraction' motif in level two, but with a difference (fig. 6). Here, the player begins in an area of small isovists, which is a simple matrix of corridors rather than a difficult maze. This area that affords little visual information gives onto a spiral of long, wide corridors, which have larger isovists, especially at their corners. As the corridors spiral toward the central exit, the visual fields naturally contract, and this contraction is exacerbated at the centre due to the narrower corridors. Here, however, the expansion-contraction only happens once, and not repeatedly as in level three.

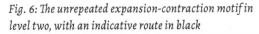

Fig. 6: The unrepeated expansion-contraction motif in level two, with an indicative route in black

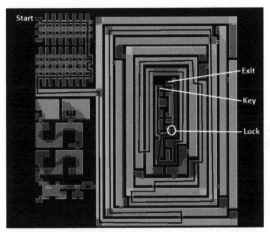

The idea of the second level's morphology giving rise to 'a rhythm' may be a misleading analogy. Because throughout 6-3 the expansion-contraction rhythm is repeated continually, or almost continually, and at a local level, we are justified in examining the most efficient route as indicative of the level's overall rhythm. However, lost a player gets, this rhythm is maintained because the seven swastikas form the core part of the level. But describing the unrepeated expansion-contraction of the most efficient route in level 2 as the level's isovist rhythm is incorrect. In fact, it is only the rhythm of one, or possibly a small number of, possible routes through the level. For example, this rhythm may be disrupted if the player enters the secret maze in the bottom left corner, which, incidentally, contains another possible Nazi-related cartographic image in the sideways 'SS.' But while this may disrupt the rhythm it does not affect the overall pattern that the morphology lays down. Whether the player becomes hopelessly lost, eventually finding the exit after much backtracking, or the player chooses to explore the entire level to collect every item and kill every guard, the entire session will be broadly characterised by this global rhythm because of the low isovist area for the entrance and exit and because of the spiral of decreasing isovist area that separates them. The rhythm will not be as keenly felt by the player who does not take the most efficient path, but nor will it be obliterated completely.

Level three's locally repetitive morphology means that its isovists are relatively uniform across the level. We only get 'blue' areas when we leave the swastika core that constitutes most of the level. Other levels, however, tend to have a lot of smaller isovists and relatively few large ones. That is, the player spends more time with little visual information than with a lot. This is central to the game's sense of pace and surprise.

The combination of areas with large isovists and small isovists leads to variation not just in the way the environment reveals itself to the player but also in the kinds of threats the player faces. Unlike in more contemporary first person-shooters, in *Wolfenstein 3D* the player is generally safer at points with large isovists. This is because, apart from bosses, enemies do not have long range weapons. The only time a trooper or dog, the two most common enemies, has an advantage over the player is when the player does not see them coming. However, large isovists do mean that the player is open to attack from multiple directions simultaneously. Smaller isovists create tension because enemies can easily ambush the player around corners, behind doors or from alcoves, but the player can generally concentrate attention in just one or two directions. Different features that give rise to low isovists such as doors, corner and alcoves, while they all contribute to tension by maintaining a sense of threat, all affect the pace of the level in different ways. Doors that close behind the player were a good way in early first person-shooters to divide up space and thereby increase performance speed, but they also led to a particular kind of rhythm, requiring players to come to a complete standstill in order to open them. Corners also slow the player down, though not to the same extent. The player may also naturally slow down at junctions to decide on which way to go. But the player may pass through corridors flanked by alcoves, such as the one in the centre of 6-1 very quickly (fig. 7). The kind of exhilarating tension felt in passing swiftly down a corridor with multiple alcoves is of a very different character to the anticipatory tension felt before opening the door to an unseen room. The constant tension felt in 6-1's alcove corridor might be contrasted with the oscillation between tension and release that defines the rhythm set up by the 'swastika arms' in 6-3.

Fig. 7: Level one isovist areas with quickest route in black

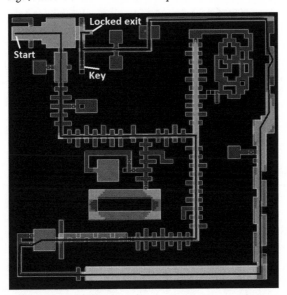

Visual and Axial Integration

The isovist analysis of 6-3 suggested that the abiding rhythm of the level is one of increasing and decreasing visual fields. But this is a purely local analysis, describing what can be seen by the player at particular points throughout the level. But while locally all of the swastikas in the level are almost identical, giving rise to this regular rhythm, globally they are very different. That is, each occupies a different place in the configuration of the level as a whole. The relative position of each swastika shows up if we look at the decision points and dead-ends of the level on a simplified graph of the level. The graphs used here are a version of the justified graph as put forward by Hillier and Hanson (1984). The method outlined in Hillier and Hanson is to take each room in a house as the base unit of the graph. Then take one of these rooms, usually the entrance way, as the root point, and represent on a graph the interconnections in the house. The graph is a visual representation of how each room fits into the overall configuration from the point of view of a particular root space. Here, rather than taking rooms as the base unit, decision points are taken as the base unit. There are two kinds of decisions in the level, crossroads and junctions. Crossroads offer the player three paths to choose from, plus the path used to access the crossroads. Junctions offer the player two paths to choose from. The graph also shows dead ends, where the player must return on the same path. This kind of graph should give us a visual representation of how each decision point fits into the overall configuration of the level. Figures 8 and 9 show the level represented with two graphs of this kind. Figure 9 shows all of the decision points and dead-ends between the entrance and the key. Figure 9 shows all of the decision points and dead-ends between the key and the exit.

Fig. 8: Graph showing interconnections in 6-3 between entrance and key

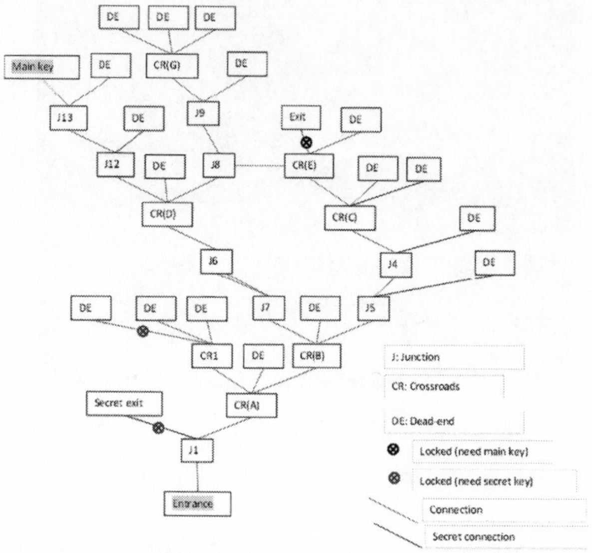

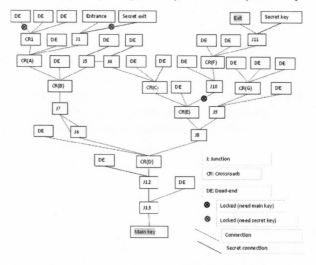

Fig. 9: Graph of decision points for 6-3 for level after the main key has been found

There are two routes between the entrance and the key that do not involve any doubling back. This is due to the 'ring' that links B, C, E and D. Of course, there are many more routes that do involve doubling back, usually a short distance, but slightly longer in the case of J8-J9. If we look just at this graph and imagine that each path has an equal chance of being taken, then the chances of the player reaching the key by either route without doubling back at least once is less than one in a hundred. There are, of course, features of the level that reduce these odds somewhat. For example, several of the decision points are between hidden and visible doors, and in these cases the player is more likely to choose the visible door. However, the odds are nevertheless in favour of the player making choices that do not lead directly to the main key. The player may even make the same wrong decision more than once, since many of the level's spaces look similar. The chances of this kind of error are mitigated by the fact that guard's bodies remain after the guard has been killed and therefore mark a particular space as one that has already been visited. Besides the possibility of making wrong decisions, the player may also purposefully make a decision that leads away from the 'main' path. Frequently dead-ends contain treasure, weaponry and ammo. Getting the key is the only necessary goal to progression, but the player may have many other more exploration-orientated goals. Therefore, there are two reasons why the player may not take the most direct path between the entrance and key: the number of decision points between these two points and the confusion this engenders, and the benefits and pleasures of exploring off the main path.

Indeed, 6-3 makes such exploration likely. If we think of this graph as showing a series of decisions, we can assign different 'levels' which quickly show the distance in terms of decisions between the entrance and particular decision points. The key is nine levels from the entrance, which is almost the maximum distance. This provides the player with many opportunities to become lost or to explore before the key is found. The player, then, may visit many or all of the points on the graph, and may visit them more than once, before finding the key. However, since the player must find the key to proceed through the level (whether through the main or secret exit) there are certain points that the successful player must see at least once. These are the ones marked Entrance, J1, CR(A), CR(B), CR(D), J12, J13 and Main key. On the ring we have two routes that do not entail doubling back. These either take in J7 and J6 or J5, J4, CR(C), CR(E) and J8. All of the other spaces may be visited but are not necessary for progression. The likelihood is, of course, that at least some of them will be visited, but every player who completes this level will certainly see the first set of points and will have at least a one in two chance of seeing the second set. We can use the same method to describe the decisions facing the player between the key and the main exit, and the graph for this is shown in fig. 8.

Now that the rest of the level is accessible the player must go from the main key location to the main exit or to the secret key, which is located near to the main exit. As with the first phase of the level, the departure point and the destination are a large number of steps apart; indeed, in this case the exit is at the furthest level from the departure point. However, at this point the player will have seen much of the level already and therefore may be less likely to get lost. Also, many of the secrets may already have been discovered, and so the player may take a more direct route to the locked door at CRE-J10. Again, there are two routes that do not double back. Just focusing on the crossroads, the first must take in at least D, E and F. The alternative, longer route must take in at least D, B, C, E and F.

If we look at the level in total, we can identify A, B and D in the first phase and D, E and F in the second phase as crossroads that the player must pass through. C is likely to be seen at some stage because it is on one of the optional routes in each phase. G is not on any of the main routes, and so may be missed altogether. This justified graph method can show the relative importance of particular decision points with respect to a root point, in this case the entrance for the first phase and the main key for the second phase. This gives us a set of local measures. However, it has been argued that a feature of 6-3, due to the abundance of junctions and crossroads, is that the player is likely to become lost or to explore off the main path over the course of the level. It might be useful, then, to describe the distance of each point not only from some root point but from every point. This would give a measure of how 'central' a particular point is in general and would therefore be a global measure. One way of doing this would be to draw a justified graph with each decision point as a root. Instead of this laborious process, Hillier and Hanson (1984) put forward the idea of integration. This method takes a particular model of space that divides the space into discrete, interconnected units and then calculates the average number of steps from each point to every other point in the system. This provides us with the permeability of the system, or the relative accessibility of each of its spaces. If we do this with the above justified graph we get the graph in fig. 10.

Fig. 10: *Integration on decision points in 6-3. More integrated points have warmer colours*

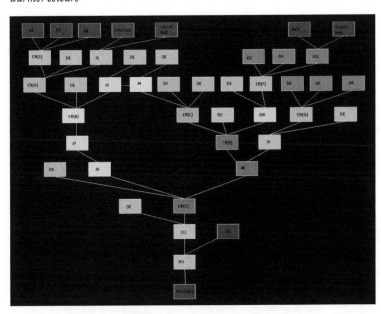

Note that even though the layout for this graph is the same as the justified graph in figure 9, here integration is being calculated in terms of the number of connections required to link each decision point to every other decision point. That is, it is not measuring the closeness of each point to one particular point but the 'centrality' of each point in terms of the system in general. This gives a sense of how accessible a particular point is in general, without taking account of the player's starting point or the position of game goals. It is unsurprising that those points on the ring are highly integrated as they are generally accessible. The further we go from the ring the more segregated are the decision points. The entrance, both exits and both keys are highly segregated, meaning that there are on average a lot of decision points between the player and these areas. Note that D, the only crossroads that must feature in both phases of the level, is highly integrated. Therefore, both the placement of locks and keys and the configuration of the level make D a pivotal point in the permeability of the level.

As mentioned, integration measures the average number of 'steps' from each point to every other point. These 'steps' may be of any kind of unit. In the above example, a 'step' is the connection between one decision point and the next decision point or dead-end. However, we might also define a step in metric terms – that is as distance in feet or metres – as the connection between turns or as any other kind of spatial relationship. Using decision points as the unit for calculating integration seems intuitive, since choice of paths is an integral part of both mazes and videogames. But by modelling the space in different ways we can arrive at other measures which may capture other features of videogame maze navigation.

The two most common ways of modelling space in space syntax research is through visual graph analysis and the axial map. Visual graph analysis extends the concept of the isovist, which describes local visual properties, to describe the global properties of a system. In the example of the simple corridor in fig. 4, isovist area showed us the visual field from particular points along the corridor. Another way of saying this is that the isovist of point A describes all points that are one visual step away from it. It is in this sense a local measure. But we might also think of points that are two steps away from A. These points cannot be seen directly from A, but can be seen by other points in A's isovist. In the same way we can describe all points in a spatial system as a certain number of visual steps from A. Visual integration is a measure of the depth of every point in the system from every other point in terms of visual steps (Turner, 2004). Fig. 11 shows the same corridor system as seen through visual integration analysis.

Fig. 11: Visual integration for simple corridor

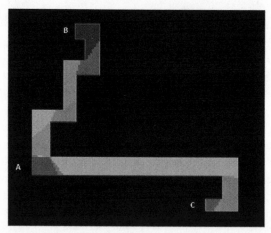

Here, the 'central' point A is highly integrated. In a simple corridor like this, the more central points will naturally be visually closer to all points than points toward either end of the corridor. But note that, even though this is a single corridor with no branches one end of the corridor, marked C, is slightly more integrated than the other, marked B. This is because a person standing at B, because he or she is at the end of a twisty corridor, must pass through a large number of visual steps to see most of the other points in the system. A person standing at C, however, because he or she is close to the long horizontal corridor, gets to see much of the system without having to pass through many visual steps. This demonstrates how even in a relatively simple system asymmetries arise in terms of visual integration.

While visual graph analysis focuses on visibility, the axial map focuses on movement. This is a model of the space based on the fewest lines necessary to connect all of the spaces in the system. With this model it is possible to find integration values for each line in a similar way, using interconnections of lines rather than inter-visibility of points. Fig. 12 shows the same corridor as an axial map, with the integration values depicted through line colour. We get a similar result, with lines near the centre of the corridor more integrated than those at the periphery.

Fig. 12: Axial map for simple corridor

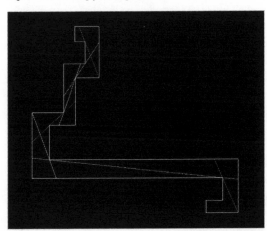

What is the benefit of modelling a spatial system in these ways to measure integration? Most space syntax studies look at the relationship between integration and aggregate movement in real-world spatial systems. The movement that can be attributed to the configurational properties of a spatial system has been termed 'natural movement' (Hillier et al. 1993). High correlations have been found between visual integration and movement patterns in public buildings (Hillier/ Tzortzi 2006; Turner/Penn 1999; Lu et al. 2009). The axial map has more often been used with respect to street systems, where integration has been found to be a good predictor of pedestrian movement (Penn 2001). Little empirical work has been done with respect to game spaces, though studies have repeated correlations between movement patterns and integration on the axial line from the real world in virtual environments (Conroy 2001) and in *World of Warcraft* (Blizzard Entertainment 2004; Ch/Kim 2007). However, without further empirical investigations claims about the relationship between configuration and player behaviour need to be treated with care. It is important to be mindful of how both local aspects of a gamespace and the particular demands and affordances of the game interact with the space's global configuration.

It must be emphasised that integration is generally used in space syntax to analyse systems in which many users are making journeys from multiple departure points to multiple destinations, for example on city streets and in art galleries. Because integration tells us about the accessibility of the space in general, it fails to take account for the way in which a space might privilege certain journeys and not others. This does not matter so much where users are engaged in different kinds of journeys, since their personal motivations tend to cancel each other out. But in games there tends to be a much more prescribed set of journeys, even in relatively complex spaces like 6-3. It is unlikely therefore that in a level like 6-3 integration will tell us much about player's movement patterns. For example, points like A, J11 and the Main key are found to be highly segregated spaces. This would suggest that there will be little player movement here. But clearly any successful game session must take in these spaces. We would expect a more integrated space like C to attract more movement. However, as we have seen, it is not on a compulsory path and therefore it may be ignored completely. However, permeability may still be a relevant factor in describing how the level's morphology structures player behaviour when the player becomes lost or engages in exploration-orientated behaviour.

Fig. 13: Visual integration (left) and axial integration (right) for level 6-3, with swastikas marked 1-7

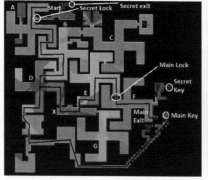 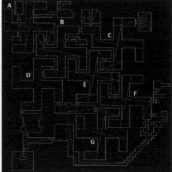

As with the decision points graph, integration on both the visual graph and the axial map is found to be highest around the ring comprising B, C, E and D (fig. 13). However, the visual graph appears less sensitive to this ring as an integrator as it has C, which is on the ring, as less integrated than G, which is off it. The axial map has D, B and C as containing the most integrated lines. This differs from both of the other graphs, which have a highly integrated E and relatively more segregated

C. The axial map's privileging of C is easier to see if we just display the 10% most integrated and the 10% most segregated lines, as in fig. 14.

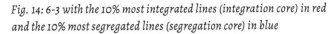

Fig. 14: 6-3 with the 10% most integrated lines (integration core) in red and the 10% most segregated lines (segregation core) in blue

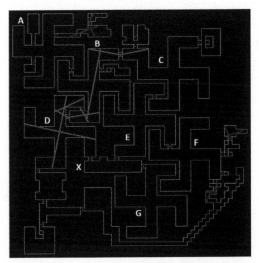

Here we can see more clearly that the integration core comprises all of D and parts of B and C. Fig. 13 also shows the most segregated lines in three areas: the room in the bottom right where the secret key is found, the room near the entrance where the secret exit is found, and the small area near where the main key is found.

Fig. 15a-b: Visual integration (a) and axial line integration (b) with connection made between F and lower corridor system

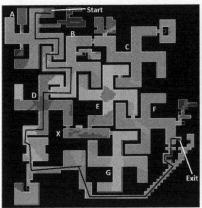

We can examine the effect of the level's configuration on integration values by changing the connections in the system. We might suggest that D is highly integrated due to the fact that it is the only gate to the lower corridor. To test the importance of this we can make a connection between the lower corridor and F and see how this affects integration (fig. 15a-b). In this revised version of the level the visual integration core shifts slightly to the right, with E and F becoming slightly more integrated due to the passageway opening up between F and the lower corridor. But the effect is not marked, and D remains a highly integrated space. On the axial map the effect on the integration core is even less, with just a slight movement into C. More noticeable is the effect on the segregation core, with the extra connection to the lower corridor obviously making the lower corridor more integrated.

Perhaps more important than the fact that it is the only 'gateway' to the lower corridor, D has a large number of connections to other subsystems. It is connected directly to B (by two doors) and, through the short central corridor X, to E and G. B has one more connection than D, but it connects to more peripheral areas and so these connections do not contribute as much to its integration values. If we disconnect B and D and add a connection between B and E instead, then we get a big shift toward the topological centre both in terms of the visual and axial integration core (fig. 16). Now E connects up directly to three swastikas and indirectly to two more. At the same time D becomes considerably more segregated because the player must now pass through E in order to access it.

Fig. 16a-b: Visual integration (a) and axial line integration (b) once the connections between B and D have been removed and a connection between B and E inserted, changing the integration across the system

This method of experimenting with connections between sub-systems allows the critic to think about how a particular level works by thinking about how it might work with a different configuration. But it may also be useful in the design process, giving an insight into the character of a level without building and testing it. Of course, this theoretical analysis could not replace the empirical investigation of play-testing and interviews with players but it may help to provide initial clues as to how different configurations might give rise to different experiences by making certain areas more accessible and others less so.

What these integration analyses demonstrate is that even though locally in terms of visual information the swastikas provide a regular beat, globally they each have their own character due to their placement within the system as a whole and the interconnections they allow. Because the more integrated areas are relatively close to all other points in the level we would expect players exploring the level or players becoming lost in the level to revisit these areas again and again, making them an important 'landmark.'

Conclusion

This chapter has attempted to describe two ways in which level 6-3 in *Wolfenstein 3D* articulates meaning. On the one hand, as an Easter egg its form interpellates and helps to construct a certain kind of *Wolfenstein 3D*-fan who can see down into the game. On the other, it structures player experience in the game by alternating areas of high visibility with areas of low visibility in a steady rhythm and, through its system of choice points between sub-systems, privileging certain areas and isolating others. Space syntax is suggested as a means of understanding the relationship between the morphology of a spatial system and player experience in the system. Future research would benefit from more empirical research through analysis of player traces and interviews with players to understand in greater detail the effect of configuration on player behaviour and pleasure.

Referencens

Batty, Michael (2000): Exploring Isovist Fields: Space and Shape in Architectural and Urban Morphology. in: *Environment and Planning B: Planning and Design* 28/1, 123-150.

Benedikt, Michael (1979): To Take Hold of Space: Isovist Fields, in: *Environment and Planning B: Planning and Design* 6/1, 74-65.

Blizzard Entertainment (2004): *World of Warcraft*, PC: Vivendi.

Cho, In O./Kim, Young O. (2007): The Relationship between Spatial Configuration and Spatial Behavior in Online Game Space, in: *Proceedings Sixth International Space Syntax Symposium*, ed. by Ayse S. Kubat, Özhan Ertekin, Yasemin İ. Güney and Engin Eyüboğlu, spacesyntaxistanbul.itu.edu.tr/papers/longpapers/104%20-%20Cho%20Kim.pdf.

Conroy, Ruth D. (2001): *Spatial Navigation in Immersive Virtual Environments*, PhD-Diss., University College London, thepurehands.org/phdpdf/thesis.pdf.

Hillier, Bill/Hanson, Julienne (1984): *The Social Logic of Space*, Cambridge, MA: Cambridge UP.

Hillier, Bill/Tzortzi, Kali (2006): Space Syntax: The Language of Museum Space, in: *A Companion to Museum Studies*, ed. by Sharon Macdonald, Oxford: Blackwell, 282-301.

Hillier, Bill/Penn, Alan/Grajewski, Tadeusz/Xu, Jianming (1993): Natural Movement: or, Configuration and Attraction in Urban Pedestrian Movement, in: *Environment and Planning B: Planning and Design* 20, 29-66.

id Software (1992): *Castle Wolfenstein 3D*, PC: Apogee Software.

—— (1993): *Doom*, PC: id Software.

—— (1996): *Quake*, PC: GT Interactive.

Kirby, Bill (1992) *MapEdit*, gamers.org/pub/archives/wolf3d/utils/maped41.txt.

Kücklich, Julian (2005): Precarious Playbour: Modders and the Digital Games Industry, *The Fibreculture Journal* 5, five.fibreculturejournal.org/fcj-025-precarious-playbour-modders-and-the-digital-games-industry.

Kushner, David (2004): *Masters of Doom: How Two Guys Created an Empire and Transformed Pop Culture*, London: Piatkus.

Lu, Yi/Peponis, John/Zimring, Craig (2009): Targeted Visibility Analysis in Buildings. Correlating Targeted Visibility Analysis with Distribution of People and Their Interactions within an Intensive Care Unit, in: *Proceedings of the Seventh International Space Syntax Symposium*, ed. by Daniel Koch, Lars Marcus and Jesper Steen, doi.org/10.1068%2Fb130016p.

Midway Games (1992): *Mortal Kombat*, Arcade: Midway Games.

Penn, Alan (2001): Space Syntax and Spatial Cognition. Or, Why the Axial Line?, in: *Proceedings of the Third International Symposium on Space Syntax*, ed. by John Peponis, Jean Wineman, & Sonit Bafna, discovery.ucl.ac.uk/3419/1/3419.pdf.

Robinett, Warren (2003): Foreword, in: *The Video Game Theory Reader*, ed. by Mark J.P. Wolf and Bernard Perron, New York, NY/London: Routledge, VII-XIX.

Rockstar North (2001): *Grand Theft Auto III*, PS2: Rockstar Games.

Sega (1994): *Streets of Rage 3 (Bare Knuckle III)*, Sega: Sega Genesis.

Stoddard, Samuel (2005): *The Apogee FAQ*, Version 7.2w, rinkworks.com/apogee/s/2.8.6.1.shtml.

Turner, Alasdair (2004): *Depthmap 4: A Researcher's Handbook*, discovery.ucl.ac.uk/2651/1/2651.pdf.

Turner, Alasdair/Penn, Alan (1999): Making Isovists Syntactic: Isovist Integration Analysis, in: *Proceedings of the Second International Symposium on Space Syntax*, pdfs.semanticscholar.org/92d9/115762df6d1e404adc96a47d1ac040cbdfdb.pdf.

Combinatorial Explorations
A Brief History of Procedurally-Generated Space in Videogames

Mark J.P. Wolf

The worlds of videogames have grown from single screens of graphics to vast worlds, some of which are too large to ever be fully explored by a single person despite many hours or even years of gameplay. As a quote from Michael Toy – one of the authors of *Rogue* (A.I. Design 1983) – indicates, new experiences are what make games replayable, and keep players interested in a game; and exploration and navigation are among the most basic kinds of experiences afforded by videogames:

> The sad discovery for authors of text-style adventures is that it is not that fun to play your own game. You already know all the solutions to the puzzles. The greatest part of *Rogue*, and the part I still wish for as I look at the gaming scene today, is that it made a new world every time. The game was just as hard to win the second time as the first (qtd. in Anonymous 2009).

The procedural generation of videogame spaces not only keeps a game fresh for players, but even for the game's creators, who merely determine the parameters of algorithms which will automate the production of game space. In one sense, the virtual spaces in which videogames' events take place are all procedurally-generated, since they do not exist without the aid of the electronics which produce them; by 'procedurally-generated,' then, we mean the production of significant game content which varies from game to game, and which changes gameplay. At the same time, however, exchanging handcrafted, human-designed locations for algorithmically-generated ones does have certain drawbacks and limitations of its own.

The first procedurally-generated content in videogames could be considered games with randomized content; in *Spacewar!* (Russel 1962), for example, the hyperdrive feature would make the player's ship disappear and then reappear elsewhere at a random location. This demonstrates one of the difficulties in defining procedurally-generated space; for example, if the locations of stars in a star-

field are randomly generated, and the positions of the stars are what define differences in a game's spaces, then one could argue that different spaces are being
generated procedurally.

The first game with unambiguously procedurally-generated space, then, would
be *Rogue*, one of the most popular mainframe games of the early 1980s. Inspired
by William Crowther's text-based *Colossal Cave Adventure* (Crowther/Woods 1977)
and the table-top role-playing game *Dungeons & Dragons* (Gygax/Arneson 1974),
Rogue was a series of dungeon rooms that the player wandered through, defeat-
ing monsters, collecting treasure, and looking for food. In order to provide variety, the rooms and the pathways connecting them were procedurally-generated;
according to another of the game's authors, Glenn Wichmann (qtd. in Anonymous
2009),

> [w]e originally wanted something very freeform, where a room could be anywhere,
> and there could be any number of rooms. We couldn't figure out how to do it. We
> ended up settling on a nine-room tic-tac-toe grid. Then there was the 'mars bug' –
> sometimes rooms just would not connect. It took us a long time to figure that one
> out, and we ended up with a number of frustrated players who were having great
> games and suddenly could not go to the next level because there was no way to
> get to the staircase.

The randomness present, then, was still within rather tight parameters, and the
randomized placement of monsters, treasures, and food also contributed greatly
to the replayability of the game. Another game dependent on randomized elements and layout was *Stellar Track* (Atari 1980) for the Atari 2600. This *Star Trek*-in-
spired resource management game had the player jumping from quadrant to
quadrant, using phasors and photon torpedoes to destroy alien vessels. Each of
the 36 quadrants was made up of 64 sectors, creating a playing field grid of 48-by-
48 positions. Each position could contain the player's ship, or an enemy ship, or a
star, which acted as a barrier to travel. Because the placement of stars was randomized in every game, along with the positions of enemy ships and refueling
star-bases, each game was a new challenge, again due to randomized content.

Randomized content was the key not only to making each gaming experience
unique and different, but also to make much larger worlds than what could be fit
into relatively small amounts of computer memory. The landmark space trading
game *Elite* (Braben/Bell 1984) featured a universe of eight galaxies each with 256
planets, in a program of only 22 kilobytes (Noyes 2006). Each planet's position,
composition, commodity prices, and name was procedurally-generated, from
numeric seeds fed through an algorithm. But while the starships and other objects
were visible from space, one did not get a sense of exploring a more earthlike loca-

tion, one with vast tracts of explorable land. This would come with the advent of fractal landscapes.

Fractal Landscapes

In 1975, Benoit Mandelbrot discovered fractal geometry, a branch of geometry that involved shapes that were self-similar at different scales, and that appeared to be able to generate forms like those of natural phenomena (such as fern branches and mountain ranges, which involve copies of the same patterns at different scales). Three-dimensional game graphics were improving and moving from wireframe graphics to filled-polygon graphics, which could be used to present landscapes with a first-person perspective. Emerging from Industrial Light and Magic's work with fractal graphics for the 'Genesis Effect'-sequence in *Star Trek II: The Wrath of Khan* (Meyer 1982), *Rescue on Fractalus!* (Lucasfilm Games 1984) used procedurally-generated fractal landscapes (fig. 1); terrain with geometric mountains of varying heights and randomized terrain helped to create more detailed landscapes than the low-resolution graphics were otherwise able to suggest, as well as their movement in three-dimensional space as the player's vantage point flew across the surface, looking to land and rescue stranded pilots while avoiding aliens and alien fire. Fractal technology would again be used in *Koronis Rift* (Lucasfilm Games 1985) which featured rovers driving over fractal landscapes which were essentially mazes, and *The Eidolon* (Lucasfilm Games 1985a), which inverted its fractal mountains to create a mazelike cave interior. *The Sentinel* (Crammond 1986) also used simple fractal-based landscapes and boasted 10,000 levels, stored in less than 70 kilobytes, and *Starflight* (Binary Systems 1986) used fractal landscapes for its 800 different planets.

Fig. 1: Screenshots from various versions of Rescue on Fractalus!

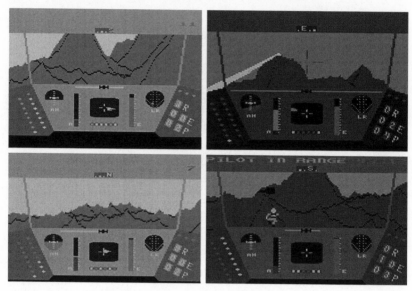

While initially offering the thrill of three-dimensional landscapes that varied from place to place, the landscapes of these early games were basically just fields of polygons set at different angles to produce a surface with simple mountains, variations which could quickly grow tiresome in their similarity – quantity over quality, as some critics have pointed out (Priestmann 2013; Cham 2014). By contrast, the procedurally-generated two-dimensional underground tunnels seen in a cutaway side view in *Exile* (Irvin/Smith 1988) seem more varied and interesting, and they also include customized hand-designed sections, something which would have been very difficult to include in fractal-based landscapes. There is likewise more direct interaction with the game's spaces in *Exile* than in the other games, demonstrating that despite their graphical detail and aesthetic value, their functionality as interactive elements was severely limited, at least within the limitations imposed by the relatively small amounts of memory and slow processing speeds available at the time.

Also, fractal terrains with their varying slopes can limit accessibility and randomly make certain areas impassable, and it is difficult to ensure that enough of a map will be accessible without limiting mountain heights and valley depths which would homogenize a landscape. Over the years since the early games discussed here, a number of different methods for generating fractal terrains have been developed, and a survey of these techniques can be found in *A Survey of Procedural Terrain Generation Techniques Using Evolutionary Algorithms* (Raffe et al. 2012). The authors compare different techniques, along with their advantages and disadvantages, and appropriateness to the needs of different games genres and their needs concerning terrain (for example, flight simulators do not need to ensure accessibility, but may instead require terrain that looks realistic from an aerial perspective).

The uniqueness of fractal landscapes is merely mathematical in nature; hand-crafted locations, by contrast, often have specific attributes that together create a distinct personality that turn a space into a place. Player activities in spaces left to procedural generation also tend to be more repetitive in nature; theme and varia-tions, rather than new themes. Prices, commodities, and names may change, but trading, shooting, and being shot at remains pretty much the same. Of course, such games can still be fun; and they tend to be more replayable, with individual games also taking much longer than in hand-designed worlds, due to their greater expansiveness. For some types of games, then, the tradeoff is a worthwhile one. *Captive* (Mindscape 1990), for example, had procedurally-generated planets and bases (65,535 of them), and the game received 91% ratings – by *Amiga Format* (in December 1990) and *Zzzap!64* in (January 1991) – and was listed as the 31st-best game of all time by *Amiga Power*. Also, games like *Elite*'s sequel, *Frontier: Elite II* (Braben 1993), were so detailed, with three-dimensional graphics and spaces, along with the possibility of freeform play, that they were competitive with games using handcrafted locations.

Another reason for procedural generation was due to the memory restrictions of earlier games, when available memory was still measured in kilobytes. With the arrival of optical disc storage around the late 1980s and early 1990s, graph-ics improved, and handcrafted worlds became much larger – *Myst* (Cyan 1993) is the best example of a successful handcrafted world of the time. While procedural terrain generation would continue to be used, increased storage capacity would allow more flexibility, and more detail could be stored and used, allowing more combination of handcrafted content and procedural generation.

Greater Storage Capacity and Faster Processing Times

With optical discs and hard drives with greater storage capacity, more RAM, and faster processing times, procedural generation would be able to provide more detail in real time, and in an increasing number of areas. MicroProse's *Civilization* series of games, which began in 1990, used procedural generation for the produc-tion of maps, allowing players to choose between general types of terrain, like con-tinents, archipelagoes, pangaeas, and so forth. The smaller scale details change, while the overall form remains consistent with the type of terrain chosen, and it is these variations in small details that keep the games fresh. But procedural generation is not appropriate for every area of a game, since quite often such material lacks the deliberate design that one finds in material handcrafted by an author.

When procedurally-generated content is combined with handcrafted material, the results can be large worlds which have more a deliberate feel in their design. In the mid-1990s *Advanced Dungeons & Dragons: Slayer* (Lion Entertainment 1994) and *Virtual Hydlide* (Technology and Entertainment Software 1995) were released, each of which had worlds that combined handcrafted material with procedural generation. *Slayer* used repeated wall, door, and window elements in a procedurally-generated dungeon which the player explored from a first-person perspective, and which included other features like moving platforms activated by wall buttons and a map that could be consulted, and that filled in gradually as the dungeon was explored (and of course, monsters, torches, and objects were randomly encountered along the way). Players could customize the dungeon as well, choosing the number of levels (10 to 20), Monster Numbers (Few, Handful, Lots, Too Many), Treasure Availability (Poor, Comfortable, Rich, Filthy Rich), Poison Strength (Annoying, Sickening, Deadly, Lethal), Food Availability (Starving, Healthy, Well Fed, Stuffed), Monster Theme (Variety, Mundane, Magical, Undead, Bug), Trap Frequency (None, Few, Lots, Too Many), and Potion Availability (Some, Some More, Lots, Tons).

While choosing the settings for *Virtual Hydlide*, the player is asked to select from "Create world randomly" and "Create world from code," a potentially confusing choice, since code is just as involved with procedural generation as anything else. This choice refers to the fact that the designers of *Virtual Hydlide* created over 20 maps for the dungeon levels and over 20 maps for the overworld, and these maps could be randomly selected and combined to form dungeons, combining handcrafted locations with procedural generation. If a new world was created, the player would be given a ten-letter seed representing that world, which could be reentered later if the player wanted to return to that world. This kind of reusable seed also reminds us that 'procedurally-generated' does not necessarily mean 'randomly-generated,' despite the fact that many such procedures involve randomization. Thus, in addition to the application of randomness to spatial construction, procedural generation can also be seen as a kind of data decompression. A game that I wrote for the TI99/4a computer in the early 1980s, for example, had a cave maze that took 100 screens to display. I managed to compress the data by dividing each screen into twelve tiles (with pathways leaving various sides of the tiles), and each type of tile was represented by a letter so that each of the hundred screens could be represented by twelve letters of text. This would be an example of something procedurally-generated which does not involve randomness, and combines handcrafted locations with procedural generation.

Some games combined various landmasses and buildings to produce procedurally-generated towns. *The Elder Scrolls II: Daggerfall* (Bethesda Softworks 1996) had a landmass of 62,394 square miles, with 15,000 towns and a population of 750,000. Criticisms and complaints of the monotony of the world (Blancato 2007) led to a much smaller (only 0.01%), but more handcrafted world for its sequel, *The Elder Scrolls III: Morrowind* (Bethesda Softworks 2002). Increased memory capacity can help to solve the problem of repetition in two ways; games can include more handcrafted interchangeable elements to be used in procedural constructions, or a greater number of algorithms can be used to add parameters to randomization as well as generate higher levels of detail. For example, *Pixel City* generates dozens of random buildings in various styles to keep the cities that are generated from looking repetitive (Young 2009). Other city generators, like *Subversion City Generator* (Introvision 2011) also plan city layouts based on waterways, bridges, and major and minor avenues, before filling them with buildings, creating more realistic urban landscapes.

The spaces of individual buildings and dungeons can also be done through the recombination of handcrafted building units. Games from the *Diablo*-series, for example, are noted for this technique. Three different floor plans of "Cathedral"-Level two from *Diablo III* (Blizzard Entertainment 2012) show how handcrafted building sections are recombined to create different arrangements which randomize gameplay (fig. 2a-c). While the repetitions in such designs are more evident from a top view, they may be less so from a first-person point of view, especially if the building interiors have randomized elements and décor.

Fig. 2a-c: Three different procedurally-generated floor plans from Diablo III

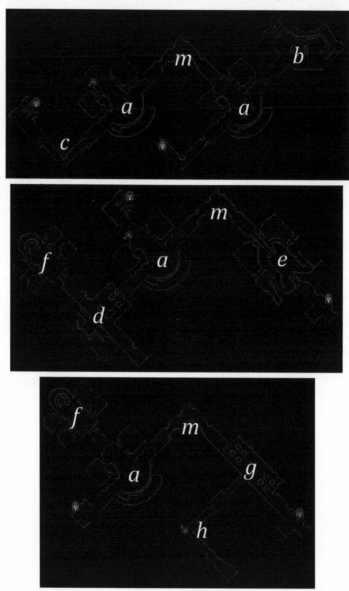

Interestingly, another consequence of greater storage capacity is how the constraints that programmers had to work under out of necessity, due to the lack of available memory, have now become something of an artistic challenge. Programmers taking up this challenge attempt to make as detailed worlds as possible fit within small amounts of memory, relying heavily on procedural generation and the faster processing speeds, which are able to decompress data, do fractal calculations, and run algorithms much faster than did the computers of the 1980s and 1990s. *Noctis* (Ghignola 2000), for example, features a three-dimensional, texture-mapped explorable universe of billions of stars and planets, all generated by a program smaller than one megabyte. Regarding the programming behind the fourth version of *Noctis* from 2003, Ghignola stated in an interview:

Its 'engine' is a mixture of sparse libraries. Planets and stars, for example are textured as pre-projected spherical maps. I don't know how many remember Quicktime [sic] VR, but I guess Wikipedia might have an article on that for those who never heard of it. QTVR worked by projecting a scene (a composite photograph) over a virtual, spherical screen, splashed on the physical flat screen. Well, *Noctis* planets work the other way around: they get a rectangular raster image and wrap it around a sphere. This is convenient in terms of speed because, if you can tolerate losing realistic, perspective aberrations when the sphere is significantly off the center of the viewport, the spherical map can be entirely precalculated, resulting in a rendering that was very fast even on my 486 of those times. The reverse (projection of the inside of a sphere) was used for skies on the surfaces of planets. Then there was a polygon engine taking care of drawing the heightmap constituting the surface itself. The polygon engine was pretty simple, but again pretty fast: it didn't even perform depth buffering (I doubt I could find enough memory for the buffer anyway), it just relied on the painter's algorithm and minimal hidden surface removal of one-sided surfaces. It was optimized enough that it could afford texture mapping of arbitrary-angled polygons, at about 1 division every 16 pixels. Where more detail was a good idea, such as to simulate grass on terrains, an additional texture layer was overlaid to the 'ground' texture, in a sort of very simple kind of bump mapping. The 256-color palette was split into four gradients having 64 brightness levels each, which finally enabled blur effects; in particular, the 'vimana drive' effect seen while traveling through interstellar medium was obtained by using an off-center blur filter over a persistent canvas. In practice, the effect was repeated each frame without clearing the previous frame, leaving trails whenever an element moved through the screen. I don't sincerely remember much about the shading of polygon surfaces, but I guess it was plain-color shading, driven by the angle of incidence of light sources. What more? One nice addition was the use of concentric, semitransparent lines to create halos around the light of stars, in such a way that – in my idea of that time – would mimic more the effect of light passing through an organic eye, rather than a camera's lens flare (Szymanski 2012).

Ghignola has revised the program in subsequent releases (and continues to work on the program; *Noctis V* is currently in the works as of mid-2019), and although the *Noctis* games are not commercially distributed, they have attained a following and are considered art games.

Another example, from Germany, is *.kkrieger* (.theprodukkt 2004), a first-person shooting game with detailed graphics and elaborate interiors (fig. 3a-d). Among its various procedural techniques is box modeling, in which 3-D primitives (like cubes, spheres, or cylinders) are subdivided with each section being replaced by more detail, a repetitive process which bears some similarity to the iterations involved in the production of fractal imagery – according to their website, some of the game's models and textures take hundreds of steps to create when the game is run. Through box modeling, texture mapping, and interactive lighting, the game uses only 97280 bytes of disk space and is able to produce a world which would normally take hundreds of megabytes to store. The small size of the game, however, does not mean that it could have produced at an earlier time when less memory was available. The many steps and processes used by procedural generation algorithms require more processing time, and faster processors for the game to operate; *.kkrieger*'s system requirements include a 1.5GHz Pentium 3/Athlon or faster, 512MB of RAM, and a GeForce4Ti (or higher) or ATI Radeon8500 (or higher) graphics card supporting pixel shaders 1.3, preferably with 128MB or more of VRAM. Thus, the small amount of memory used must be made up for through processing speed.

Fig. 3a-d: .kkrieger

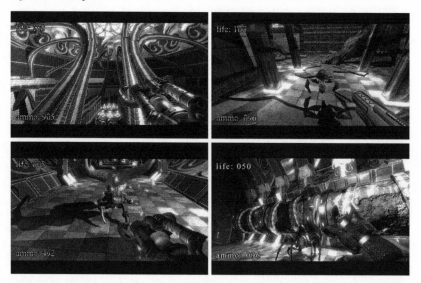

Greater storage is also necessary for games which generate and output large amounts of world data during their world creation. *Slaves to Armok: God of Blood,*

Chapter II: Dwarf Fortress (Tarn Adams 2006) – usually referred to simply as *Dwarf Fortress* – is a work still in progress, which generates all the terrain of its worlds, along with maps for elevation, temperature, rainfall, drainage, vegetation, and salinity. Mountains are eroded by rivers, and plant and animal populations are added, as well as races of sentient beings. Weather modeling even tracks wind and humidity and creates fronts, clouds, storms, and blizzards. Once the material world is generated, a historical timeline is generated, with thousands of characters being born, living lives, and dying, and events being recorded, so that in "Legends" mode, one can find a year-by-year list of the major events for every character's life, where they lived or wandered, who they fought, outcomes of conflicts, descendants, and so forth. Players can choose how much history is generated before the world is ready for their characters to inhabit. Like *Rogue*, graphics are two-dimensional and text-only (the Code Page 437 character set originally used for IBM PC computers) and appear in 16 available colors.

Generating three-dimensional terrain, the racing game *Fuel* (Asobo Studio 2009) provides players with 5560 square miles of fully-explorable terrain, for which the company received a *Guinness Book of World Records*-certificate for the largest playable environment in a console game (Fahey 2009). On one hand, the game is a good example of some of the graphics that procedural generation can achieve, underscoring the fact that it involves much more than simply randomness, but instead a set of parameters within which plausible objects and landscapes are generated; and these rules can be quite complex and elaborate ones, which, when they are balanced and adjusted just right, can create scenes which would be difficult to tell from handcrafted ones – movies have used similar techniques; Pandora, the planet in *Avatar* (Cameron 2009) was largely procedurally-generated. On the other hand, good graphics are not enough to make up for too much repetition of elements. As Marsh Davies noted in EDGE Online:

> Importantly, however, realism is not the aim – and cannot be for a world which hopes to serve as the basis for a game. Making a world realistic is not the same as making it interesting, a rule to which a game like Fuel stands in testament. Its recreation of the American wilderness was both beautiful and credible moment-to-moment, but empty and repetitive in aggregation, the terrain never quite feeling suited to the purpose of racing (Davies 2011).

While the procedural generation found in space trading games acted as a kind of backdrop for actions which were themselves typically quite repetitive (buying, selling, trading), three-dimensional worlds usually must be far more interactive for the player. Racing games like *Fuel* allow players to travel all over the landscape exploring, but beyond that, interaction is usually rather minimal. But more fully interactive procedurally-generated worlds were appearing as well.

'Infiniminer,' 'Minecraft' and beyond

The procedurally-generated world to receive the most publicity today is probably Markus Persson's *Minecraft* (Mojang 2009). Inspired by *Dwarf Fortress*, as well as Peter Molyneaux's *Dungeon Keeper* (Bullfrog Productions 1997), and especially *Infiniminer* (Barth 2009), from which *Minecraft* borrows heavily for its ideas, visual design, gameplay mechanics, and procedural-generation techniques. *Infiniminer* (fig. 4) appeared in late spring of 2009, but work on it was discontinued after source code was leaked, and other games besides *Minecraft*, including *Fortress-Craft* (ProjectorGames 2011), *CraftWorld* (2.0 Studios 2011), and *Ace of Spades* (Jagex 2012) also used and modified code from the game. Other games inspired by *Mine-craft*, such as *3079* (Phroot's Software 2011) and *Cube World* (Picroma 2013), have a similar look and feel as well.

Fig. 4: Zachary Barth's Infiniminer

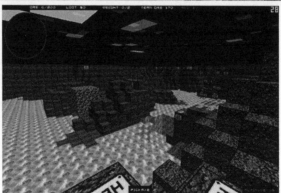

Games like these deal with the problem of repetition by moving it to a smaller scale; instead of the same trees or buildings, their worlds are composed of variations of blocks combined in endless ways. This granularity also allows users to build and destroy more easily, since construction and destruction is simplified down to the appearance or disappearance of blocks. While the graphics of these games are simpler and more stylized (something which the retro movement in gaming has made more acceptable to contemporary audiences who are used to photorealistic graphics), the possibilities inherent in the interactivity available far outweighs the aesthetic tradeoffs for many gamers. As such, space trading and exploration games have continued to evolve, with procedurally-generated planets and other locations in games like *FTL: Faster Than Light* (Subset Games 2012) and *Starbound* (Chucklefish 2016). Perhaps the most ambitious procedurally-generated locations are the millions of planets in *No Man's Sky* (Hello Games 2016). As Sean Murray (qtd. in Parkin 2014), one of the creators, put it:

> We are attempting to do things that haven't been done before... No game has made it possible to fly down to a planet, and for it to be planet-sized, and feature life, ecology, lakes, caves, waterfalls, and canyons, then seamlessly fly up through the stratosphere and take to space again. It's a tremendous challenge.

When older games revealed planets' surfaces, it was little more than a series of fractal mountains and bodies of water; even Noctis only featured rudimentary plants and rock structures. The planets of *No Man's Sky*, however, have lighting conditions based on the type of nearby star and positioning in orbit, and plants and animals involved in ecosystems, all of which are animating as you fly through the scenery, a level of detail previously only seen in handcrafted environments in games. Because the universe generated for the game is unexplored, even making a demo for the game posed problems not usually encountered in other games. According to Murray (2014):

> To give you an example of some problems, we planned out what our demo was, and then we had to find somewhere in the universe to set it. So I flew around for quite some time, a couple of days, looking for a planet that particularly suited it. So I had to pick that planet, but also find another planet that was nearby that I was going to fly to, and kind of engineer this situation where there was going to be things to fight in between. And then you actually end up having to deal with really weird things like the time of day on the planet it starts from, and what animals are going to be out at the time of day, and what time of day it is on the planet you land on. We wanted that to be daytime, and that's really hard to plan, and it just doesn't happen that easily. It was quite a fun little problem to have. Whereas, for any other game, you would be constructing something for months especially for E3. When

Ubisoft shows off what *Assassin's Creed* is like, it has specifically made that entire demo for that show. We don't have that control, which is really good, but also really crazy.

Other works-in-progress promise detailed universes of near-infinite size, such as Shamus Young's *Project Frontier*, Miguel Cepero's *Procedural World*, and Josh Parnell's *Limit Theory*, each with their own aesthetics and approach to procedural generation. What all these games suggest is that when it comes to the creation of vast videogame spaces, and the content within that space that defines it, we are seeing a shift in which 'handcrafted' will not refer to specific content or partic-ular instances of objects and locations so much as to ranges of possibilities and sets of parameters within which many variations of the required content can be generated. What parameters cover, how they are set, what settings are possible, and how different sets of parameters are linked to each other, determining ranges and limiting outcomes, will be the main ways of combining human hand-crafting with algorithmic construction and randomness. Open-world sandbox games have already made other games seem more limited in their interactivity, but so far the narratives they generate during gameplay are much weaker due to the wide range of possibilities to be accounted for. But as artificially-intelligent agents improve, and potential of story structure and world structure are explored and realized, we will likely see the quality of emergent narratives rising as well.

For games to move in the direction of procedurally-generated content is quite natural when one considers how much of the complexity of the physical universe is due to procedural processes. As fractal mathematics and the study of cellular automata has demonstrated (Wolfram 2002), simple rules and concepts can gen-erate complex structures, like a seed growing into a tree or strands of DNA guid-ing the development of the human body. Videogame worlds grown by algorithms are increasing in their complexity, and just as players explore these worlds, their designers are exploring the nature of worlds and their representations. While they will never reach the elegance and ingenuity of the procedural processes found in the natural world, their striving to imitate them can make us all the more appre-ciative of the universe around us and its combined simplicity and complexity.

References

2.0 Studios (2011): *CraftWorld*, Windows Phone: Xbox Live.

A.I. Design (1983): *Rogue*, PC: Epyx.

Anonymous (2009): The Making of Rogue, in: *EDGE*, July, 3rd, edge-online.com/features/making-rogue/2.

Asobo Studio (2009): *Fuel*, PS3/Xbox 360: Codemaster.

Atari (1980): *Stellar Track*, Atari 2600: Sears.

Barth, Zachary (2009): *Infiniminer*, PC: Zachtronics Industries.

Bethesda Softworks (1996): *The Elder Scrolls II: Daggerfall*, PC: Bethesda Softworks.

———— (2002): *The Elder Scrolls III: Morrowind*, PC: Ubisoft.

Binary Systems (1986): *Starflight*, PC: Electronic Arts.

Blancato, Joe (2007): Bethesda: The Right Direction, in: *The Escapist*, February 6th, escapistmagazine.com/articles/view/video-games/issues/issue_83/471-Bethesda-The-Right-Direction.

Blizzard Entertainment (2012): *Diablo III*, PC: Blizzard Entertainment.

Braben, David (1993): *Frontier: Elite II*, Amiga/Atari ST: GameTek.

Braben, David/Bell, Ian (1984): *Elite*, PC: Acornsoft.

Bullfrog Productions (1997): *Dungeon Keeper*, PC: Electronic Arts.

Cameron, James (2009): *Avatar*, Film: USA.

Cham, Brian (2014): The Next Space: Procedural Generation as Indicator of Technological Possibility, videogamesftvms2014.wordpress.com/tag/procedural-generation.

Chucklefish (2016): *Starbound*, PC: Chucklefish.

Crammond, Geoff (1986): *The Sentinel*, PC: Firebird.

Crowther, William/Woods, Don (1976): *Colossal Cave Adventure*, PDP-10: Crowther/Woods.

Cyan (1993): *Myst*, Macintosh PC: Brøderbund.

Davies, Marsh (2011): Building Worlds with a Single Click, in: *EDGE Online*, July 6th, edge-online.com/features/building-worlds-single-click/3.

Fahey, Mike (2009): Fuel is the Biggest Console Game Ever, in: *Kotaku*, May 22nd, kotaku.com/5265942/fuel-is-the-biggest-console-game-ever.

Ghignola, Alessandro (2000): *Noctis*, PC: Ghignola.

Gygax, Gary/Arneson, Dave (1974): *Dungeons & Dragons*, Pen&Paper: Tactical Studio Rules.

Hello Games (2016): *No Man's Sky*, PS4: Hello Games.

Introvision (2011): *Subversion City Generator*, PC: Introvision.

Irvin, Peter/Smith, Jeremy (1988): *Exile*, BBC/Electron: Superior Software.

Jagex (2012): *Ace of Spades*, PC: Jagex.

Lion Entertainment (1994): *Advanced Dungeons & Dragons: Slayer*, 3DO: Strategic Designs.

———— (1995): *Virtual Hydlide*, Sega Saturn: Sega.

Lucasfilm Games (1984): *Rescue on Fractalus!*, Atari 5200: Atari.

———— (1985): *Koronis Rift*, Atari800/C64: Epyx.

———— (1985a): *The Eidolon*, Atari800/C64: Epyx.

Meyer, Nicholas (1982): *Star Trek II: The Wrath of Khan*, Film: USA.

Mindscape (1990): *Captive*, Amiga/Atari ST: Mindscape.

Mojang (2009): *Minecraft*, PC: Mojang.

Murray, Sean (2014): *No Man's Sky: The Story, Gameplay, and Multiplayer Explained*, youtube.com/watch?v=tYoGN2zgXQU&t=65.

Noyes, Emma (2006): David Braben: From Elite to Today, in: *Gamespot*, November, 22nd, gamespot.com/articles/qanda-david-braben-from-elite-to-today/11 00-6162140.

Parkin, Simon (2014): No Man's Sky. A Vast Game Crafted by Algorithms, in: *MIT Technology Review*, July 22nd, technologyreview.com/news/529136/no-mans-sky-a-vast-game-crafted-by-algorithms.

Phroot's Software (2011): *3079*, PC: Phroot's Software.

Picroma (2013): *Cube World*, PC: Picorama.

Priestmann, Chris (2013): Why It's Best to Be Cautious around Procedurally Generated Indie Games, *Indiesstatik*, December 8th, indiestatik.com/2013/12/08/procedural-generation.

ProjectorGames (2011): *FortressCraft*, Xbox 360: Xbox Live.

Raffe, William L./Zambetta, Fabio/Li, Xiaodong (2012): A Survey of Procedural Terrain Generation Techniques Using Evolutionary Algorithms, in: *WCCI 2012 IEEE World Congress on Computational Intelligence*, June 10th-15th, goanna. cs.rmit.edu.au/~xiaodong/publications/ptg-raffe-cec2012.pdf.

Russel, Steve (1962): *Spacewar!*, PDP-1: MIT.

Subset Games (2012): *FTL: Faster Than Light*, PC: Subset Games.

Szymanski, David (2012): Interview with Alessandro Ghignola (aka 'Alex'), in: *Videogame Potpourri*, May 9th, homeoftheunderdogs.net/game.php?id=2950.

Tarn Adams (2006): *Slaves to Armok: God of Blood, Chapter II: Dwarf Fortress*, PC: Bay 12 Games.

.theprodukkt (2004): *.kkrieger*, PC: .theprodukkt.

Wolfram, Stephen (2002): *A New Kind of Science*, Champaign, IL: Wolfram Media 2002

Young, Shamus (2009): *Procedural City*, shamusyoung.com/twentysidedtale/?p=2940.

Authors

Espen Aarseth is professor of game studies and leader for the Center for Computer Games Research at the IT University of Copenhagen. He holds a Dr. Art. from the University of Bergen, where he was trained in literary theory. He is editor-in-Chief of *Game Studies*, and is currently directing an ERC Advanced Grant project, "Making Sense of Games" (MSG). The first videogame he played was *Speed Race* in 1974; game.itu.dk/members/espen-aarseth.

Sebastian Domsch teaches Anglophone literatures at the University of Greifswald, Germany. He holds a PhD from Bamberg University, and a Habilitation from the Ludwig-Maximilians-University in Munich. His major fields of interest besides videogames are contemporary literature and culture, graphic novels, the history and theory of literary criticism, Romantic literature and 18th-century literature. He is the author of a book in the series on "Future Narratives" on videogames and narrative, *Storyplaying: Agency and Narrative in Video Games* (de Gruyter 2013), which marked his return to the medium after nights spent playing the original *Doom* games. Since these days teaching, administration, and kids have largely consigned him to the ninth circle of gaming hell, AKA idle games, he is desperately trying to come up with a way to turn them into a viable academic research subject; ifaa.uni-greifswald.de/domsch.

Teun Dubbelman currently holds the position of associate professor and is vice-director of the School of Games and Interaction at HKU University of the Arts Utrecht, Netherlands. With fifteen years of experience, he is considered an expert in interactive narrative design research and education. Dubbelman received his Ph.D. at Utrecht University, with a thesis on narrative game design. He was a Fulbright Scholar at the Massachusetts Institute of Technology, working in The Singapore-MIT GAMBIT Game Lab. His recent work focuses on the topics of design pedagogy, narrative game mechanics and design for change; hku.academia.edu/TeunDubbelman.

Mathias Fuchs is currently directing a three years research project on the "Shifting of Boundaries between the Ludic and the Non-Ludic." He is a member of the Institute of Culture and Aesthetics of Digital Media at Leuphana University in Lüneburg, Germany. Having worked as a game designer and a scholar in game studies, Mathias analysed and experimented with pictorial and textual representations of space, with space transformations and 'Warp Zones'. His most recent publication is a book on *Phantasmal Spaces. Archetypical Venues in Computer Games* (Bloomsbury Academic 2019); leuphana.de/universitaet/personen/mathias-fuchs.html.

Stephan Günzel is Professor for Media Theory at the University of Applied Sciences Europe in Berlin, Germany, and currently chair of the Media Studies program at the Technical University of Berlin. His research interests include spatial and image theory, digital games as media and almost any aspect related to the notion of space; these days in particular the implications of AR-, MR- and VR-media. His point of entry into the topic of spatiality was his dissertation in philosophy, in which he investigated Friedrich Nietzsche's relation to geography. After being a passionate gamer on the Commodore 64 in the early 1980's, he quit playing with software and switched to electric guitar, thereby missing out the first wave of first-person shooters. When he then got the chance to study games academically in 2005, he got hooked on *Doom 3* and decided to write his habilitation in media studies on *Egoshooter* (Campus 2012). He found the first bachelor program for Game Design at a private university in Berlin in 2014; stephan-guenzel.de.

Bjarke Liboriussen is Assistant Professor in Digital and Creative Media at the University of Nottingham Ningbo, China. His interest in the relationship between games and space began with a PhD that explored how landscape aesthetics and architectural theory could be applied to virtual worlds. Since then he briefly worked for Copenhagen Business School by interviewing architects about innovative uses of virtual worlds in their architectural practices. His current research focuses on gaming in China and on the creative industries in China. His research has been published in journals such as *Convergence, Games and Culture* and *Game Studies*; nottingham.ac.uk/news/expertiseguide/international-communications/dr-bjarke-liboriussen.aspx

Paul Martin is an Assistant Professor in Digital Media and Communications at the University of Nottingham Ningbo, China. His interest in space in games began with a doctoral dissertation on space and place as expressive categories in games. His current work is on meaning in games, Chinese esports and game studies as a field. He was a founder member of the Chinese chapter of the Digital Games Research Association and currently serves as its president. A list of his current publications is available at ningbo.academia.edu/PaulMartin and nottingham. edu.cn/en/internationalcommunications/staffprofile/paul-martin.aspx.

Sebastian Möring is assistant professor in European Media Studies – a joint study program of the University of Potsdam and the University of Applied Sciences Potsdam, Germany – and head-coordinator of the Digital Games Research Center (DIGAREC) at the same place. His research focuses on the philosophy and aesthetics of computer games, in-game photography, and representations and functions of climate in computer games. Sebastian earned his Ph.D. from the Center for Computer Games Research at the IT University of Copenhagen with a thesis on the metaphor discourse in game studies and researched existential structures of computer games as a postdoc at the School of Creative Media, City University of Hong Kong. He got involved with space and computer games in his master's thesis which dealt with an analysis of the fear structure of computer games from a Heideggerian perspective. He is involved with the Gamephilosophy Network, organizer of the annual conference Philosophy of Computer Games; sebastianmoering.com.

Souvik Mukherjee is an assistant professor and the head of the Department of English at Presidency University, Kolkata, India. Souvik received his Ph.D. from Nottingham Trent University, UK, in which he wrote about videogames and storytelling. He is the author of two monographs, *Videogames and Storytelling: Reading Games and Playing Books* (Palgrave Macmillan 2015) and *Videogames and Postcolonialism: Empire Plays Back* (Springer 2017). His research interests span across a range of topics related to videogames and (the) Digital Humanities such as temporality, telos, spatiality and empire. Souvik is currently working on ancient Indian boardgames. A committed ludotopian, Souvik was inspired by Stephan Günzel, Mathias Fuchs and Michael Nitsche in thinking about videogame spaces in connection with temporality; presiuniv.ac.in/web/staff.php?staffid=1.

Michael Nitsche works as Associate Professor in Digital Media at the Georgia Institute of Technology, Atlanta, USA, where he works on issues of hybrid spaces and what we do in them. He uses Performance, Craft, HCI, and media studies as critical approaches to explores this borderline in digital media. He directs the Digital World and Image Group and is involved with various interdisciplinary research centers. Nitsche's publications include the books *Video Game Spaces* (MIT Press 2009) and *The Machinima Reader* (MIT Press 2011), co-edited with Henry Lowood. He is also co-editor of the journal *Digital Creativity*; homes.lmc.gatech. edu/~nitsche.

Niklas Schrape is senior strategist at the social media agency, Granny in Berlin, Germany. He studied communication, psychology and sociology at Free University Berlin and social and economic communication at the Berlin University of the Arts. He earned his Ph.D. from Film and Television University Potsdam with a thesis on the rhetorics of political computer games. Until 2015 Niklas was member of the "Innovation-Incubator" at Leuphana University in Lüneburg; leuphana.de/ dfg-programme/mecs/personen/alumni/dr-niklas-schrape.html.

Stephan Schwingeler is Professor for Media Studies at HAWK University of Applied Sciences and Arts, Hildesheim, Germany. His first book deals with the topic of space in videogames and is one of the first art historical publications in the field of game studies. His Ph.D. thesis and second book examines the practices and strategies of game art and artistic videogame modification from the perspective of art history and media theory. In the last couple of years, he was also Professor for Game Design at mAHS Stuttgart and was responsible for running the GameLab at the Karlsruhe University of Arts and Design. Among other exhibitions and events, he was responsible as a curator for the exhibition „ZKM_Gameplay" at the internationally renowned ZKM|Center for Art and Media in Karlsruhe. His exhibition "Global Games" presents videogames as political media. His other curated exhibitions include „New Gameplay" (Nam June Paik Art Center, South Korea), „Digital Games" (Ludwig Forum, Aachen, Germany); hawk.de/de/hoch schule/organisation-und-personen/personenverzeichnis/stephan-schwingeler.

Karla Theilhaber is the Executive Producer at Experimental Game in Berlin, Germany. She coordinates all running projects using the company's production pipeline, Gamebook. She has been working in digital and creative industries in Berlin, Konstanz and Düsseldorf, where she managed museum exhibitions and events (such as 'A MAZE'), and produced websites, apps, and games at digital agencies and game development studios. Her research focuses on spatial concepts in videogames and videogame development in the GDR. She has pursued a history of the only GDR game console 'Bildschirmspiel 01' through interviews of people involved in its production. For this project, she has consulted collectors, experts, as well as extensive visual and text material of archival research to pursue an understanding of objects as agents telling their own story.

Daniel Vella is a lecturer at the Institute of Digital Games at the University of Malta, where he teaches classes in digital game studies, player experience and narrative in games. He received his Ph.D. from the IT University of Copenhagen, where he focused on developing a theory of ludic subjectivity. His current research interests include the phenomenology of virtual world experience, aesthetic theory and digital games, and space and place in games. His work has been published in jour-